INDIANA'S WAR

THE CIVIL WAR IN THE GREAT INTERIOR

Series Editors
Martin J. Hershock and Christine Dee

Ohio's War: The Civil War in Documents, edited by Christine Dee
Missouri's War: The Civil War in Documents, edited by Silvana R. Siddali
Indiana's War: The Civil War in Documents, edited by Richard F. Nation and
    Stephen E. Towne

FORTHCOMING:

Kansas's War: The Civil War in Documents, edited by Pearl T. Ponce
Michigan's War: The Civil War in Documents, edited by John W. Quist
Wisconsin's War: The Civil War in Documents, edited by Chandra Manning

INDIANA'S WAR

The Civil War in Documents

~

EDITED BY RICHARD F. NATION AND STEPHEN E. TOWNE

Ohio University Press

Athens

Ohio University Press, Athens, Ohio 45701
www.ohioswallow.com
© 2009 by Ohio University Press
All rights reserved

Printed in the United States of America
Ohio University Press books are printed on acid-free paper ∞ ™

16 15 14 13 12 11 10 09   5 4 3 2 1

Cover art: Eleventh Indiana Volunteers Swearing to Remember Buena Vista, at
Indianapolis, May 1861. *Courtesy Indiana Historical Society*

Library of Congress Cataloging-in-Publication Data
Indiana's war : the Civil War in documents / edited by Richard F. Nation and
Stephen E. Towne.
    p. cm. — (The Civil War in the great interior)
Includes bibliographical references and index.
ISBN 978-0-8214-1847-5 (pb : alk. paper)
    1. Indiana—History—Civil War, 1861–1865—Sources. 2. United States—History—
Civil War, 1861–1865—Sources. I. Nation, Richard Franklin. II. Towne, Stephen E.,
1961–
E506.I456 2009
977.2'03—dc22

2009023497

To our mothers Marian:

Marian Goodlet Dewar Nation (1923–2002)

and

Marian Kleinsasser Towne

Contents

One

The Politics of Slavery 6

Two

The Election of 1860 and Secession 27

Three

Choosing Sides, Making an Army 43

Four

The Front Lines 62

Five

The Home Front 87

Six

Race, Slavery, and the Emancipation Proclamation 104

Seven

The Battle to Control State Government 125

Eight

The Morgan Raid   146

Nine

Dissent, Violence, and Conspiracy   155

Ten

War's End   190

Illustrations

Series Editors' Preface

The Civil War in the Great Interior series focuses on the Middle West, as the complex region has come to be known, during the most critical era of American history. In his Annual Message to Congress in December of 1862, Abraham Lincoln identified "the great interior region" as the area between the Alleghenies and the Rocky Mountains, south of Canada and north of the "culture of cotton." Lincoln included in this region the states of Ohio, Indiana, Michigan, Wisconsin, Illinois, Missouri, Kansas, Iowa, Minnesota, and Kentucky; the area that would become West Virginia; and parts of Tennessee and the Dakota, Nebraska, and Colorado territories. This area, Lincoln maintained, was critical to the "great body of the republic" not only because it bound together the North, South, and West but also because its people would not assent to the division of the Union.

This series examines what was, to Lincoln and other Americans in the mid-nineteenth century, the most powerful, influential, and critical area of the country. It considers how the people of the Middle West experienced the Civil War and the role they played in preserving and redefining the nation. These collections of historical sources—many of which have never been published—explore significant issues raised by the sectional conflict, the Civil War, and Reconstruction. The series underscores what was unique to particular states and their residents while recognizing the values and experiences that individuals in the Middle West shared with other Northerners and, in some cases, with Southerners.

Within these volumes are the voices of a diverse cross-section of nineteenth-century Americans. These include African Americans, European immigrants, Native Americans, and women. Editors have gathered evidence from farms and factories, rural and urban areas, and communities throughout each state to examine the relationships of individuals, their communities, the political culture, and events on the battlefields. The volumes present readers with layers of evidence that can be combined in a multitude of patterns to yield new conclusions and raise questions about prevailing interpretations of the past.

The editor of each volume provides a narrative framework through brief chapter introductions and background information for each document, as well as a timeline. As these volumes cannot address all aspects of the Civil War experience for each state, they include selected bibliographies to guide readers in further research. Documents were chosen for what they reveal about the past, but each also speaks to the subjective nature of history and the decisions that historians face when weighing the merits and limits of each piece of evidence they uncover. The diverse documents included in these volumes also expose readers to the craft of history and to the variety of source materials historians utilize as they explore the past.

Much of the material in these works will raise questions, spark debates, and generate discussion. Whether read with an eye toward the history of the Union war effort, a particular state or region, or the Civil War's implications for race, class, and gender in America, the volumes in The Civil War in the Great Interior help us consider—and reconsider—the evidence from the past.

Martin J. Hershock
Christine Dee

Preface

The Civil War was far more than a series of battles. Before the guns of war blazed, a generation of men and women argued about the place of slavery and of African Americans in the politics, economics, and social fabric of the nation and of the state of Indiana. The war itself affected almost every aspect of the lives of Hoosiers, from the material conditions of their lives to the emotional conditions of their hearts. And the repercussions of the war would continue on, the war serving as a touchstone of values and meanings for another generation.

Issued on the eve of the sesquicentennial of the Civil War, this reader aims to collect the diverse voices of Civil War Indiana. Included within its pages are the obvious protagonists, like Governor Oliver P. Morton and Senator Jesse D. Bright, but also a pantheon of the nearly forgotten from all walks of life and political persuasions, from indigent wives of soldiers to Hoosiers who fought for the Confederacy. Much of the focus in the collection is on the political divisions in the state, but with an emphasis on unveiling how those political divisions affected ordinary people on all sides. A second emphasis that begins and ends the book is on the racial values of Hoosiers and how that shaped their response to the war.

The documents as transcribed here are as close to the originals as possible. Even when offensive to modern ears, we have retained the original wordings of all pieces. *Sic* has been used as little as possible; when clarity demands it, the editors have provided spelling and grammatical corrections within brackets. To permit the inclusion of the widest possible range of documents, some of the longer ones have been edited, with omissions indicated by the use of ellipses. We believe that the original intentions of authors have never been altered.

Uncited biographical details that appear in the headnotes of the various pieces are primarily drawn from notes that accompany the archival collections from which the source is drawn and from the manuscript population census of the United States.

Three archives have provided the bulk of the previously unpublished material for this book. The first is the Indiana State Archives, Commission on Public Records, which we have shortened in the text to Indiana State Archives. The second is the William Henry Smith Memorial Library, Indiana Historical Society, which we have shortened to Indiana Historical Society. The final is the Manuscripts Section, Indiana Division, Indiana State Library, which we have shortened to Indiana State Library.

Acknowledgments

This project began when Christine Dee and Marty Hershock invited Richard to prepare a volume on Indiana, and much appreciation goes to them for that invitation. Richard contacted Steve early in the project, recognizing that Steve's strength in the history of Indiana during the Civil War would be a valuable asset.

Any historical project depends on the archivists who preserve and make accessible the myriad of historical documents from the past. In no instance is this more true than with an anthology of primary documents. Researchers on Indiana are blessed with a host of fine archives and professionals in them who have done stellar work in making their collections available. Any work on Indiana government leads to the Indiana State Archives, where Alan January provides reamarkable guidance. The largest collection of Indiana papers is at the William Henry Smith Memorial Library at the Indiana Historical Society, with a staff too numerous to list in full: especially noteworthy were Paul Brockman, Emily Comstock, and, as always, Wilma Moore. Across the street at the Indiana State Library, the manuscript collection is not as large but is filled with gems; we thank Elizabeth Wilkinson, now at Purdue, and Marcia Caudell. The newspaper collection at the Indiana State Library is extraordinary and, until his regrettable departure, overseen by the incomparable Darroll Pierson, who, as always, has been of immense help. Around the state, other archives provided key documents: the Lilly Library at Indiana University (thanks to Saundra Taylor); the archives at Wabash College (appreciations to Beth Swift); and the Friends Collection at Earlham College (hat tip to Tom Hamm). Thanks also to DeAnne Blanton of the National Archives and Records Administration in Washington, DC, and Jennifer Duplaga of the Kentucky Historical Society. Thanks to the LaPorte County Historical Society and the Wells County Historical Society for giving permission to use letters in their holdings. Special thanks to Neil Frisch, Robert Butikas, and Barbara Miller and Marilyn Swander for allowing us to present documents in their private possession.

The outside readers for both the proposal and the draft manuscript provided important pointers. Christine Dee and Marty Hershock have been wonderful series editors, and Gillian Berchowitz at Ohio University Press has been forgiving of our miscues.

Eastern Michigan University helped provide important support for the project through a Spring/Summer Research Grant and by funding a research assistant, Jennifer Stadjl. Jennifer transcribed a number of the documents in this piece, with far greater accuracy than Steve or Richard, and we appreciate her efforts. Many of Richard's colleagues at Eastern encouraged his efforts, and Steven Ramold answered key questions from time to time.

The Research Leave Committee of University Library at Indiana University–Purdue University Indianapolis granted research time to Steve, for which he is extremely grateful.

In personal thanks, Richard would like to acknowledge his sister Marilyn and her husband Daryl, who have housed him on many of his trips to the Hoosier state; this project could never have been completed without their immense kindness and hospitality. His friend Gib Chew also provided much-appreciated lodging. Richard also would like to thank his children, Isaac and Elijah, for excusing his repeated absences from home, and Debbie, who not only tolerated the absences that bore so heavily on her but provided immense support and some serious proofreading to make the volume possible. Steve would like to thank his son, David, and parents, Marian and Edgar, for their forbearance.

Introduction

$\mathcal{T}$HE TWO MAIN ISSUES that drove the Civil War—slavery and the right of a people to determine their own institutions—had animated politics in Indiana from its territorial stage. Indeed, both issues played roles in pushing Hoosiers toward statehood, as the citizens of the Indiana territory attempted to wrest control of their homes from federal oversight, a federal oversight that included persons—William Henry Harrison and others—who sought a means to introduce slavery into the territory. When Hoosiers sat down to write Indiana's first constitution in 1816, they provided for universal white male suffrage. But the delegates to the constitutional convention also made clear that they wished to forbid slavery, to keep African Americans and slaveholders from the state: "There shall be neither slavery nor involuntary servitude in this state, otherwise than for the punishment of crimes, whereof the party shall have been duly convicted. Nor shall any indenture of any negro or mulatto hereafter made, and executed out of the bounds of this state be of any validity within the state." They emphasized the finality of that decision in making that clause the only portion of the state constitution that could not be amended: "But, as the holding any part of the human Creation in slavery, or involuntary servitude, can only originate in usurpation and tyranny, no alteration of this constitution shall ever take place so as to introduce slavery or involuntary servitude in this State, otherwise than for the punishment of crimes, whereof the party shall have been duly convicted."[1] As interpreted by the Indiana Supreme Court, slavery was effectively banned in Indiana, and by 1830, there were only three slaves recorded in the state.

Without much migration from New England and New York, the strength of sentiment opposing slavery in Indiana came primarily from two groups, one of migrants from New Jersey and Pennsylvania and the other of Southerners, including a number of Quakers from North Carolina. The Southerners settled in the hilliest parts of the state, in the south-central portion, but they were almost as prevalent throughout the central third of the state, from Terre Haute to Richmond. Northern Indiana saw more settlement from the Middle Atlantic states, with some New Yorkers and New Englanders, as did both the southeastern and southwestern portions of the state. By the mid-1830s, there were strong German migrations to the southeast and southwest and eventually a thriving German community in Indianapolis as well. Nevertheless, Indiana emerged from its pioneer period with a higher percentage of its population born in the United States than any other state in the Old Northwest. Moreover, compared to other free states, Indiana had the largest percentage of residents born in slaveholding states.[2]

These Southerners were not primarily from plantation regions but from hilly and mountainous areas, especially of Virginia, North Carolina, and Kentucky. Their investment in the institution of slavery was slight, and they voted against the institution when they crossed over the Ohio and chose to make their homes in a territory and then a state in which slavery was forbidden. While some Southerners who arrived in Indiana during the territorial stage may have hoped to turn the bottomlands of the Ohio and Wabash into plantation lands, the majority of Hoosiers, despite their Southern origins, had no such aspirations. As one editor put it in 1824:

> Most of you who settled in Indiana under the territorial government were emigrants from those states where you could say "My ears are pained, my soul is sick, with ev'ry day's report and outrage with which the earth is fill'd." You saw the land of freedom with an anxious eye.—You braved the difficulties of removing; you endured the hardships and underwent the privations of settling in a country, where you no more expected to witness these scenes of inhuman barbarity inflicted on the unfortunate and unoffending descendants of Africa.

He added: "What if there are small defects in our constitution? If there are it shuts from our state the sooty slave, and his sable master."[3] Antagonism toward slaveholders reinforced the general antislavery response, which was primarily rooted in an extreme antiblack sentiment: the best society, according to this view, was homogenously European in origin.

Yet not all Hoosiers were so adamantly racist in their beliefs. At the core of the antiracists were African Americans themselves. By 1850, there were 11,262 African Americans in the state, out of a population of nearly a million.[4] Some Quakers also played leading roles in the abolitionist movement in Indiana. But many Quakers, having quit a slave society, believed the stain of slavery was washed from their hands, and in this idea they were joined by many of their neighbors who had also emigrated from the South. Baptists often refused to associate with Kentucky Baptist Associations that condoned slavery.[5] There remained among many Hoosiers an underlying sense that slavery was wrong, even though many of them were undeniably racist. Hoosiers of European descent may have generally believed that Africans were inferior, but many did not believe that inferiority meant that slavery was the legitimate fate of Africans. Even many Hoosier abolitionists did not embrace the equality of the races. But Hoosiers who believed that the gulf between the races was wide and that they were morally removed from the stain of slavery could often be found compromising away the liberties of Africans, even while professing that slavery was wrong.

Abolitionism, in other words, was never a strong movement in Indiana, even as certain Hoosiers like George W. Julian and Levi Coffin gained national recognition for their abolitionist efforts. Abolitionists were able to shape some of the conversation by the 1850s with their relentless focus on the sinfulness of slavery, but many Hoosiers could agree that slavery was sinful without agreeing that they had an obligation to end it.

Other things mattered more, like the Union and the success of their political parties. When they emerged in the 1830s, both the Whigs and the Democrats were predicated on building a national coalition in order to achieve power in the federal government. The issue of slavery potentially divided both parties, both of which preferred it off the table. And Southerners in each party repeatedly used the threat of division to win concessions from the Northerners in their party. For Southerners, protecting the institution of slavery was more important than maintaining national power; they held in reserve the right to secede if necessary. Hoosiers of both parties confronted a dilemma: how to make concessions to the Southerners on the national level while retaining the loyalty of a constituency ambivalent about slavery in order to win state and local elections.

Likewise, preserving the Union seemed to many Northerners to necessitate accommodating the institution of slavery. For Northern Democrats, Andrew Jackson's famous 1832 Nullification Crisis toast—"Our Federal Union: It must be preserved"—served to justify their willingness to find a middle ground on the issue of slavery, even while, like Jackson, they condemned those who used the threat of secession to coerce them. Hoosiers of both parties had come to believe in the Union as the best preserver of liberty and prosperity. The Union was, to Hoosier Jacksonian Tilghman Howard, the "greatest guarantee" of "the liberty of the people."[6] Condemnations of abolitionism often focused on its potential to divide the Union. Without the Union, there could be no liberty. In their racism, Hoosiers ignored the fact that slavery was a denial of the liberty of African Americans.

Hoosiers were tied into the Union through both family and economic connections. Because of their diverse origins, Hoosiers often had relatives from both sides of the Mason-Dixon line. Moreover, the nature of economic life in the Middle West tied them to markets both North and South. Well into the interior of the state, much surplus produce was sent to New Orleans; the spring floods saw many Hoosiers floating on rafts laden with goods down to the Ohio and then on to the Mississippi and New Orleans. New Orleans remained an important market through the Civil War, but goods were also traded up the Ohio and points east. The completion of the National Road in the 1830s provided a key connection to the east from central Indiana, and by the early 1840s, the Wabash and Erie Canal began to route northern Indiana traffic to Lake Erie and eventually New York City. By 1860, a number of east-west rail lines had been completed through the state, tying Hoosiers to the east coast.

The central part of the state benefited from these developments, as commercial agriculture in that region began to rival and even surpass agriculture in the bottomlands of the Ohio, the Wabash, and their tributaries. West-central Indiana saw the most growth, with intensive grain production and livestock. By 1860, much of northern Indiana was still emerging from its frontier period, and it remained forested and wet; drainage projects had just begun to claim fertile land for the region's farmers. Southern Indiana, outside its fertile valley lands, did not support as intensive agricultural production, and many of the region's farmers made a more modest living from the hilly lands. Hoosiers in all regions were primarily farmers; Indiana was one of the most rural of the free states.

In 1850, only 4 percent of Indiana's population lived in urban areas, defined then as cities with a population greater than 2,500. Most of these urban residents were located in the small Ohio River cities like Madison, New Albany, and Evansville. By 1860, the railroad played a role in substantial urban growth in the interior, with small cities like South Bend and Fort Wayne growing dramatically; Indianapolis, already the second-largest city in 1850, more than doubled in population in the next decade. Evansville and New Albany continued to grow as well, although other river towns like Lawrenceburg and Madison slowed or even declined. By 1860, urban dwellers accounted for 7 percent of the state's population, and many were employed in the emerging manufacturing sector, increasingly tied to the national economy.

Despite these ties and devotion to the Union, many Hoosiers, especially those of a Democratic stripe, also held the notion that the government that was most local was more responsive to the will of the people and thus less likely to engage in programs that were inimical to the great mass of the people. The federal government should not be a positive force in society, acting to improve the lives of its citizens, but a negative force, prepared to counter factions and cabals that threatened the people's liberties. While some Hoosiers retained hope that their state governments could act to improve lives, many in the state had become disheartened by the failures of the internal improvement projects of the 1830s. The failure of these projects—championed by many Hoosier Whigs, but supported by many in the Democratic Party as well—in the wake of the Panic of 1837 had shifted the balance of political power in the state toward the Democratic Party. To cling to power locally, even many Hoosier Whigs limited their support of government reform and economic growth programs. Hoosiers considered such policies well suited to an agricultural society. Through the Civil War, the state Democratic Party shaped its policies primarily around the needs of small farmers, paying less direct attention to ethnic minorities and the urban working class than it did in many other Northern states. In the end, Hoosier Democrats in particular could agree that for circumstances particular to a certain locale, it was best to leave regulation to the people of that locale, acting through their local and state governments. Few in the North actively embraced slavery as a positive good, but until the rise of the Republican Party, most Northerners believed that some accommodation of slaveholders was necessary.

By 1860, about 1,350,000 people lived in the state of Indiana, including about 11,428 African Americans—their numbers had barely grown during a decade in which African Americans in Indiana faced the increasing likelihood of being claimed as fugitives from slavery.[7] The reaction of Hoosiers of European descent to the rise of the Republican Party and then the Civil War would be molded by two factors: racism and devotion to the Union. The most racist among Hoosiers would oppose the Republican Party and support the right of the South to secede. Strong feelings for Union might compel other racist Hoosiers to support the North, even as in an earlier period Unionist sentiment may have compelled other Hoosiers to resist abolitionism and even the Republican Party.

When Hoosiers marched to war, most did not do so to end slavery. They marched to preserve the Union. Some of the small minority of Hoosiers who sought the abolition of slavery did volunteer for the ranks, but not always—many of the state's abolitionists were Quakers and other pacifists. Beyond the pacifist Quakers, many of those who stayed home did so because they believed, long before it was policy, that the aim of the war was to end slavery and that such an effort was a tyrannical abuse of federal power over fellow Americans' right to govern their own local institutions.

ONE

The Politics of Slavery

*L*OCATED JUST ACROSS the Ohio River from the slave state of Kentucky, Indiana was never geographically far from the institution of slavery. Slaveholders and their slaves sometimes laid over at the various river towns along the Ohio, planters and enslaved Africans transited Indiana bound for the slave state of Missouri, and Africans stealthily entered the state in search of freedom, settling in the scattered African American communities or moving on to Michigan and Canada, with their more secure promise of freedom.

In Indiana these African Americans could sometimes find assistance, notably from other African Americans who had preceded them and from scattered communities of Quakers among whom those African Americans had often settled. The Underground Railroad was rarely as organized as its name implies, nor was it often literally underground, despite tales of tunnels and caves. Generally it referred to a loose network of associates who could direct freedom-seeking individuals to like-minded folks further north. Such Hoosiers, especially among the European American community, were few and far between, but sufficiently aware of each other that they could provide an avenue of escape for African Americans fleeing slavery. But for every Hoosier, black and white, who assisted these fugitives, there were others who saw the opportunity to gain rewards. Most Hoosiers, however, aided neither African Americans nor the slaveholders and their agents.

Resident African Americans primarily settled in the southern half of the state and often near Quaker communities. Ohio River counties saw some of the highest concentrations—although the four counties east of Evansville did not—and counties with sizeable urban centers attracted others. Some African American communities were rooted in the migration of these Quakers and others who had come North and brought those they held in bondage with them, freeing them upon arrival in Indiana. Other African Americans had been legally freed in the South and had made their way to a place where the danger of being dragged back into slavery was not so great. Many other African American residents were fugitives from the institution of slavery. African Americans gathered in both rural and urban communities—where there was one family, there were likely to be several—to provide common assistance against what was generally a racist society. About 15 percent of the state's African Americans lived in the heavily Quaker counties of Randolph and Wayne and another 15 percent in the Ohio River urban counties; the rest were scattered primarily in the southern half of the state.¹ Many of these communities did get some support from sympathetic whites—generally Quakers—suggesting that the ability for African Americans to survive in Indiana was not a measure of how welcoming the state was to African Americans, but merely an indication that a few sympathetic whites could make all the difference.

For many Hoosiers of European descent, the best society was one with neither African Americans nor slaveholders; many white Hoosiers had left the South to escape that society. The society they created in Indiana prohibited slavery but placed severe restrictions on African American residents: they could not vote or hold office, their testimony could not be admitted against a white, and their children could not be educated in the public schools. For years, efforts to exclude all African Americans from the state had failed. In 1851, however, a new state constitution was written, and a controversial article excluding further African American migration to the state was proposed. This article was submitted separately to the voters, and it overwhelmingly won approval.

That many Hoosiers were out-and-out racists did not mean, however, that they supported the institution of slavery. On the national scene, slavery became the central political question during the Mexican War, when David Wilmot, a Democratic congressman from Pennsylvania, introduced an amendment to an 1846 appropriation bill for the Mexican Cession, an amendment that forbid slavery in the territories thus acquired. Five of seven voting Democratic congressmen from Indiana assented to Wilmot's Proviso, as did the two Whig congressmen, and all seven Democrats voted for the amended appropriation bill. The Proviso did not pass the Senate, where both Hoosier Senators, Democrats Edward Hannegan and Jesse Bright, opposed it, but the damage had been done to the Democratic Party, revealing a fracture at the national and state levels that Democrats would work hard to repair for the next fourteen years. Some Hoosier Democratic leaders, like Jesse Bright, would continue to protect the institution of slavery—one in which Bright was personally invested with slaves in Kentucky—as a means of holding together the alliance of Northern and Southern Democrats. The antipathy that many ordinary Hoosier Democrats felt toward slavery and slaveholders, however, meant that a mild antislavery position had popular local appeal. Democratic politicians who understood these antipathies would joust with Bright and others in winning the support of Hoosier voters.²

For most Hoosiers, however, the primary concerns that maintained party lines were the issues of state politics—fixing the internal improvements debacle, regulating banking, and moving toward a better public education system, among others—and the success with which party leaders responded to voters' concerns in those areas. For this reason, only a small fraction of Hoosiers were ever attracted to either the Liberty or the Free Soil Party. While the Liberty Party was clearly abolitionist, the Free Soil Party focused more on keeping African Americans and slaveholders out of the territories; Free Soilers gained over 5 percent of the Indiana vote in 1848, but despite having native son George W. Julian as their candidate for vice president in 1852, their vote slipped to just over 3 percent. For most Hoosier Democrats, the new Northern Democratic proposal of popular sovereignty, which left the issue of slavery to the residents of a territory, seemed the best middle ground: with their preference for settling political questions at the local level, Hoosier Democrats could appreciate leaving the issue to the territories' voters.

The petition of California to enter the Union in 1850 reinvigorated the debate and revealed that the issue of slavery threatened to destroy not only the Democratic Party but the Union as a whole. A political compromise fashioned primarily by Southern Whigs and Northern Democrats had five main features: the admission of California as a free state; the establishment of Texas's boundaries; the creation of New Mexico and Utah as territories organized under popular sovereignty; the passage of a stronger fugitive slave act; and the end of the slave trade, but not slavery, in the District of Columbia. For many Hoosier Democrats, the Compromise of 1850 was a solid affirmation of the principle of Union. For Hoosiers with strong abolitionist sympathies, the Fugitive Slave Act of 1850, which greatly streamlined the process for recovering fugitives from slavery and criminalized the act of assisting such fugitives, made the Compromise unpalatable. For Hoosier Whigs, who had tried, as had the national party, to encompass both abolitionist and proslavery tendencies, the Compromise helped push the party toward its demise.

The Compromise of 1850 created a momentary unity among Hoosier Democrats. The Democrats swept the 1852 elections and selected a popular governor, Joseph Wright, who vied with Jesse Bright for leadership of the party. But that unity was threatened when Stephen A. Douglas introduced his Nebraska bill, which placed the issue of slavery in Kansas and Nebraska under the formula of popular sovereignty, thus repealing the Missouri Compromise, which had forbidden slavery in Kansas and Nebraska. Anti–Nebraska bill sentiment in national affairs and the temperance movement at the local level brought a wide variety of disaffected Democrats, Whigs, Free Soilers, and Know Nothings together as the People's Party, which swept to victory in the 1854 election, ending Democratic dominance in the state. In 1856, the Democrats retained the governor's office and regained control of the lower house of the legislature. For state and local offices, the People's Party continued to fuse what was known nationally as the American (Know Nothing) Party and the Republican Party.

Any unity in the Hoosier Democratic Party evident in its 1856 victories disappeared with the presentation to Congress of a proslavery constitution, popularly called the Lecompton Constitution, for the proposed state of Kansas. Every Democratic congressman from the state voted for the Lecompton constitution. A broad swath of Hoosier Democrats, however, believed that the Lecompton Constitution did not represent the actual will of the majority of Kansans. The popularity of the anti-Lecompton cause began to drive a wedge between the Northern and Southern wings of the Democratic Party. President James Buchanan (1857–61), a Northern Democrat with a considerable willingness to concede to the South, tapped the like-minded Hoosier Democrat William English to find a middle ground that would keep Northern Democrats like themselves in the party but address Southern concerns. English drafted a compromise, called the English Bill, that gave the voters of Kansas a chance to vote on their proslavery constitution once again. Even with English's compromise, Hoosier Democrats edged towards splitting.

By 1858, the opposition to the Democrats in Indiana had thrown off the label of People's Party, discarding many of its anti-immigrant features and embracing the national Republican Party. The *Dred Scott* decision of 1857 had strengthened concerns that the real threat from slavery was the power of slaveholders and that their next move would be to legalize slavery in the North. Republicans believed that Kansas's fate to be a slavery state would be the North's fate as well. Although not as strongly abolitionist as many former Free Soilers would have liked, the Republicans stressed the need to keep the territories free and to limit the power of the slaveholders: "It is a question of whether the slave oligarchy shall rule, or whether the people—free people shall govern."[3] The moderate course of the Republicans served them well when the news of John Brown's raid on Harpers Ferry reached Indiana in 1859. Many Hoosiers, even in the Republican Party, equated abolitionism with fanaticism.

Brown's raid, though, captured the imagination of Hoosiers in a way that few of the political machinations that preceded it had done. Throughout most of the 1850s, the opinions Hoosiers held had remained abstractions, but the news from Harpers Ferry crystallized the concerns. Racism had prevented many Hoosiers from feeling much sympathy for the enslaved African, but the genius of the Republican Party was to paint slavery and slaveholders as threats to Northerners, too.

Much of the debate over slavery of the 1850s had been limited to those politicians and editors most engrossed in national affairs. For ordinary citizens in the early 1850s, "the temperance question is the most exciting topic that is agitating the minds of many of our citizens."[4] Temperance, which clearly separated the Democrats from the Whigs and then the Republican (People's) Party, was the partisan issue at the state level, with Democrats opposing the moralizing of their opponents. Beyond politics, for most Hoosiers the 1850s were spent at the ordinary rhythms of their lives, working, participating in their communities and churches, and tending and loving their families. That a great civil war loomed was at most a momentary fear that flitted through their minds.

ESCAPING SLAVERY THROUGH INDIANA

Jermain Loguen escaped from slavery in Tennessee in 1834 and eventually settled in Syracuse, New York, as a minister, teacher, and abolitionist. Loguen published his account twenty-five years after the escape, when slave narratives had become a popular genre. Here he recounts part of his perilous journey through the state of Indiana with his companion John Farney. The dangers began as soon as they set foot on Hoosier soil, or rather, the danger remained even though they were on free soil. Loguen—he took this name once he became a free man—clearly invents some dialogue, but his presentation provides an apt description of the nature of the Underground Railroad in the state. Loguen and Farney moved from the Ohio River to Corydon, continuing to wander until they found a sympathetic Quaker family in Washington County. They went on to Salem and then to a small African American community in Jackson County before moving through Indianapolis and out of the state.

The travellers now went along on the ice, leading their horses in Indian file, Jarm a little ahead. They left the Kentuckian foaming and swearing like a bedlamite, and kept their eyes intently upon the ice to see if it bent beneath them. Passing the center of the River, they felt safe, and for the first time raised their eyes to the opposite shore. When they started, that shore was scarcely perceptible through the milky atmosphere, but now a small village was visible a little distance from it, and three or four men were standing there, looking at them. The number of men soon increased to five or six. The fact was, that a light horse or two only had been led over, and it was still considered perilous for a heavy man and horse to venture.

As the travellers approached the shore, their color began to be seen.

"They are niggers," said one of the villagers.

"They are brave fellows, any how."

"I'll bet they are slaves running away. Let us take them up and get a pile."

"Agreed! D—n the the [*sic*] niggers! We don't want them on this side!"

When they arrived at the bank, they were six or seven rods from these men. Now they had their feet upon free soil, it become a question what to do. A word or two only was said about it, when Jarm drew out his well loaded double barrelled pistol, and said, 'Let us fire!' John also took out his pistol, and they both pointed in the air, and each discharged both barrels. The report awoke an echo on both shores, and was heard at a great distance.

"Pshaw!" said one of the citizens, "they can't be slaves."

"They are free niggers," said another, "who have been to Kentucky to spend the Holidays with their friends, and have returned in a frolic."

"Slaves never acted in that way," said another.

"They are drunk," said another, "or they had not dared come over on the ice."

A brief colloquy of that sort dispersed these wiseacres into the village, with the exception of a colored man—who was shocked by the proposal to arrest and return them to slavery. He remained when the rest were gone, and went immediately to the young men.

"What are you firing your pistols for?" said he.

"We have been travelling many days to get to a free State, and we are free now. We fired our pistols to express our joy that we were safe from our pursuers, who we think we left not far behind."

My dear fellows, you are little safer here than in Kentucky, if it is known you are slaves. Your pursuers will follow and take you here, and there are bad men enough to help them do it. Did you see those men standing with me out there?"

"Yes."

"They thought you were slaves, and agreed to take you back to your masters. But when you fired, they concluded you were free colored men, coming home in a frolic, after the holidays in Kentucky. Travelling on horse back, and shooting pistols in that way, made them so confident you were freemen, that they did not think it worth while to ask you any questions."

"I thought this was a free state?"

"It is called a free State—but the laws allow slaveholders to hunt their slaves here, and hold them, to take them back."

"Where, then, can we be safe? We cannot go back to slavery—we had rather die."

"Yes, and somebody will die before we go back," said John Farney, driving a ball into his pistol.

"There is no place in the States where you can be safe. To be safe, you must get into Canada. I am sorry to say that the only power that gives freedom in North America, is in England."

"How can we get to Canada?"

"Follow the North Star—do you know the North Star?"

"Yes."

"Have you any money?"

"Yes."

"There are those in the free States who will do what they can for you. Your danger is in falling upon enemies. It will not be safe to stop here a moment. Take that road, and go to Corridon, a small village about twenty miles from here, and enquire for a man by the name of—. He is an abolitionist, and will keep you and tell you what next to do."

$\sim$

"What do you think of the case now?" said John, after they mounted and rode out of the hearing of their white friend.

"Bad—bad enough. But we are in great luck, after all."

"How is that?—twenty miles to a friend, hungry and sleepy, the horses tired—and in good luck?"

"It is evening—we had been off our guard entirely, and lost, had we been earlier; we were exactly in time to find the friend who just left us; our shooting saved us again and dispersed our enemies; the night covers our pursuers with darkness or sleep, to give us a chance to get out of their way. It is astonishing how lucky we have been. But we must not go twenty miles to-night. Our future safety depends much on our horses; and to go that distance, after all they have done to-day, is too much for them."

"We had best stop for the night at the first place that seems safe. We shall soon find if there is danger, and no small force will attempt to disturb us."

In this manner they talked until they came in front of a small Dutch groggery, with a tavern sign before it, about eight miles from the spot where they landed in Indiana. Here they stopped, as ordinary travellers. If there were any accommodations in the house, they were already occupied, and their lodging was a little empty log barn—their provisions for themselves were furnished from their saddle-bags, and their bed was the bare plank beside their horses. They slept soundly on the hard timber, and took an early start for Corridon, twelve miles distant—where they arrived about eight o'clock in the morning.

They were not long finding the person to whom they were directed. He was a true hearted colored man, ready to advise and assist them to the best of his means. They spent the day with him. It was the Sabbath, and gladly would they have accepted it as a day of rest. But the certainty that the hounds were behind them, rabid for their blood, robbed them of the quiet necessary to repose. Their horses, however, whose strength had been so well tested, knew no danger, present or absent, and rested away their weariness.

The colored brother who entertained them, from absolute poverty, had grown to be a man of substance, notwithstanding the prejudice and injustice of pro-slavery men and laws. From him they received valuable information in regard to their condition in the free States, and advice to get out of them into Canada. But he knew little of the country. The most he could do was, to tell them they would find a valuable friend in a Mr. Overrals, of Indianapolis, about two hundred miles distant, as he supposed, in a north-westerly direction—but could say nothing of the intervening country and its inhabitants.

At midnight, the fugitives took the last lunch with their hospitable friend, and mounted their horses for Indianapolis. They were soon lost in an immense forest through which their path lay—and for three cold days and nights wandered about without food enough to sustain life, and without sight of human faces, other than the roving hunters, in whose camps they slept at night. Their path in the woods was circuitous and angular, and covered with snow—therefore they were mis-led from a north-west to a north-east coarse, and were travelling towards Kentucky. On the third day from Corridon, weary and hungry beyond endurance, they come into a country where white men lived, which was partially cultivated—but the inhabitants refused them food. Such was the extremity of their distress from hunger and cold, that their courage abated, and they began to talk of returning to Kentucky.

In this extremity, they came before a log house and asked for food. The landlord looked at them a moment with an expression of unutterable kindness, and said:—

"You are very hungry?"

"Yes."

"How long since you have eat anything?"

"We have eat very little for three days."

"Come in, and my wife will get you a breakfast."

Reverend J. W. Loguen, *Rev. J. W. Loguen, as a Slave and as a Freeman; A Narrative of Real Life* (Syracuse, N.Y.: J. G. K. Truair, 1859), 302–19.

1852 AFRICAN AMERICAN EXCLUSION VOTE

In 1852, Hoosiers voted on a new state constitution, and they were given the opportunity to vote separately on Article 13, a provision of whether African Americans would be permitted to settle in the state.

Section 1. No negro or mulatto shall come into or settle in the State, after the adoption of this Constitution.

Section 2. All contracts made with any Negro or Mulatto coming into the State, contrary to the provisions of the foregoing section, shall be void; and any person who shall employ such Negro or Mulatto, or otherwise encourage him to remain in the State, shall be fined in any sum not less than ten dollars, nor more than five hundred dollars.

Section 3. All fines which may be collected for a violation of the provisions of this article, or of any law which ay hereafter be passed for the purpose of carrying the same into execution, shall be set apart and appropriated for the colonization of such Negroes and Mulattoes, and their descendants, as may be in the State at the adoption of this Constitution, and may be willing to emigrate.

Section 4. The General Assembly shall pass laws to carry out the provisions of this article.

Indiana's Constitution of 1851, Article 13—Negroes and Mulattoes.

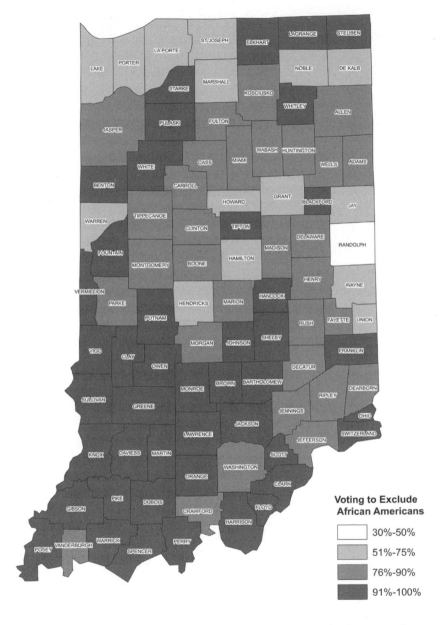

**Voting to Exclude
African Americans**

30%-50%

51%-75%

76%-90%

91%-100%

Indiana Election Returns, 1816–1851, compiled by Dorothy Riker and Gayle Thornbrough. Indiana Historical Collections, vol. 40 (Indianapolis: Indiana Historical Bureau, 1960).

INDIANA'S LEADING ABOLITIONIST

A year after Wayne County's George Julian was the nominee for vice president on the Free Soil ticket opposed to the extension of slavery, he declined an invitation to attend the twentieth anniversary celebration of the American Anti-Slavery Society. His letter was probably written to be read aloud at the convention. It downplays the differences between Julian's position and that of William Lloyd Garrison, one of the most radical of the prominent abolitionists. John Freeman was a free African American who settled in Indianapolis in the 1840s; in 1853, a Missouri slaveholder, under the provisions of the new Fugitive Slave Act, claimed Freeman as his slave. Freeman was forced to make extraordinary efforts to prove his freedom, laying bare the onerous nature of the Fugitive Slave Act.

Centreville, Ind.
Nov. 18, 1853

Wm Lloyd Garrison,

Dear Sir;

I have received your letter of the 10th inst. inviting me to be present at the twentieth Anniversary of the formation of the American Anti-Slavery Society, to be held in Philadelphia, on the third and fourth December next. . . . Most gladly would I be with you, and avail myself of the catholic invitation of your society to occupy its platform "untrammeled in regard to thought or speech." Nothing could afford me more heartfelt gratification than to embibe afresh the resolute purpose and martyr spirit of our great movement, by a friendly communion with its heroes; and it is therefore with unfeigned regret that I find myself precluded by other engagements from attending your celebration.

The object of your society is "the speedy and eternal overthrow of chattel slavery in our land." The magnitude of such a work requires a faith in those who undertake it commensurate with its achievement. They must have faith in Providence, in Rectitude, in the triumph of the Right through the sincere strivings of men. . . . If we really believed in the truths to which we subscribe in words; if, in our judgment, we could find but "one strong thing in this earth, the *just* thing, the *true* thing"; if we could fully realize that justice is omnipotent and that slavery and every other refuge of his *must* perish, because opposed to the beneficent ordainments of the universe; and if men every where would acknowledge and practically apply these truths, humanity would be redeemed from its woes, and the millennial day would be ushered in upon the world. . . . For myself, I believe the Providence of God, availing itself of the blindness and wickedness of men, is hastening on a great crisis in the history of our country; and that the cause in which we are engaged is passing through a transition period from a feeble and unpopular to a powerful and dominant movement among the great forces that are shaking the world.

This opinion is based upon facts which to some indicate the decline of free principles. The passage of the Compromise measures, now more than three years since, and the decree which simultaneously went forth that there is no higher law than the wicked enactments of men; the preaching of multitudinous heaps of lower law sermons, and the joining hands of Castle Garden politicians and atheistical doctors of divinity in the endeavor of to dethrone Jehovah and inaugurate the Devil in his stead; the holding of grand union meetings throughout the country after the union had been already saved by the nostrums and plasters of its political doctors; the calling out of the army and navy by the federal authorities to assist in the return of a fugitive slave, and the effort to drag from the grave of tyranny and foist into our jurisprudence the infernal doctrine of constructive treason; the cold blooded conspiracy of the whig and democratic parties last year at Baltimore, against republicanism, humanity, and God; the recent case of John Freeman at Indianapolis, and the reeking villainy of the Marshall of Indiana in stripping the body of his victim so that a Christless squad of perjured miscreants and kidnappers might swear according to the pattern, which they did. . . . [M]any kindred facts which I might name are not the tokens of disaster to our movement but the sure prophecies of its triumph. As the natural fruits of the slave power, appealing to the hearts and consciences of the people, they were demanded by the times; for it has been said truly that wrong institutions must grow to their full stature, and display all their diabolical enormity, before men will engage earnestly in the work of their overthrow. We should not desire to have Satan act with a prudent circumspection, and enlist the world on his side or disarm its opposition by disguising himself in the drapery of decency. Let him show his cloven foot and make palpable the fact that he *is* a devil, and his empire will be subverted.

Herein should the enemies of slavery thank God and take courage. We have unmasked the dragon. We have shorn it of its long permitted inhumanity from the right of search and compelled it to stand up in its unveiled ugliness before the judgment seat of the world. The Slave power has itself become a most efficient helper in its own destruction. Its unhallowed rule has at length set the world to thinking, its great heart to beating, and its great voice to agitating. The Anti-Slavery spirit has pervaded our literature, and millions of hearts, in the old world and the new, are now throbbing responsive to the sufferings of the American slave. . . . It is remorselessly breaking into fragments the great political parties of our country; and at the same time extending its dominion into the churches and hierarchies, which it will either purify or scatter to the four winds as a preliminary to the formation of other systems, wherein shall dwell righteousness. These facts, and the glorious future of which they are the promise, should animate us with courage, constancy, and an unfaltering faith in our continued labors for the oppressed. You, I am sure, and those who constitute the American Anti-Slavery society, will not be blinded or disheartened by the irregular ebb and flow of political currents, or by facts which drift about upon their surface, but you will penetrate beneath it, to those great moral tides, which underlie, and heave onward, the political, the religious, and the whole framework of society.

With an assured trust in the triumph of the Right, I am,

Yours very truly,

Geo. W. Julian

George W. Julian Papers, Indiana State Library, Indianapolis.

DEMOCRATIC THOUGHTS ON THE COMPROMISE OF 1850

As debate raged over the slaveholding status of Kansas and Nebraska in 1854, Jeptha Garrigus, who had immigrated to Parke County from New Jersey, wrote to his congressman, John G. Davis, to convey his point of view. Garrigus was an early settler of Parke County and the patriarch of a large family of moderate means. His views on slavery in the territories were common among many Hoosier Democrats who sought to reconcile their personal antipathy to slavery and African Americans with their willingness to open the territories to slavery.

Gallatin Ia. Feby 25—1854—

Friend John, yours of the 11 inst came to hand some Days ago. I had one of my splls on me, and could not answer It then and do not know that my head is clear anough at this time to answer you as I ought, but will try, if I understand the compromise of 20—it prohibets slavory north of 36.30— and the compromise of 50— leaves the subject of Slavory to the people forming the state when admitted into The union, now, if the two compromises do not clash let them Both stand for the sake of peace, if they do clash, do not Touch or meddle with the compromise of 50— it cannot harm the north, or benafit the South to repeal the compromise of 20— for I do not believe that Slavory ever will be wanted By the people north of 36.30— as I believe Slaves are not Profitable north of a cotton growing country. therefore I do not think the compromise of 20— worth contending about, at any rate toulch not the compromise of 50— if I lived in the south I would not care for the compromise of 20, as I do not believe It any be[n] afit to the South, I am a northen man with southern Principels, I do not believe the north have any right to meddle With the subject of Slavory, the South have just as much right to go north and steal horses, as the north have to go south and steal Negroes. These in short are my opinions, you may show this if you chuse to do so, to some good Southern democrat. As for our friend Jesse D. [Bright] he is Joined to his idols let him alone, This from the Old Jersey Blue

Jeptha Garrigus

John G. Davis Papers, Indiana Historical Society, Indianapolis.

THE NEBRASKA BILL

For many Hoosier Democrats, the establishment of the principle of popular sovereignty in the territories was more important than what they perceived as the very slight risk that slavery would actually be established in those territories, as this Democratic editorial makes clear.

THE NEBRASKA BILL.

This bill is not yet acted on in the House of Representatives. As it passed the Senate, it gives to the people of the territories of Nebraska and Kansas the right to make all their municipal laws. The conferring of this right is much disapproved of by some who have fears, that those who shall inhabit them will not be able to form such laws as they may need.

Those who are opposed to this power being conferred on the people make Slave legislation the cloak to cover their opposition to the bill. These same people are hard to pleas. They are always growling about the Slave power in Congress, and when it is proposed that Congress shall put the whole matter out of its hands, they are still disappointed. We think it right that the national government should abandon the notion that it upholds Slavery in the Territory south of thirty-six and a half degrees. We believe the public sentiment of this Nation is against Slavery and rightfully so. It is a great evil, one that the South is as tired of as the North; but the people do not want the Negro population freed among them. We believe the passage of these bills, will ensure the early settlement of the territories and their admission into the Union as free States. But if we should be disappointed and the people of these territories should adopt slavery it will be their fault and not that of the National government, or of the other States.

Time will prove that all the opposition arises from a desire to restrict the inhabitants in their rights to self-government. Every attempt to return power into the hands of the people, has its sturdy opponents. It is but a few years since a powerful party in this State contended the people ought not be entrusted with the election of their Judges. But fortunately for the human character wherever the people exercise most directly the greater number of govermental functions, their government is cheapest and best. The extension of the right of suffrage has at every step met with determined opposition and yet it has always proved to be a blessing, and none of the troubles promised by its opponents have been realized. We hope that these bills will be so amended, in the House, that the qualification for voters shall be as liberal as they are in Indiana or Illinois and that they shall have the selection of their Executive and Judicial officers. And when the people of the Territories shall have had the opportunity to exercise these inalienable rights, it will prove so much superior to the old apprentice system, that all will wonder that it had not been changed half a century sooner. Those who are opposed to Slavery, that now opposes the National Government washing its hands of it, hope to divide the Democratic party thereby and obtain political power. In this they will find themselves mistaken—democrats can differ on one or two measures and still maintain their unity on all of their great political principles, and at the ballot box.

Brookville Franklin Democrat, March 31, 1854.

THE PEOPLE'S PARTY

The People's Party was the name under which the Republican Party arose in Indiana. Welcoming former Whigs and Free Soilers, together with antislavery Democrats and the nativists who would form the core of the American Party elsewhere, this broad coalition presented itself less as a party than as a pure expression of the people. The People's Party successfully pursued this partyless strategy into the 1858 local elections; nevertheless, People's Party politicians hewed closely to the Republican Party line, which in 1854 was opposition to Stephen A. Douglas's Nebraska bill opening Kansas and Nebraska to slavery through popular sovereignty. Opponents of Douglas had come to term Northern Democrats "doughfaces": Northern men with Southern principles.

THE CONVENTION

The People's Convention meets to-day in the Court House. We have to nominate candidates for the office of Representative, Sheriff, Treasurer, Recorder, Commissioner for this, the 1st district, Surveyor, and Coroner. There should also be appointed a committee to meet a similar one from Miami, to nominate a candidate for Prosecutor of the Common Pleas Court, and one to attend a Judicial District Convention that may meet to nominate a candidate for Judge in place of Pettit, resigned. Among those proposed for the several offices a first rate ticket can be made, and it is to be hoped that no other considerations may influence the convention in their choice than a desire to secure competent officers, and such as are decided in their opposition to the Nebraska outrage. The latter should be the leading consideration, and all others considered minor and secondary.

Among those named for office on the People's ticket we have no choice. We are ready to exert our utmost ability in behalf of any respectable white man, who is not a dough-face nor a slave to his party leaders, that the convention may nominate. The only political test to be regarded is upon the questions involved in the Nebraska law, and we are ready to waive, for the time being, all other predilections.

The Convention will be free from the influence of management, or the control or dictation of leaders. The whole matter will be in the hands of the People, and if, form the whole Whig and Free Soil parties, and the intelligent and independent three-fourths of the Democracy, a good ticket cannot be formed, it is time to give up all hope of having the laws of the State honestly administered by competent men.

No man is entitled to office above another. It belongs to the People to say who their servants shall be, and it should be distinctly understood that the People's Convention acknowledge no claims in a candidate but correct political principles, honesty, and capacity, and that they will rather build up and strengthen their party with such than drag through an uncertain canvass those of an opposite character. The convention has the opportunity of offering to the people a ticket inferior to none that has ever been before the county. Let it be done, for its candidates will be our officers.

Logansport Journal, August 19, 1854.

DRED SCOTT AND KANSAS

The Indianapolis Journal *was the voice of the Republican Party in Indiana. Funded by party leaders and subsidized by public printing contracts when the Republicans were in power, its editors rarely strayed from the official party line. In this piece its editors reacted to the* Dred Scott *decision, which declared that neither Congress nor the territorial legislature had any power over slavery in a territory, and connected the decision to the problems emerging in Kansas. They raised the theme that the decision opened the way for slavery to be permitted in the heretofore free states.*

KANSAS

We publish to-day the account given by Gov. [John W.] Geary [territorial governor of Kansas] to the St. Louis *Democrat,* of the outrages perpetrated by the pro slavery or Democratic party of Kansas, upon free State citizens, and his views of the condition of affairs in that territory. From this, which is most undoubted authority, it will be seen that the statements published by the Republican papers last fall, and which the Democratic speakers and organs pronounced sheer fabrications, and dismissed with the stereotyped sneer, "Kansas lies," were strictly true, or rather less than the truth, in their exposure of the infamous barbarities practiced by the partisans of the Democracy in that country. It will be further seen that the policy inaugurated by the Nebraska bill, and affirmed by the Dred Scott decision, which makes the support and extension of slavery a duty of the National Government, will, in all probability, be consummated by the enactment of a pro slavery Constitution in Kansas. There is nothing to prevent it but the sheer force of overwhelming numbers, and that force is so skillfully diverted and broken by the recent acts of the Legislature that it can hardly be felt at all. The laws have been arranged, as all who have read them as they were published know, with a special reference to the exclusion of all Free State voters possible, and the admission of all the Missourians possible. The census is entrusted to pro slavery officers, for the Free State men do not hold a single office in the Territory, and these officers can make such registries as will answer their purposes. The control of the elections, returns, and all the duties appertaining to them, are in pro slavery hands. The Free State men have no chance but in the fairness of their enemies, and two years of war and robbery, or of oppression and insult, are pretty good indication of the sort of fairness they have to expect at such hands. It is possible that the Free State strength may predominate so far as to defeat all the advantages that the laws have given the pro slavery party, but it is not at all probable. We think, with Gov. Geary, that the chances are ten to one that Kansas will be a Slave State. If it is not, it will not be the fault of the Administration or the Democratic party. They have done their best to make it so. If made free at all it will be in spite of the impediments of Democratic territorial legislation, and Democratic encouragement from abroad to the Missourians.

Kansas a slave State—the solemn compact with the North not only abrogated but its fruits stolen by the South,—the Dred Scott decision, which makes slavery legal everywhere,—and Mr. Buchanan's Inaugural, which pledges the whole power of the Government to carry out the policy advocated by [John C.]Calhoun, leave the nation as purely a slave supporting, slave trading, slave beating nation as Algiers. Hitherto the law has kept the institution at home. It has been allowed no validity except where positively permitted by law. Now it is made an institution co-extensive with the Constitution, and it is very doubtful if the Free States, under Judge Taney's decision, can prohibit its existence within their own limits. The whole nation is now responsible for it, charged with its crimes, and blackened with its iniquities. Algiers is no worse. But the decision has only anticipated the result at which political influences were driving. We have come by a new and short road into the "Valley of the Shadow of Death," but the road we were going, and which Mr. Buchanan distinctly declared we should pursue for the four years he had the direction of our steps, was leading more circuitously, but not the less certainly, to the same point. We are now to get out the best way we can, and the

Supreme Court's decision neither increases nor intensifies the difficulties in the way. It has done nothing but give an infamous doctrine the countenance of five men, and brought the Supreme Court into a contempt that we hoped never to see manifested for so exalted a tribunal.

Indianapolis Indiana Daily Journal, March 20, 1857.

BLEEDING KANSAS AND THE LECOMPTON CONSTITUTION

The controversy engendered by the proposal to admit Kansas into the Union as a state that permitted slavery, based on elections marred by violence, boycotts, and parallel elections and conventions, demanded a solution. Adding difficulty to the entire affair was the large grant of land that Kansas sought with its admission. William H. English, a congressman from southern Indiana, headed the committee that attempted to find a compromise for the proslavery Lecompton Constitution, opposed by Republicans and many Indiana Democrats who were supporters of Stephen A. Douglas. English was friendly to the Buchanan administration and thus to accommodation to the slavery wing of the Democratic Party, whose foremost Northern leader was slaveholding Hoosier senator Jesse D. Bright. But English had marked out a position different from that of Bright and the Southern Democrats, much to Bright's chagrin: "It is to be regretted that you + I could not have harmonized on this question."[5] English was attempting to take a position that would insure that the people of Kansas would have a legitimate say on the issue of slavery (and thus pleasing many Hoosier voters as well, who believed that a legitimate vote would turn down slavery in Kansas), while not alienating the Southern Democrats. The English Bill reduced the land grant to the new state to a size consistent with that given other states, but made it available to the state only if it accepted the Lecompton (proslavery) Constitution. If Kansans rejected the reduction in the land grant and thus the proslavery constitution, they would also be rejecting immediate statehood. In an election with less violence, Kansans rejected the smaller grant and statehood. William Wick was a leading Democrat in Indiana.

Indianapolis 26 April '58

Dear Sir,

I am myself well enough satisfied with your Kansas proposition—and doubt not your good intentions. Yet it will be, for a time, quite a misfortune to party operations here, if it should turn out that those people out in K. should conclude to vote *in* the Lecompton Constitution: For it will be immediately said that as the

Republicans prophesied that the secret intention of the Dem. party was to bring in K as a slave state, by force fraud, or bribery or all together, so it has turned out that for a gift of land the corrupt fellows in K have been purchased, and also with an eye to Senatorships, & State Offices. And it may turn out that you may be held responsible to an unpleasant extent. I wish the land had been left out, or pledged to K. whenever it should become a state under any Constitution. I more wish that the bill before your Com^{ee} of Conferences acted had been laid on the table for good.

The result would have been free action in Kansas, [illegible] by land, and a most judicious postponement of admission of K as a state.

I hope you will come through safely, as to your personal interests, and that our party interest may not suffer. As to Kansas, just let him sweat.

Very truly,

Wick

William H. English Collection, Indiana Historical Society, Indianapolis.

THE SPLIT IN THE DEMOCRATIC PARTY

The question of whether to admit Kansas under the proslavery Lecompton Constitution split the Northern Democratic Party into two factions. In Indiana, the pro-Lecompton faction was led by Senator Jesse D. Bright, and in this letter, he equated the Anti-Lecompton Democrats and their leader, Stephen A. Douglas of Illinois, with the abolitionists. Bright was writing to Fort Wayne banker Allen Hamilton, a former Whig who had just been elected as a Democrat to the Indiana State Senate. An attempt had been made by the Republican-dominated legislature to replace the two Democratic United States senators with Republicans.

Jesse D. Bright
Dec. 1858
Washington
December

My old friend

I am not attall surprized to find you disgusted with the state of things that surround you now, at Indianapolis. I have had just enough experience in political affairs their, to know how to sympathize with you in the description you give of matters and things. Whether the contemptible f[a]rce of choosing a couple of Abolitionists to come here claiming to be Senators is enacted or not, all the odium and disgrace has attached from what has been already said and done, and so far as I am concerned, I wish they may be guilty of the crowning act. I care not one rush, for what, has or may be done on this subject.

I have not, nor shall I ever regard a set of men in this Country who call themselves "Anti-Lecompton Democrats," in any other light than Abolitionists, and most of them, Rotten in every sense of the term.

I count and defy the opposition of every one of them, from their lying hypocritical Demagogical Master Douglass, down to the [scrawniest] puppy in the kennel. The remittance you speak of is all right. I will give it the proper direction when received. Glad to hear from you at any time

I am Yours Truly,

J. D. Bright

P.S. To write a letter like this and mark it *private* would be cowardly. What I have here written are my opinions, anywhere + everywhere.

B

Allen Hamilton Papers, Indiana State Library, Indianapolis.

RIGHTS OF NEGROES IN INDIANA

The Brookville Franklin Democrat, *although staunchly racist in its belief that the United States was a white man's country, nevertheless recognized in 1860 some basic human rights for African Americans, thus questioning one of the basic premises of the* Dred Scott *decision that African Americans "had no rights the white man was bound to respect."*

RIGHTS OF NEGROES IN INDIANA

A case is pending, in our circuit court, wherein a resident negro is the plaintiff and white men are defendants. The action is brought by the negro, James Hays, against George W. Kimble and others, white men, for damages sustained by the plaintiff. During the present term of the court counsel have sprung the question as to the right of a negro to maintain an action against a white man in this State. The complaint is such as is usually filed in such cases. The defendants, by counsel, made a motion to rule the plaintiff to security for costs; and as the foundation for this motion make the following showing:

"George W. Kimble and others,

    vs.   Civil action.

James Hays,

George W. Kimble, one of said defendants, personally comes into open court and says that the plaintiff is a pure negro, of pure negro blood, born and raised in North Carolina, and he, therefore, prays that he may be required to find security for costs herein; and in default thereof that this suit and action be dismissed.   G. W. KIMBLE

Sworn and subscribed to in open court, February 10th,
1860.   JOHN M. JOHNSON, clerk."

To sustain this motion defendants' counsel insist, that inasmuch as the Supreme Court of the United States have decided that negroes cannot become citizens of the United States; that they were not considered as a portion of *the people* at the time of making the Declaration of Independence and at the time of framing the constitution of the United States; and were forbidden to immigrate to this State by our present constitution, that they cannot be recognized either as citizens or people in contemplation of law and consequently have no right to sue white men in this State.

On the other hand, counsel for the plaintiff admit the full force of the decision in the Dred Scott case—that negroes cannot become citizens of the United States; and that the plaintiff is a "pure negro of pure negro blood," that his race were not included in the phrase *"the people"* at the making of the Declaration of Independence and framing the constitution of the United States; and that immigration of that class of persons is prohibited by the thirteenth article of the constitution of the State of Indiana. But, they insist, that inasmuch as the defendant does not aver that the plaintiff has immigrated to this State since the adoption of the present constitution that so far as that prohibition is concerned it can have no weight in the case at bar. And that, admitting the plaintiff to be a full blooded negro, he is still entitled to maintain this suit; that our constitution intended to afford protection to every branch of the human family; and that the plaintiff is included in the class of persons mentioned in section twelfth of the bill of rights which is in the following language:

> "All courts shall be open; and every man, for injury done to him in his person, property or reputation, shall have remedy by due course of law," &c.

That the plaintiff is *a man* and included, in the generic term, by that section of the constitution, and not necessarily denied his civil right to maintain this action because he is not a *citizen* nor one of *"the people."*

The statute is silent as to the rights of negroes to maintain suits in our courts. Plaintiffs and defendants are denominated *persons* and not *citizens* nor *people*. So that the question is not solvable by any statutory enactment, but left to such construction as the courts may give as to the rights of negroes to maintain suits. The motion, to rule the plaintiff to costs in this case, has been denied, and exceptions taken to the ruling of the court. If this case be taken to the supreme court we shall, then, be judicially informed whether a negro has or has not civil rights which the laws of this State will protect. We confess that we do not sympathize, as abolitionists do, with the colored population; but, at the same time, think it unjust to allow white men to oppress negroes with impunity. The points in this case will be given, if a trial be had, which will show that to deny the right of the plaintiff would be a moral outrage.

Brookville Franklin Democrat, February 24, 1860.

JOHN BROWN

Clinton County farmer James Messler articulated an attitude typical of many Hoosiers who opposed slavery, but could not condone Brown's attack on Harpers Ferry. Earlier in his life, Messler had flatboated on the Mississippi, coming into direct contact with slavery.

March the 22nd 1860

Dear Brother

I received yours of the 15th inst the day before yesterday and was glad to hear from you again— We have fine weather here now the farmers very buisy plowing Neil has his Oats ground broke and has commenced sowing he is going to put in ten acres of Oats and fifteen acres of flax and ten acres of corn. John will finish braking for Oats tomorrow if it does not rain he is going to sow eight acres of oats and four acres of flax and intends putting in about twelve or thirteen acres of corn— John is not very well at the present—

You asked me in one of your letters some time ago what I thought about the hanging of John Brown. I think it was just and necessary. I do not defend slavery but as long as slavery exists according to the laws of the United States so long must we put up with it—I believe that Brown ment good but he could not accomplish a little good without a great deal of harme—Brown and his confederates have lost their lives with other their oponants and what good has it done the slaves[?] not any it has drawn the cords of their bondage tighter—I can not but think that Brown was slightly deranged but still I think he deserved hanging as he has been the cause of several lives being taken and if he had been spared perhaps he would have done more harme—and another thing it was necessary that there should be an example to deter others from doing the same—

This has been a very warm day and the snow is melting fast and if it dont turn colder the snow will all be gone by tomorrow night and then we will have to take the mud again—no more at present.

Your brother
Jas. W. Messler.

Messler Family Letters, Indiana State Library, Indianapolis.

TWO

~

The Election of 1860 and Secession

$\mathcal{T}$HE ELECTION YEAR of 1860 opened with the reverberations of John Brown's raid still ringing. For many Southerners, the raid and the conflicts over Kansas had reinforced the perception that no one in the North, not even the Democrats, could be trusted. In April, the Democrats met in Charleston; Stephen A. Douglas was the likely nominee, but he lacked the two-thirds majority needed for the nomination. Most Southern Democrats believed Douglas was insufficiently supportive of the institution of slavery, and when Douglas was unwilling to commit more strongly to slavery, the Charleston convention ended without a nominee, with several Southern delegations walking out before the conclusion. When the Democrats met again in Baltimore, Southern extremists again walked, but this time Douglas was able to gain a nomination from the remaining delegates. The Southern Democrats then nominated John Breckenridge for president and Joseph Lane, who once resided in Indiana, as vice president. The Democratic split was echoed in Indiana, thanks to a number of Hoosier Democrats, notably Jesse D. Bright, who were closely allied with the Buchanan administration and its patronage and who tended to follow Buchanan's vice president, Breckinridge. While powerful members of the Democratic Party supported Breckinridge, the bulk of Hoosier Democrats lined up behind Douglas, solidifying the wing of the party headed by Joseph Wright.

Douglas and the Northern Democrats ran on a platform of popular sovereignty. The Southern Democrats stood for the continued protection of their constitutional right to hold slaves in the territories, on the basis of the *Dred Scott* decision. Some Southerners, generally former Whigs, nominated John Bell as a candidate to preserve the Union on the basis of the Constitution. Finally, Republicans in the North rallied behind a moderate candidate in Abraham Lincoln, committed to preventing the spread of slavery into the territories and limiting the power of the slaveholders in national politics. In Indiana, the contest was primarily between Douglas and Lincoln.

Indiana, like several key states, held its state and local elections in October. The results of those elections suggested that Republicans had solidified their hold on the state; together with October elections in Ohio and Pennsylvania, they foretold the likely election of Lincoln the following month. The Republicans beat back Southern talk of disunion. Lincoln was elected, with over 51 percent of the vote in the state—even if he had only had one opponent, he still would have swept the state.

Lincoln's election precipitated the secession crisis. South Carolina was the first to leave in mid-December, to be joined over the next six weeks by the rest of the states of the Deep South. Even then, some in the North believed that secession was still a bluff. Others said to let them secede: "When they have suffered the benefits of disunion about a year they will be glad to get back on any terms."[1]

Yet secession loomed as a real threat to Indiana. With Louisiana out of the Union, Indiana lost one of its most important markets, New Orleans. And the possibility that all the slave states would leave the Union marked the Ohio River as the potential new boundary between the two new nations, nations that seemed potentially on the verge of war. Some in Indiana blustered that if Kentucky were to secede, so should Indiana. An early 1861 Union meeting in Perry County resolved: "That if no concession and compromises can be obtained, and a disunion shall be unfortunately made between the Northern and Southern states, then the commercial, manufacturing, and agricultural interests of this county requires us to say that we cannot consent that the Ohio river shall be the boundary line of contending nations, and we earnestly desire that if a line is to be drawn between the North and the South, that line shall be found north of us."[2]

Republicans, who had gained control of the state legislature, sent the newly elected Republican governor, Henry Lane, to the United States Senate, and Oliver P. Morton, the lieutenant governor, became governor. The legislature passed a resolution recognizing that Southerners had a right to regulate slavery, but asserting the need to preserve the Union. Others thought it necessary to go further, as Robert Dale Owen, a former Democratic congressman and the son of New Harmony founder Robert Owen, put it, to "conciliate adverse + irritated feelings" by reaching out to moderate men of all parties.[3] In the U.S. Congress, John Crittenden had already proposed a broad set of compromise measures, the centerpiece of which was to write the Missouri Compromise line into the U.S. Constitution, prohibiting slavery north of the 36°30' line and permitting slavery south of it. The only part of the plan that even a significant minority of Republicans would concede was constitutional protection of slavery in the states in which it currently existed; Republicans refused to protect the extension of slavery in any way. A Washington Peace Conference, to which Governor Morton sent only Republicans, could do little better.[4] Compromise failed.

DEMOCRATS PREPARE A RACIST CAMPAIGN

Early in 1860, Indiana congressman William English wrote to Nahum Capen, the postmaster at Boston and thus evidently an important figure in the Massachusetts Democratic Party, to learn how African Americans were treated in that most abolitionist of states.

Confidential

Washington City
Feby 1st 1860

My dear Sir,

At the suggestion of the National Democratic Central Committee, I am preparing a document for general circulation at the approaching Presidential canvass, the object of which is to show that the Republican party are in favor of establishing equality between Negroes and white people, and I desire to procure all the information I can, tending to establish that position.

To that end, you will greatly oblige me by furnishing, at your earliest convenience, information as to the action of that party in your state upon the subject

1. Are Negroes + Mulattoes restricted from coming into your state to live? Has any effort been made to restrict them?
2. May they, under any circumstances, vote at elections?—If so, what number of this class of voters probably have your + what ticket do they vote?
3. May they hold Office? Have they held Office?
4. May they testify in the courts in cases where white persons are parties?
5. May they be jurors?—or lawyers?
6. May they intermarry with whites? Do they?

If they may do any of these things, can you furnish striking examples. And by the action of what party was the Authority given?

Please state any and all facts in addition tending to show that party to be in favor of equalizing the two races.—Such as speeches + declarations of leading Republicans, +c.—enclosing extracts + documents as far as convenient + much oblige the cause +

Your friend + obt. servt.
Wm H. English
Nahum Capen, Esq. of Mass.

N.B. What is the general character of your Colored population as to improvidence, immorality, pauperism, + crime? Is it not generally true, that they work only when employed in menial capacities under the eye + direction of white persons?

William H. English Papers, Indiana Historical Society, Indianapolis.

DEMOCRATS SPLIT

The first rift of the 1860 election occurred within the Democratic Party, when Southerners walked out of the Charleston convention to prevent the nomination of Stephen A. Douglas as their presidential candidate. Northern Democrats like the editor of the LaPorte Times *condemned these "secessionists" as extremists in the mode of the Northern abolitionists and held out their program as the middle course.*

THE SECESSION MOVEMENT.

The delegates who seceded from the National Convention, recently held at Charleston, represent the extremists of the South,—that class of Southern ultraists who think that the perpetuity of the Union is only desirable when their peculiar institution is guarded by the most positive legislation. Like the Abolitionists of the North, there is no middle ground for them. It is all one thing or nothing. It is not strange that such an element should have an existence in this country. One extreme produces another, and each will continue to recede farther and farther from a central, or conservative position. The leading object in the minds of these extremists is either lust for power, or bull-headed opposition. There are men, who are always found opposing everything advanced or sustained by others,—not from principle, is their opposition drawn, but from a desire to be pitted against something or somebody. These are just the men to be found,—and who are found—in the ranks of the Northern and Southern ultraists. Both are equally dangerous to the country. That such an element as this should have found its way into the Democratic party *is* strange. The conservatism of its principles, enunciated in State and National platforms,—obedience to all law, the retention of the provisions of the Constitution, and the preservation of the Union under any and all circumstances, being its avowed objects—presents an insurmountable barrier, to any "Union-slider," or Southern secessionist, who might desire an affiliation on other grounds. The Democratic party is better off without these hangers-on. The man who connects himself with the Democratic party for any other reason than that its principles accord with his views of right, is doing the party an injury, and is working out for himself no good. The demands of the Southern secessionists, as evinced in the Charleston Convention, are absurd. What Northern Democrat, do they suppose, could assent to the adoption of a platform asserting the right of Congressional intervention for the protection of slavery in the Territories, or for the re-establishment of the traffic in slaves on the high seas, and be sustained at home. Can any Southern man advocate both these propositions, and receive the support of the Southern people? We doubt it. The predominate element of the South is conservative. The ties that bind them to the North, are too strong to be severed by a self-destructive blow. Their rights under the Constitution are too well understood by them to be endangered by demands greater than that instrument affords. Whatever Southern politicians and demagogues may demand, the *people* of the South want their constitutional rights, and nothing more. The bolters of the Charleston Convention, we feel assured, do not represent Southern sentiment. They only represent, as we before stated, the ultraism of the South. And now that this element has been lopped off, the Democracy can breathe freer, on account of its purification.

It is well that the Democracy of Charleston adjourned without making a nomination. At Baltimore the South will have an opportunity to show her love for the Union, which no man doubts. She will then be represented by delegates upon the direct issue, now presented to her—and it is to be seen if she really demands Congressional protection, and the liberty, unrestrained by law, to swarm her shores with new importations of African slaves. The South is true to the Union and Democracy—she will prove herself to be so at Baltimore.

LaPorte Times, May 12, 1860.

DOUGLAS DEMOCRATS

Most Hoosier Democrats supported Stephen A. Douglas for president in 1860 and resented the fact that many prominent Indiana Democrats were supporters of John Breckinridge.

Bloominggrove, August 7th, 1860.

Mr. Editor:—The democracy of Bloominggrove township, met for the purpose of organizing a Douglas Democratic Club.

[list of names]

The following Resolutions were offered by E G. Glidewell and unanimously adopted:

Resolved, That in Stephen A. Douglas we have a representative man of the
National Democracy, under whose standard victory is certain; and that
we pledge to him our unflinching support and never yield until *victory
is Ours.*

Resolved, That the course of our United States Senators, Messrs. Bright and
Fitch, deserves the most unqualified condemnation; they are not repre-
senting the Democracy of Indiana in their hostility to our first choice,
Stephen A. Douglas. Their present attempt to divide and distract the
democratic party of Indiana, and boast by so doing to give the State to
that Tory candidate Abe Lincoln, will be remembered against them by us
as an attempt to rule down the Democracy who gave them the dignity
and power they now enjoy. When their present terms expire they are
certain to be blotted out and sink so low in the estimation of the genuine
Democracy that they can never be resurrected.

On motion, the Club adjourned to meet on next Friday evening.

William Parrot, President.

James Dukate, Sec.

Brookville Franklin Democrat, September 21, 1860.

"THEY WANT TO RULE US BECAUSE THEY WON'T TRUST US"

*Even before the 1860 election, Southerners broadcast threats of secession.
Republican newspapers like the* Indiana Daily Journal *of Indianapolis worked
hard to convince the party faithful not to be swayed, arguing that these threats
were one means by which the Slave Power attempted to rule despite its minority
status.*

DISUNION—WHAT IT IS, AND WHAT IT HAS TRIED TO DO

We presume no man of average intelligence in any party is surprised by the
"disunion" clamor which is just now filling the air in the absence of other more
effective noise. The experience of thirty years has prepared us for it, and the
feebleness of all other arguments against Republicanism has prepared us for an
unusual vigor and dolefulness in it. Whether it means anything more this time
than formerly is doubtful, but if it does it is the duty of all honest men to bring
its meaning out, and have the question raised by it fully and finally settled. No
good can be accomplished by yielding what we know to be our right to threats of
disunion, whether they are made merely to drive us into the concession, or really
to herald a revolution in the Government. Some time or other the question *must*

be decided whether the majority of the nation can elect the officers and define the policy of the nation, and it can be settled now just as well as four years or forty years hence. If this Government belongs to 300,000 slaveholders, and is constructed on the basis of their right to be satisfied with all that is done on penalty of its destruction, now is as good a time to learn it as any other. It is a better time in fact, for the position of those who threaten disunion is so flagrantly wrong, arrogant and treasonable, that a refusal to meet it fairly is an acknowledgement of more than their right to rule us. It is an acknowledgement of their right to despise us. "Disunion," stripped of the exaggerations of foolish or dishonest alarms, means just this, and no more: "We slaveholders are afraid that our property will not be safe under any government that we don't make or approve, and we won't stay in it if that majority won't let us rule it. We don't claim any more power than the other States, but the other States must let us have the power to satisfy us that no interference without property shall be attempted. If they don't we shall dissolve the Union. The Republicans may not interfere with our property, but we won't wait to see, for it will be a humiliation we can never endure to submit to the rule of men who claim that the government was made for their benefit as much as ours." This is "disunion" pure and simple. This is all of it, too. The most labored argument that Calhoun ever made did not state it any more clearly. The dread that any government not of their own choice will render their property insecure and cut off the opportunity of increasing its value by expansion, is absolutely the only argument or pretext that slaveholders have ever urged, or can urge, for disunion. They want to rule us because they won't trust us. To yield to a demand with no other justification, is to concede a great deal more than the control of the government. It is to concede the control over our own manhood, the annihilation of our own labor, the inferiority of our own free institutions. If this government can only be preserved by surrendering it to those who will use it, and who proclaim that they will use it, for the benefit of slavery, and the predominance of slavery over free labor wherever the two are brought in contact, it is of little value to anybody. Now we believe that even in the South there is too much good sense to justify disunion on such a pretext.—Certainly there is too much in the North to be alarmed at a disunion clamor which has no other pretext.

Indianapolis Indiana Daily Journal, October 30, 1860.

THE ELECTION OF 1860

The election of 1860 saw Abraham Lincoln sweep a majority of the votes in the state. However, in some parts of the state both John Breckinridge and John Bell got significant numbers of votes.

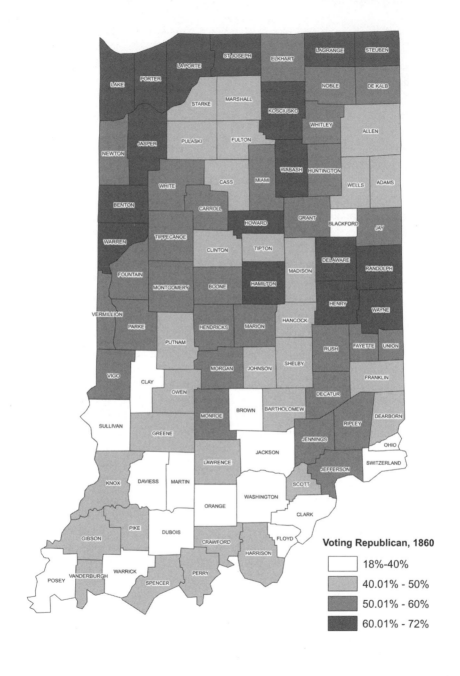

Voting Republican, 1860

☐ 18%-40%

☐ 40.01% - 50%

☐ 50.01% - 60%

■ 60.01% - 72%

Voting, Southern Parties, 1860

- 0% - 5% Southern Democrat
- 6% -15% Southern Democrat
- 16% - 34% Southern Democrat
- 0% - 5% Constitutional Union
- 6% - 15% Constitutional Union
- 16% - 23% Constitutional Union

Walter Dean Burnham, *Presidential Ballots, 1836–1892* (Baltimore: Johns Hopkins University Press, 1955).

SECESSION AS BLUSTER AND BLUFF

A leading abolitionist paper in Indiana, the Centreville Indiana True Republican *was edited by Isaac Julian, brother of recently elected Republican congressman George W. Julian. In this piece from early December 1860, the paper spied no real crisis. Two weeks later South Carolina became the first state to secede from the union.*

THE SINGLE DANGER.

What is the danger of the hour?—Not a dissolution of the Union, civil war, or anything of that sort, though now so commonly anticipated by timorous persons. The country will pass safely through the present crisis, as it has done through others very similar.—People are strangely forgetful. One year ago there was quite as much excitement as at present. The John Brown raid had inspired intense feeling throughout the country, North and South. Congress met amid fearful apprehensions as to the stability of the Union, and those apprehensions deepened during the dead lock of months duration concerning the election of a Speaker—the South blustering then as now about secession and dissolution in case the Republicans should elect their candidate for that office. Well, they *did* elect him—and what followed? Why just nothing at all unusual. So it will turn out now.

Is it not amazing that, with all our past experience, we do not at once detect in the present commotions at the South, a repetition of the old stale trick of trying to frighten us into their measures? Nor is it surprising that they again resort to it, for thus far it has hardly if ever been known to fail of the desired effect. So they are naturally "trying it on" again, with old and new variations, and with a vigor proportioned to their idea of their present emergency.

Now the real danger, and the only one, is, that they may succeed in their effort— that corrupt or weak kneed politicians in the Republican ranks may be found ready again to compromise with men who keep no compromises when made, however solemn or time honored.

Centreville Indiana True Republican, December 6, 1860.

"THE SOUTH IS MAKING A GREAT TO DO"

Once news of South Carolina's secession reached Indiana, the prospect of war became a central concern of Hoosiers. William Ross was probably a Kentucky-born commission merchant in Terre Haute. As a man who served as an agent for farmers selling their produce, he daily came into contact with the distress that secession brought to the markets.

Terre Haute Dec 23rd 1860

Dier Uncle Yours of the 10th Dec is Recd and contents noted and I must say that I was happy to hear from you and to hear that you and yours ware well

We are all well and I must say to you that times is verry close here and financial matters is closer than I have ever seen them and it is owing alltogether to politics and it is the first political panic that ever I new or heard of The south is making a great to do and for what. No other cause only because a corrupt and foul party could not rule any longer and for my part I say let them cecede if they wish I am perfectly willing and I am also perfectly willing to shoulder my musket in defense of Republican principals if it is necessary I am willing that the majority should rule whether republican or dimocrat but I am for pease if it can be had on amicable terms but I hope the north will not yeald one hairs bredth to the south[.] if nothing but war will do them let them have it and I think that they will soon get satisfied

Uncle thare is no sale here for any thing even pork is being sold on a credit The folks in Illinois was all well the last that I heard of them Brother Samuel is in Cansis I suppose but I can not tell whare as I have not heard from him sense he got thare Brother Daniel W Ross is in the United States army[.] his five years was out last May but he has not Returned yet and I have not heard from him for one year except verbal account but I think that he will be at home this winter Mother is well or was a few days ago I will now give you the price of produce in our market flower $4.50 wheat 75cts corn 20cts pork from three to four dollars[.] our city is quite healthy at this time uncle I will now close hoping to hear from you often I Remain yours verry Respectfully

William Ross

Kephart and Kidwell Family Papers, Indiana Historical Society, Indianapolis.

A POLITICIAN WRITES HIS SONS FROM WASHINGTON

From the halls of power, Richard W. Thompson, growing despondent for the cause of Union, lays out for his sons what he claims no politicians or journalists speak. A prominent Indiana politician since the 1830s, Thompson was a Whig and then Know Nothing who publicly advocated for Bell but privately admired and corresponded with Lincoln.[5] Thompson was willing to compromise with slaveholders to preserve the Union, but he became a strong Republican during the war.

Washington Dec 29. 1860

My dear Sons

I have concluded to write you a joint letter, for I have so much writing to do that I have not time to say, seperately, to you what I want to say about the condition of affairs here; and you can form but little idea of them from what is said in the newspapers. The conductors of the press belong to one party or the other, and whatever they write is prepared with a view to show that they are

right + every body else wrong—and, hence, the country is kept in ignorance of
what is actually going on. The "correspondents," who send their letters from
this city to every part of the Union, are, as a class, altogether unreliable. They
manufacture all sorts of stories—all for the purpose of magnifying their own
importance + making their papers sell. And yet these men do more to mould +
direct public opinion than any other class in the country. They have such a share
of influence over the public mind that they can write a man up or down, just
as they think best for their own interest. The politicians are completely subject
to them, and the two classes have brought the government to the very verge of
ruin. I have tried to persuade myself that there was no real danger, and that the
present storm, which now convulses the country would pass away. But my hope
of such a result becomes weakened every day, and I should not be surprised to
see the Union entirely broken up in sixty days, and a furious Civil War raging in
ninety. The difficulty doez not lie, as is supposed, in the laws passed or not passed
by the northern states, but in the belief which the southern people entertain,
that the northern people have cultivated a felling of hatred for them, because
they hold slaves. This, they think, has gone so far and has taken such complete
possession of the northern mind, that it will never be satisfied until slavery is
abolished in all the States—and, therefore, they are ready to secede from the
Union, set up a government for themselves, and maintain their position, if
necessary, by the sword. South Carolina is already out of the Union, and it is
confidently expected that Alabama, Georgia, Mississippi, Florida, + probably
Louisiana will follow the example before the 1st of February. And, if nothing
is done, in the mean time, to settle the difficulty between the sections, the
secessionists hope to have all the slave states out of the Union before the 4th of
March. Their object is then to claim that as this city is within the seceding states,
Mr Lincoln cannot come here to be inaugurated. If he then makes the attempt
they will resist it by force, + then the war will begin here, + Pennsylvania
Avenue be drenched in blood. If it comes to this, the northern men will come
here to sustain Lincoln, and then the whole country will become involved. The
South has now from 50,000 to 100,000 men under arms—with their officers
selected, + they are trained almost every day. The times are fearfully alarming
and there are no statesmen here to turn the tide. All the men here are mere
selfish politicians + look to their own political interests far more than they do
the happiness of the country. Their imbecility may cause the war to begin before
the 4th of March—for the South Carolinians say that if the President does not
order Maj Anderson to evacuate Fort Sumter, they will fire upon him + take the
fort. It is thought that they cannot take the fort very easily—but as Anderson
has less than 300 men, they may overcome him. Still if they begin the war upon
him, he will destroy a great many before he gives up—for the fort commands the

city of Charleston + bombs thrown into the city will almost destroy it. These things are horrible to think of, and yet there is imminent danger that all this may soon become reality. The northern people think that the threats of the South is all bluster—but they are deceived + misled by the politicians. If they knew the true condition of affairs, I think they would require the difficulties to be settled and the Union saved. But they do not seem disposed to inquire into it—and all may soon be lost. The administration has become contemptible + has no power to do anything:—it hobbles along like a decrepid old man, seizing upon mere expedients to keep itself from falling entirely down. It is rumored that Mr Seward has become satisfied of the danger and is about to offer a proposition of compromise. I hope he is, for he can do very much toward restoring peace. But I fear he will not go far enough. The disease has become too desperate to be removed by ordinary remedies. We shall know more about this in a few days—for it will not do to postpone it much longer, if any thing is to be done. . . .

. . . I am sorry that I couldn't be at home to spend my Christmas—but it was impossible without neglecting business here more important than any I have at home. I spent my Christmas Day in my room, as it snowed here. We have snow again + shall likely have a snowy new years day. But no body seems to enjoy the holidays here, as there is a universal panic in regard to the Union. Washington, of course, will be destroyed if it is dissolved. I hope you will have a pleasant new year + that the little ones will enjoy themselves. Tell Harry + Fannie that I will bring them a book a piece, + your sister has already bought one for Charly, called the American Family Robinson. Why do you boys neglect writing to me? You must not do it any longer—not only because it is your duty to do so, but because it is absolutely necessary that you should write more. And when you write take pains to say something about what is going on—for you *must* cultivate an epistolary style. My second sheet has given out + I must close, with kisses for your mother + the little ones.

Your affec. father

R. W. Thompson

F L & R. W. Thompson, Jr.

Thompson mss, Lilly Library, Indiana University, Bloomington.

ABOLITIONISTS AS DIS-UNIONISTS

During the secession crisis, many Hoosiers, and especially Democrats, thought that the abolitionists bore significant responsibility for the destruction of their beloved Union. Meetings across the state urged union, together with the suppression of the abolitionist program. Dubois County, with its sizeable German Catholic population, was one of the most solidly Democratic counties in the state.

UNION MEETING.

Pursuant to notice, the citizens of Patoka township, Dubois Co., irrespective of party met in Huntingburg on the 22d inst. After an artillery salute of thirty-four guns, in honor of Washington and the Union, the meeting was organized by electing Sandusky Williams, Esq. President, and B. R. Kemp Secretary.

On motion, a committee of seven was appointed by the Chair to draft resolutions. Messrs. B. R. Kemp, J. B. Gohman, Dr. Thomas Johnson, Dr. John W. Taylor, A. H. Miller, John B. Lemonds and Mormon Fisher were appointed said committee.

After a short time they reported the following, which were unanimously adopted:

> Whereas, we, the citizens of Patoka Township, Dubois County, Ind., have assembled for the purpose of expressing our opinion upon the crisis which is now agitating our country, and hastening us on to ruin, tyranny and degradation, therefore
>
> 1; Resolved. That it is now time for the people to arise in their power and take their destinies in their own hands, and thereby save the Union, if possible, for a large portion of the members of Congress are acting the part of political demagogues, regardless of the interests and welfare of their country or the wishes of their constituents.
>
> 2. That as a settlement of the pending difficulties we are willing to accept the Crittenden proposition, or any other amendment of the Constitution, that will guarantee to the citizens of every State, the protection of their property, and just rights and privileges in the Territories, and the re-capture of their runaway slaves, according to the Constitution and Fugitive slave law; and all persons acting contrary to the aforesaid laws are violating the Constitution, and deserve the severest condemnation of law abiding people and Union-loving men.
>
> 3. That those States having laws contrary to the Constitution and Federal laws, commonly called Personal Liberty Bills, ought to repeal them, and that it is the duty of every State to use all honorable means to hold the Republic together, as bequeathed to us by the revolutionary patriots, and to transmit it, unimpaired, to unborn millions, as an asylum for the oppressed of the world.
>
> 4. That we see in coercion nothing but civil war, without the accomplishment of practical good to either section.
>
> 5. That the action of Gov. O. P. Morton, in appointing the most radical men of his party, instead of conservatives (if he could not violate the skirts of his party, and appoint some others,) as Commissioners to the Peace Conference, at Washington City, is heartily condemned, as the action of

said Commissioners has retarded instead of furthering a settlement of the difficulties.

6. That Hons. S.A. Douglas, J.J. Crittenden, Wm. Bigler, and others, who have used their talents and influence in Congress, and Ex-Presidents Tyler and Fillmore, and others, in their State Conventions, deserve the heartfelt thanks of all true lovers of their country for their efforts to effect a compromise, and prevent civil war. To praise such men as we wish, we are unable to find language. Give honor where honor is due.

7. That these resolutions are for white men exclusively; we hold to no equality with the negro, and will have no social intercourse with them, for we look upon them as an inferior race, and believe the Almighty never intended the races to amalgamate.

8. That the present condition of African slavery does not afford any reason for destroying the liberties of twenty-six million of whites, and plunging them into unholy, unjust and fratracidal war, for the four million blacks, who are unable and unworthy to govern or take care of themselves.

9. That a copy of these resolutions be sent to our Representative in Congress, our Senator and Representative in the Legislature, and that the Jasper Courier, Paoli Eagle, Cincinnati Enquirer and Louisville Auzeiger be requested to publish.

The meeting was then addressed in an appropriate style by Messrs. Lemonds and Williams, after which it adjourned with three rousing cheers for the Union.

S. Williams, Pres't.

B. R. Kemp, Sec'y.

Jasper Courier, February 27, 1861.

AN ATTEMPT AT COMPROMISE

Amid the secession crisis in early 1861, moderates called a peace conference in Washington to attempt to compromise and assuage Southern slaveholders' fears. Indiana's delegates reported to Governor Morton.

Washington City

Feb 21/1861

Hon O.P. Morton

Dear Sir:—I have written you several times since our arrival here, but the veil of secrecy which the South (+ weak men of the North,) has thrown over our deliberations has prevented that full report which under other circumstances I should have felt it my duty to make.

I have been expecting to hear from you + to have your views, but I suppose your official duties, with the diversion created by the Pres [?] riot, has engrossed your time.

We are now and have been for the last 5 days in full discussion of the various *Peace* propositions before our body. The Debate is exceedingly able and interesting and should have been placed in possession of the public. The debate closes tomorrow at 1 oclock and then we commence voting on the various propositions, say twenty, now before us. We vote by States, and where a delegation is divided the minority have the right to place their vote in the Journal.

My impression now is, that a majority of the States will recommend certain amendments to the constitution, with an alternative proposition that if Congress fail to prepare the specific amendments, they shall request the several States to call a general Convention. I think the vote on the above will stand 12 to 8. I *dont know* how Inda. will vote finally. I *hope* we shall be a unit. I can only speak for myself, and that is to say that I have as yet seen no reason to change my position. I *may* as a last resort vote to recommend a genl. convention, but I shall not do this unless I feel assured that it will be acceptable to the moderate men from the Border States.

I shall probably speak tonight—We have thus far done all in our power to procrastinate, and shall continue to do so, in order to remain in Session until after the 4th of March. For after the inauguration we shall have an honest fearless man at the helm, and will soon know whether the honest masses of the People desire to preserve and perpetuate our Government.

Yours truly
Godlove Orth

William Dudley Foulke Papers, Indiana State Library, Indianapolis.

THREE

Choosing Sides, Making an Army

$\mathcal{F}$ OR INDIANA, the Confederates' firing on Fort Sumter helped unite a divided state, much as it did throughout the North. If many Democrats thought that Republicans had not given peace enough of a chance, they also believed that about the Confederacy, whose choice to fire on American troops signaled their unwillingness to compromise. The first days of the war saw Hoosiers coming together to express their outrage about the Confederacy. Even Republican newspapers conceded "the indications of the past few days show that with all their hostility to Mr. Lincoln's political views, the heart of the Democracy beats as warmly for the country as it ever did," adding, "there will be no more Republican or Democrat henceforth, till the country is at peace."' Men flocked to sign up for military service.

Many of the concerns about the Ohio River being the border between the two nations came to naught when Kentucky remained in the Union. Much of the Upper South joined the Confederacy after Lincoln called up troops to put down the rebellion, but most of the slave states bordering the free states remained in the Union (and western Virginia would break off from Virginia to rejoin the Union). While Kentucky would remain the home of many Confederate sympathizers and see much fighting during the war, it would serve as a buffer between Indiana and the Confederacy. And since Kentucky remained in the Union, much of the bluster about Indiana or parts of it seceding quickly faded.

The vast majority of Hoosiers publicly supported the Union, as evidenced by enlistments. Those whose support for the Union appeared lukewarm often were pressured publicly. "To Preserve the Union" was the rallying cry, and any mention of the issue of slavery was quickly disavowed by most Union men, Republican and Democrat. Democrats who supported the war found their political faith in the Union in the words and actions of Andrew Jackson: "Our Federal Union. It must be preserved." For moderate Republicans, the Union helped distance their position from that of their abolitionist colleagues; for all Republicans, the Union could provide a common ground to unite the North. Those in the North who opposed the war, though, shared a belief common in the Confederacy: they believed the purpose of the war was to end slavery.

In the heady days early in the war, most Douglas Democrats could be found supporting, with varying degrees of warmth, the war to preserve the Union. But supporters of Breckenridge in the 1860 election formed the core of those opposed to the war. There were exceptions: Senator Graham N. Fitch of Logansport had joined Jesse Bright in supporting the Southern Democratic ticket, but, after his Senate term ended in March 1861, he fought as the colonel of the Forty-sixth Infantry Regiment. Fitch's Senate colleague Bright, who remained in the Senate, embodied the Hoosier opposition to the war. Bright was eventually expelled from the Senate, and Governor Morton, in a show of unity, replaced him with former governor Joseph A. Wright, a Douglas Democrat who had struggled with Bright for control of the Indiana Democrats for many years.

The breadth of Hoosier support for the war is evident in the ease with which the state initially raised troops. Within days of the first call for troops, Indiana's quota of six infantry regiments was filled, with far more willing left behind. Six additional regiments were quickly formed, first for Indiana service and then in federal service. By the end of June, ten more infantry regiments were authorized, and by the end of August twelve more. Sixteen more were authorized before the end of the year. Of these fifty regiments, forty-three were mustered in by the end of 1861, joining four cavalry regiments and nine artillery batteries; all told, around 50,000 Hoosier men were under arms by the beginning of 1862, out of a population of 204,000 white men aged fifteen to forty in 1860.[2] The fervor of enlistment was not matched by munitions on hand; accountings in the first month of 1861 had identified a few hundred weapons statewide.[3]

By the summer of 1862, thirty more infantry regiments, three more cavalry regiments, and ten more artillery batteries were authorized. By now, the belief that it would be a quick fight had subsided and so had some of the enthusiasm for the war. The horrors had become more evident with battles like Shiloh. Moreover, concern about the Republican administrations of Lincoln and Morton had reduced the enthusiasm of Douglas Democrats for the war. The state nearly met the August 1862 quota for troops, and the state administration decided to draft only in those townships, approximately a third of the state, in which voluntary enlistments lagged behind the quota proportion, to the tune of 6,060 men. By the time the draft could be organized, more than half this number had been induced to enlist, leaving a draft of 3,003 men, spread over more than 300 townships. By 1863, the federal government had taken over the raising of recruits under the Enrollment Act of 1863. Between more than 40,000 volunteers and the earlier surplus of troops offered by Indiana, the state was not subject to a federal draft until July 1864, when the president called for 500,000 additional troops, with Indiana to supply over 25,000, nearly half of whom were drafted men and substitutes. A final call for nearly 23,000 men in December 1864 led to nearly 2,500 men being drafted.[4]

About 197,000 Hoosiers are believed to have fought in the Civil War, although that number undoubtedly includes a number who reenlisted in a different regiment. No more than 2 percent were conscripts. The desire to preserve the Union, coupled with bounties and other inducements provided by local governments eager to avoid the infamy of needing a draft, meant that most men volunteered. Men who avoided voluntary enlistment, if draft figures are correct, were often physically handicapped or had hardships—such as being the only son of aged parents or the sole parent of young children—that would preclude their enrollment in the army. A drafted man could also avoid service by furnishing a substitute to serve in his place, or pay a $300 commutation fee to the government. Immigrants, especially those who were Catholic, were the most obvious category of men to avoid enlistment; one of the reasons to emigrate to America was to avoid conscripted armies. Many such immigrants were Democrats as well, but they hardly fit the image of the typical Southern sympathizer. Most true Southern sympathizers not only avoided enlistment but probably avoided the draft as well: at least 2,500 men did not answer the three calls statewide, representing about 15 percent of those drafted. But with nearly 200,000 men in arms, out of a population of eleven-to-fifty-year-old men that numbered only 306,000 in 1860, it is clear that Indiana stepped up to the cause.[5]

THE WAR BEGINS

Even as war began, concerns about traitors at home were not far from the minds of Republican editorialists.

WAR BEGUN!

Civil war has been commenced. The forces of the seceding States have attacked Fort Sumter. Without waiting even for an attempt to supply the Fort with provisions, they have begun a conflict which may last for years.—They have determined that no peaceful separation shall be made. Without provocation, with no motive but the humiliation of the National Government, they have attacked our fort, and by to-morrow may massacre Major Anderson and his garrison. They have gathered nearly 10,000 men to attack 70.—They have erected miles of batteries against a single fort. They have multiplied the means of attack till a fight has become hardly better than a murder. And feeling themselves strong enough to overpower the little force that has waited patiently in maintenance of the honor of the nation in their dangerous position, they have begun the war. They have not been assailed. They have not been threatened. No coercion has been employed, or even menaced. Nothing was asked but that provisions should be sent in for the sustenance of starving men. Humanity would allow a little band of seventy soldiers the means of preserving life, when duty and honor forbade their deserting their post. But humanity, peace, and national duty, have all been unavailing to avert a mean and murderous attack. The little fort and its handful of men are standing alone against thousands.—This is the honor of traitors, the humanity of seceders. The news we have received makes it sadly probable that before twenty-four hours have passed the national troops in Fort Sumter will be either murdered or prisoners. If the result fulfills this apprehension there will be a terrible reckoning for those who have provoked the conflict. Traitors here may glory in the defeat of their Government and the murder of the defenders of their honor, but the time of settlement will come. We heard more than one or two or three men last night rejoicing in the prospect of the massacre of Major Anderson and his band.—They were already laying out a plan of submission to the seceded States, and the adoption of their government. They made no concealment of their satisfaction that the nation was to be beaten, dishonored and broken. Such men are traitors, and the meanest of traitors. It should be the duty of the people to protect themselves and their government against such men. If we must fight the seceding States let us at least have no traitors at home. If Anderson holds out, as the latest news indicates he may, and the reinforcements of the government can effect their purpose, we shall have a chance to learn such infernal scoundrels that fighting their own country is not a pleasant operation.—They need the lesson badly, and we trust they may learn it speedily.

Indianapolis Indiana Daily Journal, April 12, 1861.

"I NEVER SAW SUCH EXCITEMENT IN ALL MY LIFE"

War fever touched everyone in Indiana. The war occupied all thoughts and influenced all actions. Thirty-nine-year-old Charles Peddle was Pennsylvania born and a machinist for a railroad.

Terre Haute Indiana
April 21, 1861

Dear John,

I suppose that you are all in a ferment of excitement in Philada as we are here and everywhere, from what I can see and hear. We are all afraid that Washington will fall into the hands of Jeff Davis. The secessionists so far appear to be carrying everything before them. We have sent two companies, about 200 men from this place and other companies are organizing. I am about joining the home guard, one company of which intends purchasing their own weapons (Sharps Rifles) and I shall probably enter their ranks. Four companies are being raised of home guards two of which propose going to war if needed, the other two, the Sharps

Rifle men among them, will stay at home except in extraordinary cases. We look for squally times along the Ohio River as Kentucky no doubt will go with the balance of the slave states. A steamboat loading here for New Orleans was ordered to cease loading and it is the intention to stop all trade with the South from the states north of the Ohio.

Great fears are felt here that Missouri will go out. If she does, I think there will be Civil War in St. Louis, as there's a good many loyal citizens there. It is pretty hard to say when this matter will end. I suppose we will all have to contribute blood or means in the cause of our country. That was a most dastardly thing of the Baltimore mob in firing on the Massachusetts and Pennsylvania troops. How does Bill feel about the war? Does he talk of enlisting? I never saw such excitement in all my life as exists now in the public mind. About 8 or 9 of our Railroad boys have gone and more will go if required. We have intelligence that the wires are down between Harrisburg and Washington. The women folks about town today are engaged making flannel shirts for the men who went from here and who are still at Indianapolis.

We are all tolerably well just now. I'm afraid that this war will interfere with our contemplated trip to the East. With many thanks for your kind favors in the shape of papers and with love to May and the babies.

I am your
Brother Charles

Peddle Family Letters, Indiana State Library, Indianapolis.

FORT SUMTER AND THE CALL TO ARMS

In the wake of Fort Sumter, a special session of the Indiana legislature was called into session. Horace Heffren, Democrat from Washington County, nominated a Republican to be Speaker of the House in a show of unity in support of Union.

HOUSE OF REPRESENTATIVES.

Wednesday, April 24. 1861.

REORGANIZATION OF THE HOUSE.

Mr. Heffren. Mr. Clerk, scarcely four months since, you and I met in this Hall as members of two opposite political parties. At that time the honorable gentleman from Knox, (Mr. Allen,) was selected as a candidate for Speaker of this House, by one of those political parties, and I was selected as the candidate of the other political party. Times have changed. The Union that you and I love, and we all love—the star spangled banner, which my hands and the hands of my gray-haired friend here, assisted in raising over the dome of this building, is in danger. Union and harmony and concession should now be our motto. Our coming together now falls upon a time when our country is menaced with danger, and when our homes and our firesides should be protected. It is therefore that on this occasion, I take great pleasure in having the privilege of nominating for Speaker of the House of Representatives, the Hon. Cyrus M. Allen, of the county of Knox.

The Clerk announced the order of the vote to be *viva voce,* which being taken resulted as follows:

Whole number of votes cast 88, of which Cyrus M. Allen received all.

So the election was declared unanimous.

The Clerk called on Messrs. Heffren, Gresham and Burgess to conduct the Speaker to the chair; which service being performed—

The Speaker. Gentlemen of the House of Representatives:—In this renewed manifestation of your confidence, you will accept my heartfelt thanks. The unanimity with which I have been called to preside over your deliberations during this session, evidences to me that we have come up here actuated sincerely by the desire to promote the interests of our country, the Union, the Constitution and the institutions of civil and religious liberty.

It affords me great pleasure to be able to say that we come up here divested of all party prejudices and actuated by the single, unanimous desire to promote the best interests of our whole country.

We come together under extraordinary circumstances and upon an extraordinary occasion. We have been called together by the proclamation of the Governor to consider questions arising out of the present excited state of the country. Of the reasons for that call it does not become me to say anything by way of address at this time. It is for us, when the Governor advises, to act promptly and efficiently for the best interests of the whole country.

Brevier Legislative Reports 5 (special session 1861): 6–7.

ENFORCED LOYALTY

From the first shots fired at Fort Sumter, those suspected of disloyalty were visited and even abused, with the approval of majority of the public.

We learn that John Ketler, a wealthy farmer residing on Green's Fork was visited the other day by a committee of his neighbors, to make inquest as to his devotion to the Union. He had stated some time previous (as we are credibly informed) that he had written to Gov Pickens of South Carolina, proposing to send him sixty men at his own expense to fight for "Southern rights"—hence the suspicion as to his present position. He now, we learn, declared that what he had said respecting his correspondence with Pickens was "all in jest," and that he was "a good American citizen." Some of the committee did not consider his explanations satisfactory, but they let him off in the hope that he would cease to jest about matters so serious.

Barton Wyatt, another wealthy citizen of this vicinity, we learn was also put through at Richmond in the same way, but with less tenderness. This course is right, whenever there is just cause of suspicion. "He who is not for us, is against us."

Centreville Indiana True Republican, April 25, 1861.

THE FIRST VOLUNTEERS

With the war begun, at Fort Sumter, young men across the state vied to be included in the first volunteer companies, and communities across Indiana gathered to send their boys off in style.

Liberality At Knightstown.—The citizens of Knightstown gave the volunteer company from that place over two hundred flannel shirts, and each man two blankets. They gave to Capt. Moreau a very handsome sword, and suffered none of the volunteers to pay for any thing after their enrollment. The company consists of one hundred and thirty-five men of more than average height and size, and of as fine appearance as any group that has presented itself here. When mustered into service yesterday at Camp, and it became known that some would be rejected on account of an overplus of members, a number who were selected by their comrades to stay at home, wept bitterly. They wanted to be a part of the army of freedom, and wanted to remain with their companions. When ascertaining their luck, they returned home with saddened hearts.

Indianapolis Indiana Journal, April 23, 1861.

THE EARLY TRIALS OF WAR

War disrupted the lives of many Hoosiers. Laura Ward's letter touched on two local events, and then turned to two media events of the early war, the death of Stephen Douglas and that of Colonel Ellsworth, the first Union soldier to die in the war while trying to take down a Confederate flag during the occupation of Alexandria, Virginia. She then returned to the daily rhythms of life in her Henry County town.

June 3d 1861.

Dear Sue, my kind teacher. I sit me down today to answer your kind and joyfully recieved letter of May the 18th. I am in excellent health as is all the rest of mother's family. I am glad to hear that you and Jo have such a pleasant home, and do not be surprised my friend to see me at any moment, now, for I have determined to pay you a visit at the earliest convenient period.

You ask me how the subject of war stands about here. I will answer you by relating a few incidents which are a sample of the general mind of the people. Several volunteers went from Lewisville. One of them when he went to start was followed to the depot by his wife, where she clung to him and shrieked and sobbed and refused to let him go. Four men stepped forward and took her away from him and held her and the fellow coolly got on the cars and left. Another volunteer went, who was sent back, the company being full, when he when he [sic] arrived. He came back and ever since has been trying to get news of some company that is not complete being determined, he says, to fight for his country yet.

There was one old fellow, well known as a democrat, who coolly avowed himself a friend of the South; and a banner being raised in Lewisville he threw an insulting letter at it and otherwise taunted the Reps. Immediately a large crowd collected and run him through the streets throwing stones at him and trying to catch him to hang him. The gallows were erected but he saved himself by flying to a friends in the country. They refused to let him return and he stayed there two or three days. At the end of that time there came a letter to the P. O. directed to him and bearing the Montgomery seal, and having a device of the Palmetto flag on it. Lewisville was again aroused; its citizens started after him again. He fled to Indianapolis; they followed him there. He fled once more and finding him rather hard to catch they passed sentence of exile on him; banishing him to within fifty miles of Lewisville; and the last heard from him he was 20 miles South of the State Capitol. None consider him safe yet. It does seem hard but they who are traitors to their country, and it such a country as this, deserve death.

I have heard news this evening which I earnestly hope may not be true. It is sad if it is. They say that Mr Douglas is dead. Once I would have rejoiced to have heard it, but since I have learned how firm a friend of Uncle Abe's he has been, how he has stood by him in the thickest of his troubles. I have learned to look upon him in a different light from what I used to. I have learned to respect the man who seemed to have an enemy in everyone around me and have been his firm friend ever since Mr Lincolns Inaugural Address. The news is telegraphic and has not been confirmed yet and I hope it will not be. Perhaps Mr Douglas's political career may look rather doubtful and some things he may have said and done look rather dark; I am not politician enough to know about that. I only know that when the hour of trial came and many, whose political career has been fairer than his, were forsaking the Union and the Administration and turning traitors to their country that he remained the firm friend of all; and this is sufficient to win my heart, to disarm me of all my ancient enmity, and make

me respect him I once scorned and hated. If it is true about his death, I think
Uncle Abe's heart will be sad, for I have heard that he respected him very much
and was much gratified at his friendship. And I think there will have been two
of the saddest funerals, within so short a while, at the Presidential Mansion that
there has been for a long time. Colonel Ellsworth's body was taken there after
his death. Sue I wept when I heard that brave man was dead. Many around here
wept. Oh it was so hard that with the traitor's flag in his hand and his manly
young brow flushed with the pride of victory, and his young heart burning with
love for his country in the very midst of his manhood, he should be shot down
and his life blood should flow out from that noble heart and dye the Traitor's
banner. But Sue it is God's will, and God knows best. Oh my heart was with
dear old Uncle Abe's when I heard of how he wept at the news of his friends
death and Sue I pitied him from the very depths of my soul and my tears came
faster as I read of his. But I must quit writing of such things. My letter I fear will
grow tedious and uninteresting. One subject pursued too long becomes dull.
But the war and the incidents connected with it are so interesting to me that I
can scarcely talk or think of any thing else, and that is the reason why I write on
such subjects so much. It is interesting to every one now. The first question asked
when a couple of men meet is "what is the latest news," And when the ladies
meet, too, they forget all other things and cease to talk about their new quilts,
and about how much it takes to clothe the family and how much trouble they
have getting articles of wearing apparel made up, and broach the all absorbing
theme, the one interesting topic of the war. Every one talks and thinks of the
war one half their time if not more. It is in everybodys mouth. At the table, in
the streets, rain or shine wherever two prsons meet little else is spoken of. And
so my dear friend I have good excuse for writing two thirds of my letter about
nothing else.

Well now to other subjects[.] Sue I will tell you how I am engaged in passing
of my time this summer. I plant flowers and watch them and tend them and thus
engage about one third of my time; the rest I spend in tending the garden and
helping mother; and every moment of spare time I get I instantly improve by
reading something useful or writing some of my thoughts down on paper This
last named occupation is the most pleasant to me of anything else; inasmuch as
I delight in nothing more than reading my thoughts after I have written them
down I memorize poems also and every practical book I can get hold of you
may be assured I read most thouroughly. I do not attend to my Arithmetic and
Grammar as well as I ought to; my Geography I have in requisition quite often;
always getting it whenever a place is mentioned, in connection with the war,
of which I know nothing. My Philosophy I have almost forgotten. But as the
summer advances and the flowers need less care I shall [have] a great deal more

time to devote to other studies besides those of a literary character. Now talking about literature makes me think to tell you that a literary society has been started at a school-house about a mile and a half north of here called the Swamp school-house. . . .

Well Sue, I think it is time I was drawing my long long letter to a close. I know you will become very tired of reading it. I ought not to have written so much. But when I get to talking to my friends through the medium of pen and ink I never know when to stop. So you must please excuse me for taxing your patience so long; though if you like to read letters as well as I like to write them I need not ask you to do that. There are few however who like to read letters, especially when they are lengthy and the writing is poor like it is in this one. By the by, Sue, I fear if you do excuse the length of the letter you will not excuse the poorness of the writing although I should ask you to, which I humbly do. I hear you say it done me very little good to go to writing-school last winter and get the premium if my hand write did not improve more than it has. Well my hand write improved very much, but the truth of it is I did [not] keep it improved and I am now as bad a writer as ever. But I guess that next you will be thinking that I am a long time bringing my tedious letter to a close. So I will just ask you to give my best respects to Jo and tell you to look for me every day, for I am coming Sue to pay you a visit, and then remain your friend and pupil

Laura Ward.

Thomas B. Redding Collection, Indiana Historical Society, Indianapolis.

SOJOURNER TRUTH VISITS INDIANA IN THE WAKE OF THE WAR'S START

Sojourner Truth was a noted African American abolitionist. The presence of Truth initiated a near riot; even Republicans like the editor of the Angola paper thought it best to focus on Union, rather than on slavery.

ANGOLA.

The usual quietness of Angola has been considerably disturbed this week, by the encampment of a set of wild Arabs, known as Gipsies near our town, a few days since, some of our citizens being much inflated with patriotism, came near ending their lives by the Code known only among gentlemen (as the Southern chivalry styles it,) by fighting a duel. But fortunately the the (sic) better judgement of some one was allowed to dictate, and the proceeding stopped before blood was shed, but that was nothing to be compared to what took place on Thursday night. A few days ago a colored woman by the name of Sojourner Truth, came to our town, and whether it was her intention to have spoken or not we are not advised, but it being understood that she was an advocate of the war, and the policy of the Government, some of our citizens wanted to hear her speak, through curiosity, in order to get her ideas as what the result would be to her race, but it was thought by some that she was going to deliver a flaming anti-slavery speech which ought not to be allowed at this excited state of affairs, and a general pitching in took place, which resulted in a good deal of very loud, harsh, and unfriendly talk, and has aroused a feeling in our place, which at this time should not have been known. With but few exceptions our entire community was in favor of sustaining the policy of the Government in putting down rebellion in the South at whatever cost it might be, and it had become a settled fact in the mind of every man that Slavery had been the whole cause of the disturbance, and that the negro question aught not to be raised again by any one in the north, by either black or white, but we apprehend that the trouble was as much aroused on account of the prejudice to the anti-slavery lecturer present as to the colored person, knowing her bitterness to the Constitution and the principles of Slavery. We very much deplore the condition of the public mind at this time, being aroused as it has been, by the same rights being trampled upon here in the north, that we are asking of the rebellious south "that is" freedom of speech.

Angola Steuben Republican, May 18, 1861.

JESSE BRIGHT'S EXPULSION

In December 1861, Senator Morton S. Wilkinson, Republican of Minnesota, proposed a resolution calling for Jesse Bright's expulsion from the U.S. Senate, on the basis of disloyalty evidenced in the following letter. Although Bright had written this letter before war had commenced, he had long been the nemesis of both Republicans and Douglas Democrats, and he was expelled early the next year. In August 1861, Thomas B. Lincoln had been tried for treason for this affair, but the indictment was squashed and Lincoln was permitted to go South.[6]

PROPOSED EXPULSION OF MR. BRIGHT

Mr. WILKINSON submitted the following resolution:

Whereas HON. JESSE D. BRIGHT heretofore, on the 1st day of March, 1861, wrote a letter, of which the following is a copy:

Washington, March 1, 1861.

MY DEAR SIR: Allow me to introduce to your acquaintance my friend Thomas B. Lincoln, of Texas. He visits your capital mainly to dispose of what he regards a great improvement in fire-arms. I recommend him to your favorable consideration as a gentleman of the first respectability, and reliable in every respect.

Very truly, yours,   JESSE D. BRIGHT

To his Excellency JEFFERSON DAVIS,

President of the Confederation of States.

And whereas we believe the said letter is evidence of disloyalty to the United States, and is calculated to give aid and comfort to the public enemies: Therefore,

Be it resolved, That the said JESSE D. BRIGHT is expelled from his seat in the Senate of the United States.

Congressional Globe, 37th Cong., 2d sess., 1861, 89.

BRIGHT'S DEFENSE

Defending his actions, Bright entered into the record this letter, which he had sent a constituent when the earlier letter to Jefferson Davis had become publicly known.

AT MY FARM, *September 7*, 1861

In reply to your favor of the 20th, just received, I have to say that I have been personally acquainted with Mr. Lincoln for more than twenty years, he having been at that time a prominent merchant of your city, where I was then residing, and was just entering on my career of life. He did me the favor to employ me as his attorney, and I generally attended to his legal business. The letter to which you refer is no doubt genuine. I have no recollection of writing it, but if Mr. Lincoln says I did, then I am entirely satisfied of the fact, for I am quite sure I would have given, as a matter of course, just such a letter of introduction to any friend who had asked it. So much for the letter.

You say the impression is sought to be created, on account of this letter, that I am in complicity with the southern rebellion. I have so little regard, indeed such an utter contempt for Abolitionism, which is seeking by every means in its power to "crush out" every man who dares to dissent from the policy it prescribes, that if it were merely to satisfy the corrupt partisans of that doctrine, I would not take the trouble of denying or attempting to counteract this impression. But for your sake, and the sake of such old tried friends as you, I think it due to myself to say, that I am, and always have been, for preserving the integrity of this Union. I was laboring zealously for its preservation when these men, who are now so clamorous for its maintenance, were willing to *"let it slide"* rather than abate one iota of their unconstitutional doctrine of inequality; and no man regrets more than I the present condition of public affairs, or is more anxious to see peace, unity, and fraternity restored. I do not think the policy of that party is calculated to produce such results; so far from it, the inevitable tendency of its measures, in my opinion, is to render the disruption permanent and incurable. And hence

I have opposed, and so long as my present convictions last shall continue to oppose, the entire coercive policy of the Government. I hope this may be satisfactory to my friends. For my enemies I care not.

Sincerely yours, &c.,   JESSE D. BRIGHT

J. FITCH, *Madison, Indiana.*

Congressional Globe, 37th Cong., 2d sess., 1861, 89.

REPLACING BRIGHT

Once Bright had been expelled from the Senate, Governor Morton was empowered to appoint his replacement. His eventual choice of former Democratic governor Joseph Wright served to seal an alliance between the Republicans and the Democratic faction headed by Wright, an alliance which would become known as the Union Party in the state. Terre Haute politician Thompson was the former Whig who had publicly supported Bell in the 1860 election, but was a long-time acquaintance of Lincoln. Robert N. Hudson had been the editor of the Terre Haute Republican paper.

Washington Feb. 12th 62

R. W. Thompson
Dear Col,

I have had many talks with Gov. Morton since the expulsion of Bright from the Senate, as to who ought to be his successor. I am well convinced that his personal feelings are warmly in favor of tendering to you the appointment, but strange to say he is overwhelm[ed] with letters + dispatches from Indiana, urging him to give the appointment to Joe. Wright. This surpasses my understanding, but still it is true. Over one hundred letters + dispatches have be received by him in the last few days from Indiana, + nine tenths of them ask the appointment of Wright—is not this strange?

The members of Congress had a meeting—I was present. The Gov. asked them who he should appoint, + every one excepting Julian (+ he half way consented) advised him to appoint Wright.

I would not be surprised if Wright would get the appointment. The Gov. however starts home today + will not make the appointment until he arrives.

I can not see any good to come out of the appointment of Wright—it is to time serving + I have done what I thought adviseable to prevent it.

The case which Sullivan counseled us in, was all bosh[?] & ended just where it began.

Hoping you are well I remain

Yours +c.

R. N. Hudson

Richard W. Thompson Papers, Indiana State Library, Indianapolis.

"IF THE SOUTH CAN MAINTAIN ITS POSITION ALL WILL BE WELL"

Bright was not the only Hoosier to sympathize with the South or give aid to it. Like Bright, William A. Bowles was a slaveholder who lived in Indiana—he was one of the last men to hold a slave in the state, and his wife held slaves in Kentucky. A physician, he was already notorious in Orange County for his extreme politics. He was also an owner of the famous French Lick spa. In the second letter, Joseph Cox was probably a thirty-eight-year-old Indiana-born lawyer who lived in Paoli and whose parents were from North Carolina. Cox remained in Paoli after the war. The most eminent Hoosier to fight for the South was a Franklin County native, Confederate Brigadier General Francis Shoup.

French Lick April 25th 1861

Eliza Bowles

These are days of extraordinary things in this once happy land of so called liberty Life Liberty and property and property [sic] are all in danger now. Six thousand troops have been sent to the city of Washington so it is reported by Governor and a large number of cannon have been purchased and are soon to be in battery among the people to keep them on [?tion] The republicans of Paoli have taken new courage and raised a pole which they call a Union pole and sware that fire and blood awaits the man or set of men who will attempt to cut it down or rais a secession pole, in or about the place and they also threaten to demolish commingors office if he publishes any thing against it. There is a strong feeling in this community to take it down and if the attempt is made there will be a bloody soon follow, though I do not consider there is much danger in the people about Paoli but they will be reenforced from the North with large guns as they are now doing at Caro Ill. I look to hear of despert consequinces from that quarter in a few days. The war Spirit is getting up on all sides the republicans have the controle of the State and therefore the advantages in use of the State arms and my fear is that the Douglass wing of the Democratic party will go off with the black republicans and if so our condition but you may imagine our condition but you can not realize it Kentucky will go out but too late to help us in this State if Ky had have gon out at the proper time Southern Indiana would been with her to day if not the whole State. But so it is we must take things as they come as we are not the directors of our destiny. Let war come we must pass from the present condition for in it we can not remain free and happy and if the South can maintain its position all will be well and the rising generation may look forward for happy days But if the North should happen to conquer, then this continent will be for ever doomed be a world of miserable mongerals which will prove a pest and a curse to every social relation of man kind No domestic news of the country a wet cold and backward Spring I heard from Dr Graves on yesterday all well and he reports that Mrs Caffery thinks that the scrofula is about to return on Puss and says she complains very much No letters from you 2 months has elapsed and but one letter and that came in quick time enough I have some ham, a Barrel of Beef and two barrels of flour for Mother ready but fear she will never get them as they will in all probability be confiscated by the way but I shall wait until the excitement is a little over and there is any chance I will send them My love to Mother and all inquiring friend.

I am W A Bowles

P.S. Direct your letter to Paoli Lane has got the office

⁓

French Lick Ia 1861

Genl Pillow August 18th

Dear Sir

Permit me to introduce to your favorable consideration Joseph Cox Esqr who comes South for the purpose of rendering himself useful in the cause of Southern rights. Any favors shown him well be gratefully acknowledged by your obt *servt*

W. A. Bowles

Union Provost Marshals' file of Papers Relating to Individual Civilians (RG 109, microfilm series 345), roll 31, National Archives, Washington, D C

CAMP LIFE

Early enlistees were well aware of the political dimensions of the war; here the distinction between War Democrats like Joseph Wright and Confederate sympathizers like Jesse Bright is made clear. But William Jones of the Thirty-sixth Indiana Volunteer Infantry Regiment reported on many of the mundane aspects of camp life as well. It is notable that Jones came from a Quaker family, demonstrating that some Quakers took up arms to fight.[7]

Camp Joe Wright Aug 8th (1861)

Dear Brother

As I want to write home every week, if not oftener, I thought I would take turns and write to you all for when one gets a letter it will do to let all of you know how I am getting along. ol I was never in better health than I am *now* I weighed myself yesterday and weighed 144 which is *ten pounds* more than when I left Camp

Wayne. The coat that Woodard made is now to small I can only *button* the *three top buttons* with any ease I think by New Years I will be the *biggest* of the family.

There is nothing here in camp that would interest you What I know of the only change we have had was when we changed the name of our camp from Sherman to Joe Wright one reason for changing was that being camped on Jesse O Bright farm who was and is yet a bitter enemy of *Old Joe* we thought the best thing to do was call his farm Camp *Joe Wright*

Jim Bates was down to my tent to borrow the *Broad Axe*[8] He is well so as all the other Richmond boys. Oh some of you boys at the shop ought to write a letter to Jim He has had no letter since he came here and there is nothing that makes a *soger boy* feel better than a letter from some one at home.

I wrote Will Kitson a letter several days ago I don't know whether he ever got it or not if he has why I want him to take time some of these days and answer it.

The boys belonging to *Hoover* got up a *petition* asking him to *resign* but I do not think he will do it I guess the reason is that some of the boys want to be promoted Joe Smith wants to be a Lieut and they want Ike Ogborn to be Capt If they were to make that change I don't think it would any. Oh there is not much fun down at Jeffersonville I have only been out once and that was last Sunday and me went Louisville Ky It is not the place that I thought it would be The streets are too narrow and there is more dirt on them than anything else *We* that is the staff and *Non Com* staff were all invited over to dinner at the Louisville Hotel today but as all of us couldn't go I told George to go and I would stay and keep shop They say that they had a very good time George's Brother is here and he has been on a *Man of War* and they had not seen each other for *eleven years* I do not know how long we will be here in camp Maybe for some time yet can't tell anything about it I guess I will stop gave my love to mother and tell her that I am getting along nice also to the rest of the family my respect to the boys in the shop

Brother Will

Morgan Jones Family Papers, Earlham College Archives, Richmond, Indiana.

CONSCIENTIOUS OBJECTORS

Some Hoosiers who chose not to fight did so for religious reasons, including Quakers who had formed the backbone of the abolitionist movement in the state. A significant number of them volunteered for the military, but many other Quakers, like David Marshall, stayed true to their faith.

Carthage, Rush Co., Ind.
Jno 13 1862

O. P. Morton
Gov. Indiana

It is by no means my desire to improperly intrude upon thy time which I know must in the present state of affairs be *precious,* yet being a member of the Society of Friends and fully convinced in my own mind that the doctrines of that church in regard to *all* wars are in accordance with the precepts of our Saviour, I feel like saying, in kindness, a word on behalf of myself and fellow professors, that whilst we sincerely desire the best interests of all mankind to be promoted, and especially those of our own beloved country, we cannot because of *conscience* bear arms, and therefore if we be drafted we must in being "subject to the powers that be" patiently and humbly submit to the legal penalty which a refusal must incur.

This would subject us to much suffering without promoting any cause which the government seeks to maintain. Allow me therefore in view of this fact or feature, and also because that that the most if not *all* our younger members who have not become established in our peaceable principles so fully that they could not be *induced* to bear arms, have already volunteered; to humbly suggest to thy consideration the propriety of making some provision similar to what the Governor of New York has done, whereby the members of the Society of Friends may be exempted from "military duty." The provision refered to requires a certificate of membership verified by affidavit, to be filed with the town clerk.

> With sincere desire for thy present and everlasting welfare,
> I am in much humbleness thy friend, D.M.

[penciled annotation, probably the work of Military Secretary William H. H. Terrell.]

Answer that under our Constitution citizens conscientiously and religious opposed to bearing arms are not subject to draft. The suggestion requiring a certificate from Friend of church membership is a good one and will be considered by the Governor. (When you answer this letter take it to Gen'l Noble). T.

Oliver P. Morton Papers, Indiana State Archives, Indianapolis.

A UNION DEMOCRAT'S ACCOUNT
OF DRAFT IN HANCOCK COUNTY

Despite the initial surge in volunteers, by 1862 enlistments dragged and the state chose to institute a draft in those townships that had lagged in voluntary enlistments to meet the federal quota. Democratic Hancock County had several townships subject to the 1862 draft. This sequence captures some of the kinds of events that transpired around the draft.

James Allen, of Sugar-creek township, a ranting member of the late Breck-inridge County Convention, at which Warrum and Mason received their nominations, and who calls all Union men Abolitionists, cut off his right index finger one day last week. It is surmised by some, and boldly proclaimed by others, that James had the forthcoming draft in view when the finger was cut off. We would advise Jimmy to cut off another finger, if he don't want to fight for the Union and the Constitution. As it is now, he will not be on the "privileged list," and may be drafted. (August 14, 1862)

Enrolling Commissioners will meet at the Court House, Tuesday next to hear applications for exemptions from draft. Applicants must be present and undergo an examination. (August 21, 1862)

A very large number of people were in town on Tuesday last. That was the day appointed for examinations for exemption from draft, and the news of the change of days had not reached the remote parts of the county. Several companies of "invalids" could easily have been raised from the crowd. The days now fixed for the examination is Monday, September 1. All persons wishing to be placed on the "retired list" must be present in person for examination. (August 28, 1862)

The work of exemptions, under the direction of the Enrolling Commissioner and his Deputies, Examining Physician, R. E. Barnett, and Provost Marshal L.W. Gooding, has been going on since Monday last. Up to the hour of going to press (11 o'clock A.M.) the following is the result of their work:

> In Blue-river township 51 applicants for examination and 18 exemptions granted.
> In Brown township 41 applicants and 11 exemptions.
> In Buck-creek township 52 applicants and 12 exemptions.
> In Brandywine township 48 applicants and 10 exemptions.
> In Center township 59 applicants and 25 exemptions.

From those figures it will be seen that Dr. Barnett is very careful not to grant exemptions for trivial causes. (September 4, 1862)

The Board of Examination and Exemption was just one week in session. They had a trying time in examining the cripples and those who thought they were or ought to be cripples during the war. Dr. Barnett, we believe, faithfully and impartially discharged the duties of his onerous and thankless position. He exempted no man, unless he was *undoubtedly* disabled from bearing arms. (September 11, 1862)

The Enrollment of Hancock. The following is the official statement of the enrollment of this county, as prepared for us by Commissioner Judkins. From this statement it will be seen that the county has furnished *thirty-three* and *one-fifth per cent,* of its fighting strength, while the townships have furnished as follows—Blue-river 30; Brown 28; Brandywine 31; Buck-creek 38; Center 40; Green 30; Jackson

29; Sugar-creek 30, and Vernon 35. We omit the fractions, increasing where the fraction is over one-half, and decreasing where it is less. (September 18, 1862)

Greenfield Hancock Democrat.

AVOIDING THE DRAFT

By 1864 and 1865, the supply of men who could be shamed, coerced, and bribed into volunteering proved insufficient and a draft became necessary. Some men schemed to avoid the draft; this insurance policy was particularly crafty. The 1860 census reveals interesting data on a number of these fellows. W. H. L. Noble was a married Mississippi-born railroad agent with small children. Ignatius Brown was a wealthy twenty-eight-year-old lawyer, Iowa-born and married to a Kentucky-born woman, with small children. Jacob Coffman was a thirty-year-old carpenter, married with small children. Percival Stedman was a thirty-three-year-old married father, employed by a railroad as a clerk. Kentucky-born Granville M. Ballard was twenty-seven years of age, apparently single, and employed as a teacher by the state asylum for the blind, where he lived. F. W. Hamilton may have been Frank Hamilton, a twenty-seven-year-old clerk living in a lawyer-headed boardinghouse, interestingly enough, with Horace Heffren's brother, among others. A. D. Ohr might have been Aaron Orr, who in 1860 was a thirty-four-year-old married clerk with small children.

This agreement made this 23rd day of February, A.D. 1865, Witnessed: That whereas a draft of Three Hundred Thousand (300,000) men, ordered by the President of the United States, is now pending; and, whereas our names are liable to be drawn; Now Therefore, we hereby mutually agree to pay Two Hundred Dollars ($200) each into a common fund to procure substitutes for such of us, if any, as may be drafted, it being understood and agreed that if the name of either one of us who has loaned the City of Indianapolis fifty Dollars ($50), thereby entitling himself to receive Four Hundred Dollars from said city, if drafted, shall be drawn, said sum of Four Hundred Dollars shall be contributed to said-common fund and become a part thereof, for the purpose of procuring substitutes; and it is further understood and agreed that after such substitutes are procured the residue of such common-fund, if any, shall be divided equally between us. This agreement shall continue during the war. Witness our hands the date and year aforesaid.

F. W. Hamilton	U. S. Hammond
D. R. Donough	Ignatius Brown
A. D. Ohr	Jacob Coffman
W. H. L. Noble	Percival Stedman
John Daroty	Granville M. Ballard

Lynday Brown Papers, Indiana State Library, Indianapolis.

FOUR

~

The Front Lines

*T*HE SOLDIERS and seamen from Indiana who fought to preserve the Union had many and various experiences. Soldiers marched through all the states of the rebel South, fighting scores of battles and skirmishes, occupying and pacifying a restive, hostile population, and restoring federal authority over the landscape. Likewise, men who enlisted in the United States Navy served on oceangoing ships, blockading Southern ports, chasing rebel blockade-runners and Confederate naval ships, and ferrying troops to Southern shores to reconquer the South. Many Indiana seamen served on gunboats that plied the rivers offering access to the heart of the South.

Varied as their service was, Indiana men shared numerous common experiences in their efforts to suppress rebellion. They sweated in the stifling heat on the march, they froze while bivouacked in open fields without tent or blanket, and they often lacked adequate rations to eat or safe water to drink. They died in large numbers. More than 24,000 Indiana men died as a result of their service to the United States to put down the rebellion. As nearly 200,000 men from Indiana served during the Civil War, the death rate among Indiana troops exceeded 12 percent, below the 14 percent rate of all Union troops.[1] In addition to those who died in service, many thousands more carried home serious wounds and illnesses. Many of the injured died shortly after the war, weakened by their wounds and exposure. Others suffered physical and mental pain for decades afterwards.

After the rebels fired on the United States forces in Fort Sumter, South Carolina, thousands of Indiana men and boys answered the call to arms. Women also responded to the call by participating in the war effort in the ways that mid-nineteenth-century culture afforded them. At first, many men and women were motivated by a sense of adventure—an opportunity to experience the sensations of danger. Others found motivation in a deep and abiding indignation at the rebels' actions and a patriotic zeal to preserve their country. However, as the rebels proved to be tenacious fighters and the rebellion was not soon quelled, patriotic zeal slipped away from many. But for others, the prospect of a protracted war redoubled their determination not to allow rebellion to destroy the Union.

As Indiana's population resided mainly in the countryside and small towns, most of Indiana's Civil War soldiers were farmers, farm laborers, and craftsmen.

They were young, often in their teens and early twenties, unmarried and footloose. However, many older, married men in their thirties and early forties volunteered to serve and fight. Leaving behind wives and children, these men suffered great heartbreak and sadness as the war dragged on, not seeing their beloved families, hearing only secondhand of their children's growth, progress in school, sicknesses, and sometimes death. In letters from home they read of the difficulties the women they left behind faced in managing family, farm, and other matters without them. But as their letters home often show, they felt justified in their decision to fight for their country because their country truly needed them.

Men who volunteered early in the war frequently mentioned their zeal to "see the elephant:" to experience battle, to kill rebels, and to risk being killed, all in the name of patriotism. However, after their first experiences in battle—such blood-baths as Fort Donelson, Pea Ridge, Shiloh, Iuka, Corinth, Antietam, Perryville, and Fredericksburg—their avid bloodlust often turned to a more circumspect regard for self-preservation. Soldiers whose patriotic motives remained firm none-theless began to count themselves fortunate not to be in the thick of battle. They continued to fight and fight hard, but they understood the costs.

Marching and living in camp were the chief occupations of Indiana soldiers. While the railroad and riverboats played a significant role in transporting men and equipment during the Civil War, armies in the field marched carrying their weap-ons, food, shelter, and stores on their backs, with usually one wagon per company of men. The majority of Indiana's troops fought in the vast "Western" theater of operations—from the Appalachian mountains to Texas. The Army of the Potomac, in which a small number of Indiana units served, confined itself mostly to Maryland and northern Virginia, locked in a relatively immobile but bloody stalemate with the rebel Army of Northern Virginia. Covering these vast distances in an effort to wrest the Southern states from rebel control, soldiers marched great distances—often twenty to twenty-five miles a day—during campaigns, often with the prospect of battle at the end of the march. When not marching, they frequently lay idle in camp, brushing away flies and mosquitoes, suffering from boredom and chigger bites.

More Indiana soldiers died of disease—typhoid fever, malaria, diarrhea, in-fluenza—than were killed by rebel bullets or artillery. Rural farmers with limited prewar exposure to disease may have been at greater risk when herded together in camp. Sanitary measures were primitive, and the causes of disease were poorly understood by medical professionals. As a result, men (and women) commonly drank water polluted by human feces when camp latrines were located close to wells and streams. During the winter, Hoosier soldiers sometimes went without overcoats and blankets, much to the consternation of Governor Morton. "It is a contest between human life and the regulations," he wrote, badgering military officials to cut through the red tape to supply Indiana troops.[2]

Compounding the attrition from battle and camp disease deaths, Indiana soldiers deserted in large numbers. Approximately ten thousand Indiana soldiers left their units, slipping past sentries and military police, stealing away on trains homeward or making their way on foot. Many soldiers grew disenchanted and disgusted by the protracted struggle, finding the Lincoln administration's policy of freeing Southern slaves especially distasteful. During the winter and early spring of 1862–63, when the Emancipation Proclamation was announced, the Army of the Cumberland in Tennessee (of which Indiana units formed a significant portion) lacked thirty thousand troops who had deserted. Efforts to capture deserters occupied military leaders. Many deserters went home and found shelter with family and friends, while others hid out in the forests and swamps of Indiana. For whatever reason, they wanted nothing more to do with the war.[3]

For most Indiana soldiers, and also for women who experienced life at the front, the war was a debacle to be survived. As varied as were their experiences, so too were their means of survival.

"DRUNKENNESS IS THE GREAT VICE OF SOLDIERS"

Camp life prompted a rude awakening for many inhabitants. Drinking, swearing, gambling, prostitution, and other vices shocked some observers. Henry B. Hibben was chaplain of the Eleventh Indiana Volunteer Infantry regiment and later was a chaplain in the U.S. Navy.

Paducah Ky
11th Regt Ind
October 30th '61

Mrs Emily Ross

Dear Sister

Your good and patriotic and motherly letter was received a few days ago; I sent for your Son to come to my tent immediately after I received your letter. I showed him your letter and told him that I would be glad to do all I could for him. We have a bible class and a weekly prayer meeting, which he has promised to attend.

He seems to be quite well and says that he gets along very well. Soldier life however is very hard, and I fear very demoralizing too. There are a great many men who are very profane, and it seems to me that men give way to all their passions and are worse than they are at home.

Our General however has shut up all the whiskey shops in town and it is very seldom that the soldiers can get liquor. This is a blessed thing, for drunkenness is the great vice of soldiers, and it of course unfits them for service as well as leads them to greater crimes. Our men have plenty to eat here but it is not always well cooked. and they do not sleep very comfortable of nights when it is cold. But, we expect all to have stoves for our tents in a short time. The people here are all secessionists and sympathise with the Rebels. Many of the people have fled and left their houses, fearing that we would murder them.

They seemed to think that we are savages and would devour them. I cannot conceive how intelligent people can be so ignorant and deceived about their northern brethern. We have had no fight here, and I don't know whether the Rebels will try to drive us out or not. Some think they will and others that they will not venture to attack us here. I wonder that they did not attack us long ago. We have only about six thousand here, all told sick and well, and they have 30,000 in Columbus and at parts adjacent to it. Thirteen of our soldiers have died since we left home. Typhoid fever is the principal disease. We have taken a large fine house belonging to a Rebel for our hospital, and we have Sisters of Charity to help us take care of the sick. They are very kind and attentive. The health is pretty good now. We have about thirty or forty sick.

I can't tell how long we will stay here, or when we will move forward.

I would be glad to hear from you at any time, and I will try to attend to any requests you have to make concerning your son. I will do all that I can for him, and you will please tell him to come to me for advice and assistance whenever needed.

> Believe me with esteem & respect &c.
>
> Henry. B. Hibben

Kephart and Kidwell Family Papers, Indiana Historical Society, Indianapolis.

AWAY FROM HOME

Even when soldiers were encamped only a few miles away from home, the stress of separation pained Hoosier families and tried marriages. A German-born Jackson County recruit in the Fiftieth Indiana Volunteer Infantry regiment bickered with his wife by mail. As the war moved on, new heartaches appeared. Bad news like the death of a child grieved the soldiers and undermined their will to fight. A birth could reinvigorate their hope. Soldiers also often vented against their neighbors who remained civilians. The letters are translated from the original German.

> Camp Hefhern [Heffren]
>
> Dec. 7, 1861

Dearest:

I have been waiting for over a week for a letter from you, but so far I did not get one. I don't know what the trouble is: whether you don't care for me or whether you are not permitted to write. But if I don't get a reply to this letter,

I won't write to you, either, and I won't send a cent of money home, because you promised to send me some money and you didn't do it. If you write, do it immediately, for there is a rumor that we'll leave here next week. And another thing: you can fetch my clothes at the depot in Vallonia. The uppermost pieces belong to the Nentrup boys . My coat, my trousers, vest and hat are in the package. . . . .(Unintelligible lines). There is nothing further to report except that I am well. My shoulder is again in good shape. Let me close my letter with many regards and with the hope for an early reply

Your faithful husband
Joseph Hotz
50th Regiment
Camp Hefhern
Bedford

~

Jan.22, 1863

Dear Wife:

I hope you are well when you get this letter. I received your letter of Jan. 12, when you said that you are well, but that all of you had been sick except for my child. This evening I received a few lines from Hunsaker, saying that my child died. That's a hard blow for me; nothing seems right any more, I would rather not live any more. But it can't be helped. God gave her life and he took it again from her. I know it is hard for you, but it is even harder for me . You are at home and could see her, but I'll never see her any more. When I come home again, I won't find her anymore. I always had so much fun with her and now it is all over. Do not grieve too much; you have to resign yourself to it as must many other parents. You must remember that other parents also see their children die. I wished I could be with you now, then it would not be so hard for you. I hope that the war will be over soon, so that I can see you again. I wish I could be discharged and maybe I could with the help of Dr. Worth in Browntown. You or your father could talk with him. You can tell him that I broke my shoulder and also a rib; tell him, that sometimes I can hardly stand it. Ask him whether he can get me discharged; I'll pay him well for it. Let me know why Karoline died. Tell the doctor that we already lost one family member in the war and that your father is unable to work. That's all for today.

Your loving husband unto death
Joseph Hotz.

~

Collierville, Ten.
July 15, 1863

Dearest wife:

I hope this letter will reach you in good health, as is the case with me. I received your letter of the seventh of July and found that you bore me a son, about which I am very happy. Take good care of him and bring him up well till I get home. Give him my name if you want to. I hope I'll be able to send you money soon, because you said you did not get the last money. I can't be blamed for this, I did what I could. You wrote me a bad letter and called me a liar, about which I already wrote to you. This made me very angry. I know that the last letter I wrote to you was too hard, but I could not help myself. I was just too angry, but you must not take it too hard, for you know how I am. Im am quickly hot under the collar and then you'll have to be careful. I am sorry that I wrote you such an unfriendly letter. But don't write such a letter to me any more. You wrote that I thought you were not good enough for me and that I wanted to leave you. This never was true and never will be true. I won't act like some English villains and leave you in the lurch. It would be much too cowardly for me. You know that as well as I. You know I am too good for such behavior. You say I don't send home as much as others. They send home everything and after a week they write home for money again. By the time the next payday comes around they got 25–30 dollars from home again. That's foolishness. You know that we always need some money, because everything is very expensive here. If we buy anything we have to pay threefold for it. When you write again, write me the news from Indiana. Write always whether my child is still well. Now I like to live again and when I think of my child I forget everything else. Don't get angry and don't lose courage; I think that I'll soon be with you again because the war will soon be over.

That's all for today. Greetings to everybody in the whole house and whoever asks for me.

Your loving husband
Joseph Hotz.

~

Little Rock, Ar.
(This letter is dated Sept. 5, but undoubtedly should read Oct. 5, 1864)

Dear Wife:

I hope your health is as good as mine when this letter reaches you. I received your letter a week after you wrote it and I found that all of you were somewhat better again. I was very happy about this. Now that my son survived his illnees I think he will soon be as strong as before. I also saw that Schenk's wife died and that he was drafted. Drafting alone would not be so bad, but that his wife died is a great blow for him. I don't know what he is going to do with his children if he has to go himself and cannot afford a substitute. You say that they did not draft in our township; I wish they had done it because there are a goodly number of lazybones there with a big mouth who fight at home behind the whisky glass. It would not hurt if they had to go and would not come home any more, because there are too many villains around as it is. They don't want to work and they don't want to do anything for their country. I wished the Low Germans[4] would have to go soon, because they already made a lot of money with their bacon. They should find out how it is in the war. They would not get so much bacon to eat; they would eat crackers with maggots in them, maybe half a finger long. That would make their fatheads thinner. There is not much in the way of rumors around here, except that we are on short rations. Everything is quiet around here. We haven't gotten any money yet; regards to everybody, including Al(?) if you see him.

> Your faithful husband
> Joseph Hotz
> to Maria Hotz

Joseph Hotz letters, Indiana Historical Society, Indianapolis. Translated by Hermann G. Rothfuss.

"BOYS, I WANT YOU TO KEEP THIS"

Some soldiers tried to lead their families from afar. Here, a Hancock County father in the Fifty-seventh Indiana Volunteer Infantry Regiment provided guidance to his wife and sons.

Camp Hardin, Louisville Kentucky, Sunday Dec 29th, 1861.

Dear Wife and Children,

This evening after a very busy day I sit down in my tent to write to you again. I had flattered myself that to day, I would have an opportunity and time to write without so much hurry and confusion: but such has not been the case, and I must now write to you in the best manner I can in a crowed tent by candlelight. The most I can say is that I am well, and would feel well if I knew you were well at home. I fell much anxiety to know how you all are, and yet fear to hear from you lest I hear of your being sorrowful, sick and discouraged. Eliza, you must not be discouraged, Remember that the sun is never brighter than when it emerges from behind the darkest storm cloud. So the dark cloud which now obscures our happines may soon be dispeled and the pleasures and enjoyments of Home and the social surroundings of our children again soon be ours. Remember there is a power that is greater than ours that fixes our fate. A hand that is higher than ours determines the destiny of and elevates or depresses the fortunes of feeble mortals like we are. Remember Eliza that though it sems hard it is our duty to submit in the best manner we can to the dictates of that power and the ruling of that hand. Eliza

~~One thing I want the Boys if I should never be~~ been just now bothered)

I have an abiding faith that all will be well yet; that our Government will be sustained; that we will yet have a country, a Home, and time and opportunity allotted to us to enjoy them. Eliza, live in hope. Never despair. Duty, justice to yourself; to our children; to each other and our country, all demand that we should submit cheerfully and hopefully to the privations and troubles which we have to endure. If we can have no government: no Country; no Country no home. Now Eliza I want you to join with me, (though we are separated by many long miles our wishes may be the same.) in the consoling hope that our countries troubles may soon be settled, and Homes which are now made sorrowful because of absent ones may soon be rendered cheerful and happy by their safe return. I often think that our Country must have been guilty of some gross and flagrant outrage, for which the Great Ruler of the Universe as a punishment for our national sins ordained that the Democratic party should be permitted to exist, to bring this great calamity upon our Nation.

Boys there is one thing I want to say to you which I don't want you to forget, that is that the Democratic party is guilty of and has brought the present troubles upon our once happy but now unhappy Country; That notwithstanding repeated and continued warnings it has for many, long years persistently pursued a course and policy which lended directly to our present condition; and after rank rebellion was fully inaugurated failed to use the power of the government for its suppression until it had fastened its deadly fangs on the very vitals of our government. And then, and now with more than the hypocrisy of the Devil throw every obstacle they can in the way of a successful settlement; and afford to the Rebels all they ask; that is *to be let alone*. Now I never want you in any way to be connected with this hypocritical party, or anything which calls itself by the name of Democrat, nor assist in any of its party schemes or projects. Remember that if anything is so rotten and mean that you cant find any word to express its meanness anywhere else the name Democrat will express every characteristic of its meanness in the fullest sense. Boys I want you to keep this, and if I should not be permitted to advise you in after years, I want you in public life in future to be governed by this admonition.

Health in our camp is generally good. Troops are moveing south every day. Several long trains went down to day. I think we shall leave this week.

I suppose if you send letters to me here and the Regiment has left they will be forwarded on to where we may be. But they must be directed like the scrap I send you. If we should leave before I hear from you I shall write to you immediately upon arriving at our destination; but it takes so long I can't promise to write it like this. I think I will send my comfort[er] before we leave here as I think I will not be able to carry it, and it is worth a great deal more than it will cost to express it home. I have not had time to write to Pap nor any one else excepting what I have written to you since we have been here. Tell Mrs Bartlows that Oliver is well.

It is now late, and I shall not begin on another piece of paper tonight. Write soon.

Yours in love John A. Craft.

John A. Craft Papers, Indiana Historical Society, Indianapolis.

"WE HAD THE SATISFACTION OF SEEING THE ELEPHANT"

Soldiers were eager to see battle for the first time. After the battle of Shiloh, one of the worst bloodlettings of the war, one soldier from the Twenty-third Indiana Volunteer Infantry Regiment proudly reported his and his comrades' bravery.

Pittsburg Landing Tennessee April the 16th 1862

Dear Mother I wrote to you once since the fight but for fear that you didn't [get] my letter I thought I would write again I am well and hearty and hope when these few lines comes to hand that they may find you and all the rest of the family injoying the same good health I was in the fight on monday and I tell you that the 23rd is some pumpkins in a fight not a man flinched but all were anxious for to get a shot or two at the rebels and we had the satisfaction of seeing the elephant the texen rangers made a charge on us but we soon turned them they were 1.500 strong we killed 67 of them Brother Rodgers says that the hill side was black with them our surgeon says that he thought there was over a hundred of them killed them texen rangers kill six of our men and wounded severall others but they payed the penalty of it there was three wounded in our company one of them is a messmate of mine there names were James Davis of Austin Richard Humphrey of New Albany and John White of Baltimore MD we was not in the fight on sunday but we marched all that day slept on our arms that night and went to fighting in the morning we had killed wounded and missing fifty two Dick Lodyn and Gabe ritison have come back but did not get back in time for the fight before I would have missed that fight I would give fifty dollars there was no fear come on me and I went asleep twice on the battle field and the shells and balls a flying like hail about our heads, but the boys didn't seem to

mind it a bit more than a shower of rain the next morning after the fight was the
worst of all the dead & wounded laying all over the field On wensday we burried
4013 rebels there loss is about five to our one I seen old Johnson the rebel general
after he was killed governor Morton came down with three boats to take his
sick and wounded soldiers home he ordered divine service held in all the Indiana
camps last Sunday which was done I got to see a lot of the madison boys Jack
Grayson Mose Crawford bill nickolas bill Norris and old medlecot they are in the
6th Ind I seen Jim Baldwin day before yesterday we had a fine time a talking you
may be sure I am a looking for John every day the teams have not all come in yet
the boys want to go to corinth, Miss . . . not to finish up rebelion

Laurel fugitt are both a writing to day and we will send them in one envilope
I believe I have told you all write soon give my best to all inquiring friends tell M^rs
Kirke that I have got my wish and have seen the elephant all over give my love to
the family and take a double share yourself Write soon

James C Vanderbilt to Mary Ann Vanderbilt

tell the people that I got out of the fight without a scratch or a black eye be sure
and write soon

excuse me for not writing *sooner* for the mail didn't go out

James Vanderbilt Collection, Indiana State Library, Indianapolis.

"NO MAN NEED WANT TO WITNESS AN EXECUTION"

*Soldiers deserted in large numbers and for many reasons. One soldier in the
Twenty-seventh Indiana Volunteer Infantry Regiment reported on the execution
of a captured deserter. The Twenty-seventh was in New York City in July 1863 to
put down the New York Draft Riots.[5] "Butternut" was a term of derision used by
Republicans to describe backwoods Democrats.*

Tuesday 22d of September
On the Rapidan yet 1863

Dear Parents

We are still here in a new camp but orders that indicate a move at anytime.
My 24th Birthday I spent in as hot a place as I have picketed since being out.
Being placed in some buildings on the edge of the stream some 50 yds. across.
Having to crawl down to the buildings after night and remain secreted until the
next day night. Not a man daring to show his head without being shot. One
fellow put a hole through my haver-sack about five hundred yds. off. They have
good marksmen being Louisianians. We got water at night to do throughout
the day. Were under the range not only of their muskets but some twenty odd
cannon that commands the ford. They were firing away at us all day; but we

stood it through all day without returning a shot. Having orders not to fire
unless an attempt to crop. These are the days that tries men's nerves as well as
sould. Especially Butternuts Gizzards when there is a draft around. Last Frid;
there was a military execution for desertion in our division; there were several
thousand present and the prisoner soon passed into eternity with six bullets in
his breast. No man need want to witness an execution but if there had been
more done in the beginning of the struggle the army would have been better
off. I have concluded to keep the check a few days as Maj. Smith of the 150th
No 3 (from Po.) says their pay master will be here in a few days and I think I can
get it cashed here. We are having quite cool weather; and like fall. I hear you
have had considerable frost west. I enclose my 1st Lt's photograph also Charles
Buckinham Jr's when in N. Y. City I got a new album and now have a choice
collection. I rec'd a letter from Gertrude also one from Edwin lately which I shall
answer soon; as I have given all the news. I will cease at present.

Love to all Josiah

Josiah S. Williams Collection, Indiana State Library, Indianapolis.

FAKED ILLNESSES TO OBTAIN MEDICAL DISCHARGES

*Soldiers often intentionally made themselves sick to obtain medical discharges. A
regimental chaplain reported on the phenomenon.*

Head Quarters 84th Ind
near Franklin Tenn April 15th / 63

Mr. W.H.H. Terrell,

Dear Sir,

In resuming my accasional notes of the Condition and doings of the 84th
Reg Ind Vol,—allow me to say that the monotonous life, of which we felt
half inclined to complain in our last communication, has suffered a decided
interruption, as our present address would in some sort indicate. . . .

We have been recently favored with a visit from Drs Bosworth and Biddle, two
of Gov Morton's medical Agents at large, to look after the Sanitary Condition
of Indiana Troops. Now it is but fair to presume that there is about the same
amount of dishonesty in the army as in the same number of population in civil
life. It has been ascertained that many have disguised their age and infirmities,
until they drew their bounties and then soon began playing for a discharge Such
efforts are sometimes *successfully* played. Take two instances. We hear of a man
who gained his discharge (*honorably* of course) by swallowing tobacco—thereby
superindusing? sickness and spasms He fell down at picket posts &c, and must
be discharged. He succeeded, and then wrote back disclosing the joke on the

doctors. Another got in Post. hospital and constantly used Rhubarb, which baffled the efforts of surgeons and kept up the appearance of chronic Diarrhoea. Well, after he obtained *his* (*honorable*) discharge he revealed the secret to a friend that *he* (the friend) might "go and do likewise". Now while some such attempts are successful, not a few are discovered and discouraged by the Regimental surgeons. But when traveling physicians came along, it is not wonderful if they (the dissemblers) "pour out their deep complaint" to still further press their "dark designs", and it is well if all parties escape "without the smell of fire upon their garments".

With a high appreciation of these transient physicians, and their mission, it is not going too far to say that they are quite liable to be misled. Surgeon Boyd, on behalf of deserving ones of this Reg, was pleased a few days since, to acknowledge the receipt of a handsome donation of sanitary goods, through Mr. [Scott?] Indiana Agent at Nashville—Many thanks for kind remembrances of the loved ones at home—

The 84th has never yet been in serious action, but has always shown a willing "mind to work" when occasion requires. The Paymaster is among us and we are all feeling better. We are making war on the enemy in the way of forage. Fifty to one hundred waggons frequently go out and return loaded—the other day Maj Neff, and yesterday Col Orr, achieved a success of this kind. These expeditions Please the boys hugely. We have a fine force here—are in a good cause and have no fears of results—

Yours truly, Silas T. Stout, Chaplain 84th Ind

PS Should you publish please send me a copy—STS

84th Indiana Volunteer Infantry Regiment Correspondence, Indiana State Archives, Indianapolis.

"THE HOSPITAL IS A HARD PLACE TO BE IN"

For soldiers who remained in the army, life was hard even while in camp. A soldier from Owen County recounted life in camp. Rumors fueled a constant fear of the battle, in this case with the Confederate forces in Mississippi commanded by Sterling Price and Earl Van Dorn.

La Grange, Tennessee
January 20th, 1863

Dear Mary:

This note leaves me in good health, hoping this may find you the same and all the friends in good health. The weather today is nice and worm and everything has the appearance of spring. We have had some pretty bad weather here for the past few days which made it bad on the soldiers. About two weeks ago we had a pretty good snow the biggest one that has been in this country for many years, it was about three inches deep on the level. We had to stand on picket guard when that snow fell and we had to be in it three days, but we had to grin and bear it. If we did not have to go on picket guard we would have an easy time of it. We have our tents fixed up in the best of style and they are good and warm. We draw plenty of provision at this time. We don't draw any hard bread but we get plenty of flour. I have got to be baker in my mess and have got to baking good biscuits as good as anybody can bake. I take lard vinegar and soda with a little warm water and salt and that's the way that I make my bread, it raises pretty well. Besides all that I pressed me a bake oven and lid from an old secesh one night, that holds biscuits enough for fourteen of us at one time.

I must tell you the names of all the boys that is in my mess. James, Samuel, J. F., Dick, Timothy, Jacob Niehart, Philip Gonser, William Davidson, Jacob Stantz, John Kitch, John Hare, Jacob Fiscus and the two Hout boys. John Stantz and George W. Boon have left our mess and are in the Hospital. John Stantz has gone to Memphis and Boon is here in the city Hospital. I was at the city Hospital yesterday to see some of the boys. I saw Gabriel Hockstetter, he looks like a skeleton, he was awful sick but is getting better fast. Joseph Carmichael is in the city hospital I have been to see him every day for the last week, he has got the typhoid fever. I don't think that he will ever get well, the doctor has give him up for to die. Manoah Stantz was taken to the city hospital yesterday, he has the —— fever, tell Stantz's folks about it if you see them.

The hospital is a hard place to be in, the boys are not taken care of like they would be if they were at home, but they are taken as good care of as could be expected everything considered. They are a great many dying at this place, on an average they are about twenty-five per day at this city and about two out of our regiment per day. Our regiment is getting pretty well thinned out. Peter M. Hockstetter, John Moyier and J. J. Hout are not well but ain't bad sick.

Dear Mary I must tell you we are expecting a battle to take place here soon. It is stated that Price and Van Dorn are marching on to us with thirty thousand men. How true the report is I can't tell but one thing is certain, we have strengthened our picket guard and have sentinels every tent that our field officers stays in. I stood at the colonel's quarters last night for the purpose to give him the alarm if the enemy should make a break and come through our picket line. I want you to be of good cheer and don't apprehend any danger for I don't. I feel just as safe here as I would if I was setting by the fireside in the State of old Hoosier. The state of affairs looks gloomy and it is hard to tell which way the scale will turn yet. Old Abraham's Proclamation don't take very well and I am sorry it is so. I don't like it myself, but I would be glad if the people of the north would keep a little cool and not have quite so much politics mixed with their heroism. It is reported here in camp that Indiana and Illinois and Ohio is about to take their soldiers home. I hope to God that it ain't true. So far as home is concerned I would like to be there well enough but I don't want to come home without the war is closed, the the rebels driven into the Gulf of Mexico and the Negroes into hell. I think if that could be done it would stop the war and if that won't do it we will have to hang old Greeley and a few more of the Abolitionists, and if that don't do it I can't prescribe anything that will heal up the wound.

Dear Mary, I want you to take care of yourself the best that you can. I heard that you had moved to your fathers' and that brother Jacob had moved in the house with mother. When you write again I want you to tell me what you have done with the stock that I left on the place. I would like it if you could sell all the stock with the exception of the mules and one cow. I want you to keep them until I come back or until you hear that I am dead. I want you to write often to me, we have mail every day here and it has been about three weeks since I have heard from you. The last letter that I got I got from Sophia. Tell Miller to send me his best respects if he can't send me a letter, and tell Jacob to write for they are the only ones that I don't get letters from.

Direct your letters to Memphis, Tenn. 97th Regt. Ind. Vol. in care of Captain Robinson and I bet that it will come.

This from your affectionate husband Andrew Bush to Mary Bush. James Helligas and Samuel are well. Tell old Schultz that Immanuel is well and fat as a buck but can't butt so hard.

A. Bush

Andrew Bush Collection, Indiana State Library, Indianapolis.

WOMEN AT THE FRONT

Although mostly men left home, Hoosier women also experienced the front lines—working in hospitals, some following husbands or lovers; a small number donned a uniform to fight. Jane McKinney Graydon, an abolitionist from Indianapolis, described her situation and work in the military hospitals in Nashville, Tennessee.

Nashville Feb 23 1863

My dear Jemmie

Your letter gave me unfeign'd pleasure, particularly as it was unexpected. I received it a few days ago, and intended to answer it immediately, but for several days have been unusually busy. About the middle of last weeks one of the Hospitals was burnt down. Of course, the inmates had to be distributed among the other Hospitals. And besides, we just receive'd a large number from Murfreesboro, poor fellows, some of them paid very dear for their removal. They arrived here late in the evening, and from some cause they were suffer'd to remain all night in the cars— and it rain'd hard all night, and of course they had to suffer very much— some of them were brought in a dying condition. In 24 hours 4 or 5 died, 2 in my ward. One poor man, a Tennesseean, he was so anxious to see his wife and children, but nothing could save him. He was too far gone when he was brought in. This has been quite a day here. The celebration of Washington's birthday. The stores were closed and a large and enthusiastic meeting was held in the State House, some fine speeches were made and patriotic songs were sung. I was wishing for you today dear Jemmie. This is (a) beautiful place, or rather has been. The situation beyond description beautiful. Last evening thirty boats arrived fill'd with stores and soldiers. The house we stay at has a Portico extending nearly to the water's edge; if we happen to be out, we have a fine view of them as they pass. But this evening, one of the young ladies and myself walk'd down to the levee, to see them. It was a splendid sight, so many fine boats. I expect the horses and mules are glad they have come, as some are loaded with hay, and it is a long time since they had any. It would make your heart ache to see them. They are a poor abused species of creation.

Tuesday. I had hop'd to have finish'd my letter last night, but some company came in and there was so much talking that I had to stop. You would laugh if you could see our furniture. We have four chairs, and when there is more in the room we have to use our beds. Now dear Jemmie I want to talk to you about this Nebraska project. You know I desire your comfort and happiness, and I am afraid it will not pay for the privations and the many dangers you would incur— and as to the expense I know it will be 3 times the sum you mention. I heard a gentleman speak of the journey, and he said it was the last place a man should go for pleasure. I would much prefer your going east. Do not let anything take your mind off your studies. Did your father speak to Genl. Dumont before he left home? If he did not, get him to write to him immediately. I am very sorry you and I did not call on him. I expect Mr. Alexander this evening from Murfreesboro and when he comes we are going to see Andie. I feel quite impatient to go. How do you get along at home? Be as attentive as possible, and help your sister and Aunt Sophy whenever you can, do not let them get out of heart. I will be home after awhile. Has Mr. Marshal got a house yet? I hope it will not be long before they go to housekeeping. Tell Emma to get her Pa to get her a paper of Corn Starch, to make pies and puddings. It is so nice, and she will find it so convenient, everything is scarce in the spring. When the shoulders are smoked sufficient they had better boil one. They are so nice cold. Do not forget the Primers and Spelling Books, if you can possibly send them. I meet hindreds of contrabands,[6] and not one I have spoken to can read. How I would like to bring your sister Mary Ellen one, and one for myself. But I must stop, and go and cook up something for my poor soldiers.

Afternoon. I hope dear Jemmie you will go and see Grandma very often. I heard a gentleman at dinner say that Illinois butternots are use(d) up, that they were dead as Cock Robin. I hope so. He thinks that those in Indiana and Illinois will have to leave there, that they will be so despis'd, that they will not be able to stand it. But I must close as I want to send this off. I was in hopes I would have received a letter from your sister Mary Ellen. Remember it takes three or four days for a letter to come. There is so much delay in Louisville, owing to the immense number that is sent on. Give my love to everyone big and little, and kiss all the children, not forgetting Ella Sharpe, and get someone to kiss you for your loving

Mother

Jane Chambers McKinney Graydon Papers, Indiana Historical Society, Indianapolis.

CARING FOR THE SICK AND WOUNDED

Given the federal government's woefully incompetent medical care of troops, Governor Morton in early 1862 created the Indiana Sanitary Commission and Indiana Military Agency to care for wounded and hospitalized Indiana soldiers in the field. State agents worked all over the occupied South bringing medical supplies, clothing, and food to Indiana's sick and wounded. Mrs. E. E. George, a prominent Fort Wayne resident, volunteered her services to the Indiana Sanitary Commission in early 1863 and worked diligently in army hospitals in the occupied South to aid the dying and wounded. She herself died of typhoid fever in 1865 while with the army in North Carolina.[7] Isaac Jenkinson, a prominent Fort Wayne Republican, was an owner and editor of the Gazette.

LETTER FROM MRS. GEORGE.

Chattanooga, June 1, 1864

Mr. Jenkinson:

I left Huntsville, Alabama, on the 8th of May, about 12 o'clock at night—dark as dark nights can be. Within three miles of Stevenson we were fired into by the guerrillas, and our engineer badly wounded. Fortunately we had two engineers on the train, and proceeded with safety to this place. I stopped at the rooms of the U.S. Commission, where I received every attention in their power to render.

Mr. Turner, our agent here, procured an ambulance, and Col. Taylor, of Ohio, was my escort to the hospitals. I found want existing everywhere—want that could be alleviated by proper attention.

On Monday morning at 7 o'clock, in company with Mrs. Horner and our
state agent, I started in the hospital train for Kingston, Georgia, after a load of
wounded. Kingston is some 75 or 80 miles from this place.

We arrived in time to witness one of the saddest sights I ever witnessed. An
ambulance train brought in 1,200 wounded men. A large number were slightly
wounded, or at least in hands and feet, some with two fingers carried away,
some through the hand, &c. There were 75 with amputated legs and arms, some
wounded in the head, in fact, in every form and manner They were of the 20th
corps, Hooker's division, in which was the 27th, 33rd, 85th and 70th Indiana
regiments. They all suffered their fair share.

Col. McDougal, of the 133rd New York Inft., lost his right leg, and though
suffering intensely, was enthusiastic for his country, and only regretted that he
could do no more. A Captain Bigalow, of the 19th Michigan, died in the cars on
the way down, and three more were in a dying condition.

The report from the front was, both armies had fought hard all day, (the 30th,)
without any particular advantage on either side, the rebels falling back within
their breastworks at night.

The rebels shelled our hospital at Dallas and wounded many the second time.

I leave here to-morrow for Kingston, and shall remain there until it ceases to
be a stopping place for our wounded. I never more heartily blessed the Sanitary
Commission than I did last Monday night. Mr. Merit, our Relief Agent was here,
and he not only did honor to humanity's cause, but to the State he represents.
There is room for more men like him. He is going to open a room at Kingston.

Every foot of country here shows it is the theatre of war. I am sitting in sight
of Lookout Mountain, and wondering how our people ever scaled its summit,
and for ages to come it will be a wonder.

The 44th is here doing Provost duty. Col. Aldrich, who has just left the office,
reports his men healthy and in good condition. The Colonel is looking very well.

The rebels owe us a spite, and like to express it whenever they dare. They
put a torpedo on the railroad track between Huntsville and Stevenson the other
night, which was accidently exploded by an old horse roaming around.

The hour has expired, and wishing to be remembered to all my friends,

I remain yours truly,

Mrs. E. E. George

Fort Wayne Daily Gazette, June 10, 1864.

PRISONER OF WAR

Soldiers risked capture and imprisonment under harsh conditions. An officer
released on exchange reported to his home community through his local Fayette

County newspaper on his experiences after having been captured by forces under the command of General John Hunt Morgan. In an exchange, captured soldiers often gave oaths—their word, or parole—not to bear arms until they were exchanged with prisoners of their opponents. They were often released by their captors in the interim.

CAPTAIN BECK'S IMPRISONMENT IN THE SOUTH.

Mr. Green—Dear Sir: As many of my friends, with whom I have not had an opportunity of conversing, seem desirous of having some account of my experience and treatment as a prisoner of war, I avail myself of the offer of the use of the columns of your paper for that purpose.

I presume that the most of your readers are familiar with the circumstances attending our capture, and I will only say that we were overpowered by far superior numbers, and after giving them a gallant fight of an hour and a half, were forced to surrender. We were then on the field treated with almost every indignity, some of our men being stripped of part of their clothing, and some wounded men, although a bitter cold morning, were robbed of their boots, and several that were placed in wagons to be taken to Gen. Morgan's headquarters, froze to death after their arrival there. We were all taken to Gen. Morgan's headquarters, where all of the men and most of the officers were stripped of their overcoats and blankets, and the men forced to remain out in the open fields without any protection from the weather, and for forty-eight hours, without anything to eat. Our men were fortunate in not being held long enough to receive any serious injury from their exposure, but many prisoners taken since have died from exposure and ill treatment received at the hands of their captors.

While at Morgan's headquarters, the officers of the 2d. Indiana Cavalry were placed in charge of a Captain Murphy—a brute in human form—who treated us in the most insulting manner; in fact from his exceeding profanity and coarseness, his very presence was an insult. We were placed by him in a dirty log cabin, under close guard, where we were kept four days, with only one meal a day, and that of the very coarsest food. We were also, while at this place, robbed of all our clothing except what we had on, and our side arms, which Morgan had promised we should retain; but this was only one instance of his many villainies, for while he is making the fairest professions to your face, his minions are robbing you. From there we were taken to Murfreesboro, where we were paroled by order of Gen. Bragg, but instead of being sent within "our lines" and set at liberty, as we supposed we would be, we were again placed under close guard—a thing before unheard of in any civilized warfare. We protested against such treatment and asked to be set at liberty or have our paroles cancelled, both of which were denied us. We were then taken, via Chattanooga, to Atlanta, Ga., where we were placed in a close prison, with barred windows, and closely guarded. While here, we were visited by a good many of the officers of the rebel army, some of whom were profuse in their professions of kindness towards us, but they invariably ended in "professions"—We were also visited by many of the citizens—the general tone of whose conversation was that they were very tired of the war, and wanted to know how long we were going to fight them; hoped it would soon cease, &c. We invariably answered them that we were going to fight as long as one of them was found in arms against the Government, or until every rebel was exterminated. We found amongst the citizens and many of the private soldiers a strong Union sentiment, and all they wanted was an opportunity to espouse the Union cause. There was a large number of their own soldiers and citizens in the same prison with us, but occupying different rooms, against whom they practiced the utmost cruelty, inflicting the severest punishment for any slight offense; and many of them were brought in with chains around their necks, some of whom were conscripts who had refused to go into the army, others for having expressed sentiments favorable to the Union. Some old men, seventy years old, were brought there in chains because they had dared to remain true in sentiment to the old flag.—Our quarters here were, comparatively speaking, comfortable; but our food was of the very meanest kind, consisting of coarse corn bread and boiled beef, and occasionally boiled rice.

From Atlanta we were taken, a part of the way in freight cars, via Augusta, Ga., Kingsville, S.C., and Wilmington, N.C.,—passing through a dreary and desolate country—to Richmond, Va., arriving at the latter place on the 1st of March, and immediately placed in the notorious Libby prison, where we were forced to sleep on the floor, with no covering but ragged and dirty blankets that were actually alive with vermin. I can not picture the revolting scenes we witnessed and the terrible treatment we received in this prison, but leave you to imagine from the fact that there were over two hundred of us confined in one room, without a chair or bench of any kind to sit on, and at times our stomachs, although biting with hunger, would revolt at the food brought to us; but it must be seen and undergone to properly understand it. We were kept in this prison a little over a month, when the welcome intelligence came to us that we were to be released; and I can assure you that a shout of gladness resounded through the air when we were taken on board the "truce boat," and the "stars and stripes" again unfurled over our heads.

As for myself, I hold all questions subordinate to the great and important one of suppressing the rebellion and maintaining the Union. It is a duty we owe to mankind—to the progress of human freedom; and, more than all, it is a duty we owe to the poor white people of the South, to crush this terrible rebellion and release them from the iron despotism under which they are groaning. The worst reports that we have seen in the newspapers in regard to their sufferings, and of the scarcity of food, and the riots in consequence thereof, hardly come up to the reality.

In conclusion I will add that, before this is laid before your readers, I will again be in the field with my company. . . . I go with the hope that I, with the many others that have gone from this county, may soon return to our friends and our homes, the Union saved and our beloved country once more enjoying the blessings of peace.

Truly, yours,

Chris. Beck,

Capt. 2d Ind. Cavalry.

Connersville, May 2, 1863.

Connersville Weekly Times, May 7, 1863.

"THEM DREADFUL DAYS"

A young Marion County soldier from the Seventh Indiana Volunteer Infantry Regiment recalled the horrors of the Gettysburg battlefield.

Harpersfery V[a]

July the 18th 1863

Dear Sister

I received a fiew lines from you some days since stating that you had not been very well for some time, the Aresypelos [Erysipelas][8] in the face I believe. I hope you are well eer this.

Since I last wrote home we have had some long, hard and toilsome marches. And then Old Lee permited to escape uninjored any more. But we give him a good thrashing in P[a] which he will remember. Have you read the official despatch from Mead? He says since the rebbs crossed the river [Potomac] they have lost killed dead on the field 5,565, besides 9,730 wounded prisners,10,236 uninjured prisners, ([to] say nothing of the wounded he took across the River, which is said to be about 5,000) making in all 25, 531, which we can swear to. Then there was said to be about 5,000 deserters and 300 drowned in crossing the River, making in all Lee's loss since he has crossed the river 35,831. Besides the small arms that we captured. I saw wagon loads, one after the other, drawed of[f] of the field. I seen almost enough to have loaded a train of cars from your house to Brown's.

I have seen a great many hard battles but I believe that Gittysyburg was the most desperate sight I ever saw. On the right of where our regt fought, dead rebbs lay almost as thick as leaves on the groung and in all shapes, mangled in all kinds of sights. There is acres of ground there that is covered with dead rebbs' graves. I might fill a quire of blank paper fooscap were I so minded for seldom has any other circumstance or subject entered my mind since them dreadful days. I hope that I may never experience more such days while I live.

As I said in the commencement, we have made long and hard marches. My feet is wore of[f] up to the ancle bone. I never had such feet in my life before, but we have run Lee out in[to] V^a and have stoped to rest. And I hope [to] draw clothing. The Boys as a general thing are very raged.

I hope we may not leave this camp untill peace is declared, which I have ever reason to believe will not be long. I must tell you how the people treated us in P^a. They are not worthy of comparison with the good openhearted union people of M^d. The cleverest people that ever I saw are the loyal of Md. But the Pennsylvanians, save a fiew instances, was very stingy and penurios (were very fraid that the soldiers - - marched to death to save their country and homes from being disstroyed by a gang of thieves and cutthroats- -would burn some rails to make coffee, that they could not rest. When in M^d everything that a Union man had was the soldiers. Such men as them will be rewarded.

Well, I must close. I hope you will write soon.

John L Harding
to Mary E Harding

J. L. Harding mss, Lilly Library, Indiana University, Bloomington.

"OUR MOTTO IS, 'DEATH TO TRAITORS'"

Many soldiers became embittered toward those at home whom they considered to be sympathetic to the South and less than zealous in suppressing the rebellion. They often voiced their anger through their hometown newspapers, as well as in private letters.

ARMY CORRESPONDENCE.

Tullahoma, Tenn., July 10th, 1863.

Mr. Conn—Dear Sir: We received your kind letter, and were glad to hear from you, though we regret to hear of such a disturbance in our formerly quiet neighborhood, and the circumstances which brought it about are deplorable indeed.—To believe that any of our fellow-citizens there would be guilty of going so far into a league with the devil, and other secessionists as to wear emblems of sympathy for the rebellion, is something that we could not do if we had not the most convincing proof that it was so. This man of whom you speak as having been guilty of wearing a butternut breastpin we consider worse than the rebels we have to fight here, because he is where he has a chance to know that secessionists are wrong, and he is just as much guilty of the death of the thousands of soldiers who have perished in this war, as any other rebel who has not been in arms against us.

For him to send to us for our opinion as to which was right, him in wearing it or you taking it off of him, seems to us to be one of the most preposterous ideas in the world. If he thinks we would decide in his favor, he must be either crazy, or think we do not know what we are fighting for. Why, if we, as a company, in the discharge of our duty, were to meet one of these men with one of these emblems of treason upon his person, we would not hesitate (if it were not that military law does not countenance such extreme measures) to hang him upon the first tree we came to.

Of course, we consider that you did just right in taking the emblem off of him; we should feel very much hurt to hear that any one had been allowed to wear them with impunity. Had you killed the rebel in the attempt to take the butternut off of him, we would have justified you in it.—He may have worn it through ignorance of its real significance, but we "can't see it." We cannot see the way in which men keep themselves so ignorant in these times of light and knowledge, and the plea of ignorance make [sic] his case look so much the worse.

Our motto is, "death to traitors," let them call themselves butternuts, copperheads, peace men or whatever title they may choose; and we desire you, that is, all true, loyal men to join us in putting down the rebellion by adopting our motto and sticking to it until traitors shall be known and heard of no more. Hoping that we have given our opinion so that all butternuts can understand us, we remain very respectfully yours,

N. B Bennett, B. A. Louderback, H. C. Oliver, Thomas Athow, H. C. Sellers, Sylvanus Bishop, George Foltz, A. C. Myers, James P. Wilson, John Humes, S. W. Bennett, R. B. Reed, Samuel Lamb, J. W. Martin, P. C. Hincle, G. Martin, James Ward, John H. Grable, J. B. Graham, B. F. Elliott, William H. Jones, Alexander Sedam, J. V. Pownal, J. W. H. Louderback, M. Foltz, O.E. Filley, J. Fouts, C.A. Goodwin, J.R. Fallis, William J. Kline, H. C. Pownall, Enoch H. Jones, S. Clark, H. Grow, J. V. Reed, Robert W. Smith, S. B. Helper, Joseph Calkins, Edward Campbell, William Griswold, Daniel Smith, A. Brown, Aaron Booth, Enos Studebaker, Members of Co. E, 29th Ind. Vols.

Rochester Chronicle, August 13, 1863.

DEATH

James Marquis of the Seventh Indiana Volunteer Infantry Regiment had great plans for his future, but Ulysses S. Grant's Virginia Campaign, in the spring of 1864, claimed Marquis as one of its victims. The high casualty rate in the Army of the Potomac under Grant earned him the nickname "butcher."

Culpeper Va April 2d / 64

Dear Mother.

Your Most Welcome letter of the 27 Was duly received and read With delight. I suppose you feel proud at your new home Would have Written before this but did not know Where to direct My letters, to, not Knowing whether you had Mooved or not. We are still in Our Winters Quarters and Will be for sometime yet Withot the roads and Weather get better it has been raining and snowing for the last too Weeks and Our house smokes so We Cannot hardly stay in it.

I received a letter from Mag the Other day and she said she was going to teaching School again. I dont think she had better teach any longer, for it is to Confining for her. OH. yes I got a letter form George and Riley the Other day and he said he Was going to enlist in the Navy he told Me if I Wanted to Enlist again to go in to light Artilery. That Was the place to play soldier Boy. I think he played pretty Well While he Was in the Company. I say, While he Was in the Hospital at Washington City. Well you spoke about the Children being sick. I am sorry to hear that, but they Will get Well before long I hope.

did Daniel get My letter I Wrote to him Or not. if so Why dont he Write to Me. I Will answer all the letters that I get from home but you at home have got a better Chance to Write then I have for I am On duty Every day and night. and you see how things stands. (5) Months More and then I Can stay at home Or any place that I Want too. I think some times When I get home I Will get Married and go to Work. and again I dont think I Will, the best thing I Could do Would be to Move On that place that Bacan lived On Or the Hill. I dont know Whether I Could if I Wanted to but I Will find Out When I get home. Well I must quit for My hand trembles so I Cant Write you Must Excuse Bad Writing andspelling so good by

I Will Write soon again

From your son
Jam. G. Marquis

Pick Me Out a Good Girl

～

I wrote your mother since.

On the battle field Va.

June 5th 1864

Dear Friend Maggie

Your letter of the 20th arrived yesterday. And now it becomes my painful duty to write you all I can about your Dear Brother. I regret that you will be disapointed when I tell the truth. If it were possible I would gladly comply with your request, and send James body to you, But Maggie I was not allowed even the mournful privilege of bearing his body off the field, or seeing him burried. Military orders prohbit any person from leaving their posts in time of battle to carry off the dead or wounded except such persons as belong to the Ambulance Corps. And they are prohibited from carring off the dead until after the wounded are carried. Jas. was killed during the Ist days battle which took place on the 5th of May near Willderness Church while our division were charging the Rebels through a dense wilderness. Our Brigade had just charged a Rebel Brigade and taken many of there prisners while the rest of them were running for their lives. Jim had just captured one rebel and turned him over to the guard who were going to the rear with a squad and was pressing forward after another. About this time Some of our troops on the right, gave way and let the enemy flank us. Come in behind us and fire into our rear, this was when Jim was shot. The ball passed through the lower of his renapsack and into his body. Just to the left of the back bone, apparently passing directly through the heart. He fell, then arose to his feet and said I am wounded boys take me off, and then fell again I immediately ran to him, and spoke to him, but soon noticed he was dying. He spoke not a word once only caught his breath twice after I got to him. By this time the rebels had us almost surrounded, and we had to make a hasty retreat, to escape capture. As it was there was 8 of Co. F. captured. Consquently for the time being Jims body was left in the hands of the enemy. As soon as our division was rallied again we were moved to the left. I think however that some of our troops retook the ground that Jim was left on. If so he was burried by friends, but I know not who. All of our dead were left in the hands of the enemy that day, [unintelligible] our brigade. Also of the wounded.

Yes Maggie I would gladly comply with your request in regards to sending home Jims body, were it possible, but we are more than 30 miles to the left of whe[n] he fell[,] within nine miles of Richmond and I know no[t] where his body is, with out going & I did there is now nothing to prohibite the rebels from accupying the ground. My health is good. Cousin Theophilius F. Knowleton was killed on the Ioth of May, his body was also left in the hands of the enemy our losses have been dreadful during the campayn, but I think the Rebels loses have been equaly great. Excuse in which this is written, for I have no ink and bullets are whizzing over my head while I write.

Health and spirits are pretty good though we need rest and sleep badly.

Good Bye

your sincere friend and sympathizer

D. Holmes

FIVE

The Home Front

$\mathcal{T}$HE MOST IMMEDIATE IMPACT on the home front came from the absence of over half of all Hoosier adult men. Nowhere was this absence felt more keenly than on the farms of Indiana, where nearly 200,000 worked as farmers and farm laborers in 1860, over half the state's employed workforce of 336,000.[1] While many older male farmers remained at home, their sons and the younger men who made up the bulk of the farm labor pool were the state's primary source for troops. These farm laborers were joined by a significant number of younger landholding, married farmers who also enlisted.

Altogether, there was a significant drain on farm labor, and the male and female farmers who remained sought ways to compensate for the lack of labor. Key among these accommodations was the purchase of farm machinery, notably mechanical reapers for wheat and other small grains. These reapers significantly increased productivity: with a mechanical reaper, two workers could reap in a day as much grain as twelve workers in the past.[2] Female farmers sometimes could be found in the field, though often the women who headed farm households hired workers.[3] The war forced women to supervise the laborers they hired and to make decisions about marketing and planting. Labor shortages had less effect on the most important Hoosier grain, corn; it could remain in the field longer before being picked, so the lack of a mechanical solution was not as severe. The war years would see a slight shift away from corn and toward wheat in response to progress in mechanization. These shifting demands for goods, coupled with the loss of southern Indiana's most important market in New Orleans, brought anxiety about future prospects, especially in the early days of the war. By the middle of the war, however, the Mississippi had reopened, and the army's demand for foodstuffs raised prices for farmers. Hoosier farmers fortunate enough to have sufficient labor and capital to take advantage of the situation enjoyed a boom time, and many men reluctant to volunteer for the army reaped the financial benefits of the war, much to the chagrin of their more patriotic neighbors in the army.

For the state's small urban working class, however, the war was not so beneficial. Mechanization in manufacturing accelerated dramatically, and productivity increased in turn. Workers saw their real wages lag; despite the shortage of labor, their income rose more slowly than prices, which climbed dramatically during the war. The war was a boon to manufacturing, but less so in Indiana than in other Northern states. Within the state, manufacturing shifted from New Albany and Madison to Indianapolis and Evansville.[4]

Higher prices for both agricultural and manufactured goods were a special burden on those who had to depend on soldier's pay, which was sometimes slow in arriving. Many communities pledged to aid those whose husbands or even sons were at war, but this assistance was often inadequate and sometimes dependent on partisan politics. These difficulties discouraged many married men from enlisting. The wives of those who did enlist often sought help not just from the government, but from friends, neighbors, and kin. Many women left their homes and returned to live with their parents or moved in with their in-laws, creating frustration and conflict for these women who had previously headed their own households.

Anxiety increased dramatically on the home front, as typical roles shifted within families. The emotions were most deeply felt as many Hoosiers had to say good-bye to their sons and husbands, brothers and cousins, sometimes forever. With both disease and battles claiming many soldiers, the folks at home were in constant fear of losing their loved ones. Ill health or a lingering recovery from battle wounds added to the suspense. Many feared that they would be the recipient of a letter informing them of the death of their son or husband. And more than 24,000 Hoosier men did die.[5]

Those who remained at home were expected to do their part, although it was an expectation that was not always fulfilled. Women shifted the focus of their volunteer work from overseas missions to the soldiers and their families, and sometimes even the freed peoples. Women and men prepared boxes of goods to send to their local companies, providing foodstuffs, clothing and blankets, and the small amenities that made life at the front a little more bearable. They also raised funds for national organizations like the United States Sanitary Commission and the Christian Commission, which had taken some responsibility for the physical and spiritual care of soldiers in hospitals and in the field. Men who remained at home worked at insuring that the honor of their community would be maintained by raising funds to increase bounties, cash bonuses for enlisting, and providing aid to soldiers' families. One of the most important responsibilities of families, especially wives, was to write their loved ones. To keep the morale of the troops high, their officers preferred letters that were not filled with complaints. Men appreciated much detail of home life in these letters, as a means of keeping them connected to the lives to which they hoped to return.

At the same time, the life of home went on. The fields were planted and harvested, the work was done, children were born, children and adults died.

HEARTS SEPARATED

For young couples, war brought separation. Even before Lucius Chapin enlisted, his wife entreated him not to go. And once he was gone, the pangs of separation could be intense, especially when she was mistreated by his family, with whom she stayed for a while. Lucius's parents were born in Virginia and Kentucky and were moderately well-off farmers; Alice's father was John W. Osborn, a noted western Indiana abolitionist and editor. In 1860, Lucius and Alice were already married, but living with Alice's sister. Lucius was Quartermaster Sergeant of Company M of the Fourth Indiana Cavalry (Seventy-seventh Regiment).

Terre Haute, June 29th 1862

My Dear husband

What are you doing now about 12oclk. Oh, do you want to see *me*? I would give any thing almost to see you. I think I am better, they *all* say I *look* a great deal better, but I have such queer pains. Father came last night & brought a prescription which Dr Patrick says will do me good if any thing will. Father has gone out to Woods Mill [and] will write to you right away. & now my dear husband let me tell you I do not *verily* believe I could live & bid you good bye to go in the *Army*[.] How can you for a moment think of such a thing, can you leave *me*? *Can* you leave our babes? *No*, no, *no*, ever since the idea has got into my brain I'm like a foolish one, I cry & can't help it most all the time & still I struggle & work to help the precious promises in view. I pray & try to do so continuously for grace & patience for us *both* always, together, oh how disappointed I was to get no letter last night when they returned from the P.O. We sent over to Mr. Perry to bring over the bedstead for me[.] he at first refused because he had no order from you, they didn't urge him but after awhile he brought them, I am still as you left me in the Parlor. Father has a done a good deal to get ready at Sullivan, And heart full of desire to go ahead & for us all to help one another in all kindness, oh my husband I love you let us try to feel right and as Christians should, Uncle Jonas was just here & brought some nice cherries & a fine young Squirrel, oh, don't I want to see you though. I've a great many things to tell you but cannot write them; I think or at least before soon to be able to sit up or be moved but *God* alone has real knowledge. Did you go to Church today, please write to me *every day* and tell me what you do, wont you? & how Ally my own little Allie does & what? Solomon goes away in the morning. I don't remember where, but think to *Greencastle* Uncle Seely had a poor forlorn soldier from the Hospital with him, oh when I see such I cant consent to your even thinking of going. You wrote you should stay there some time; *I* can't spare you long can I? Though I am kindly cared for & every thing that can be thought of done, still I am not satisfied. I want my own corner & family. I will not try to tell you of

Father's movements but leave that to him. I don't know why but it seems to me there is such a heavy load on my heart it can never be removed & theres only one thing can do it; Dont imagine I only think of self I nor none of my folks think but what you have had the hardest time nearly any one ever had. I do not forget the many hours of patient kind attention you have given me. I love you for it & because you were of all the world my husband and I hope to make you a true & faithful though very weak wife until *death* shall *part us,* & now let us love one another and study what will make each other happy & that strive to do, & may *God bless us*

[handwriting shifts: has the voice of Alice's father]

We have just returned. Alice has spent a lonesome day but seems better than in the morning when we left. She is now pretty free from pain. The idea of your going into the Army b[r]eaks her heart—But I told her you certainly would not go unless you could procure such a position, as would *pay* and enable you to resign and return home if the service was not pleasant to you. It would certainly be folly for you to go on any other terms, when there are enough others to go, and there is enough to be done here to serve the country. But if you prefer going, come down, and we will endeavor to raise enough men for you to procure a commission. I have made some progress in preparing to enter with you, in the business talked of but this sheet is filled—I will write you again soon,—perhaps tomorrow. If you can do nothing to profit where you are, come to me at Sullivan

[no signature]

~

My Love, I got your Note of June 10th from Triune tonight, but although it is 12 oclk at night I must write you a few words, I love you tonight dearest—I sent you quite a long letter to Mur—this morn—there is nothing occurring here—except mother is *real* sick tonight I have just written to John to try to cheer him up a little—The news here tonight is that *Lee* with 100,000 men are across the Rappahannock and marching on Washington and Lincoln has called for 300,000 more. We of course hope it is a Canard—I am glad my darling that your whole soul seems so stayed on your Redeemer Oh may God bless and keep you Father wont listen a moment to a fear that any harm will befall you—Darling— *dearest hearts love* were you here you would see your Wifey mostly *undressed* sitting beside *"Our* Bed" *now* indeed a lonely couch to me—Could you see into my heart you would find *love* and affectionate regard so strong that your Wife would if you desired her immediately lay down this old *Pen* and would undoubtedly fall to loving her *dearie,* Would in all probability rush to his arms and never think of *Pen* again to night—possibly if the—Oh pshaw—but *where* are you? and [missing]

What manner of creature am I to write to you after this style when I know not *how* you are or where but oh my love how I should delight to have you here—to *love* you—to feel you once more *all my own* and *free,* is it possible those days are flown forever! That we shall never again enjoy the *close embrace* of wh[ich] you spoke in your late note! That the loving kiss shall ne'er be pressed again? but I wont think it I will try to trust *Our God* and if we never meet on Earth again I believe, hope and pray that in Eternity we *shall*—I love you—and only write this line to say so and to ask if you think I could I had best try to send you a [?]Boxer now—I'm more than anxious to—I'll try to say howdye do in the morn—Write all you can dear one to me—I love you for writing so often—Good night didn't Wifey make a fancy bird? Here is a kiss—Mr. Abbotts note I thought was kind—he is to fill H. Ward Beechers pulpit part of the summer—I suppose you know H.W. has gone to Europe—

I have no word from the home folks—Miss James wants me to go home with her—and talk to Mr. Williamson in regard to the business proposition—What do you think? please write very soon

Your ever loving
Alice
June 15th / 63
Destroy

First letter from Lucius P. Chapin Papers, Indiana Historical Society, Indianapolis; second letter from photocopies filed in 4th Indiana Cavalry correspondence at Indiana State Archives, Indianapolis, courtesy of Robert Butikas, Westville, Illinois.

A FATHER'S GRIEF

The worst fate for those on the home front was to lose a loved one. Here J. W. Gordon explored the meaning of his son's death. Gordon was probably Jonathan W. Gordon, a prominent Indianapolis attorney and Republican politician. His unnamed son might have been James R., sixteen years old in the 1860 census.

Indianapolis, Ind.
Feb. 8th, 1862.

My Dear Sir:

Yours of the 4th inst., came to hand this morning. I thank you for its expression of sympathy. I know it is heartfelt; and, therefore, feel its generous power to alleviate my great sorrow. I was very sick when I wrote you; and am still very poorly; for I have not slept without taking medicine, since my glorious boy gave up his life for a country that I fear is, as you say, "lost."

You Know that whatever might be used of my letter without compromising me, and with advantage to the country is at your service. By compromising me I do not mean in any political sense; but as a soldier in the army. All I said is true; and, keeping my name out of use, you may use it, as I am sure you will discretely for the country and mankind.

Let me, (if I did not), give you an extract from my boy's last letter to me, which I found in his coat pocket immediately over his heart, after it was brought home to me; and covered with his own innocent blood: It is to me his last will and testament—sealed with his blood. A nobler testament was never made, by hero or martyr. He says:

"You seem to be at a loss, My Dear Father, to understand my motives for volunteering; but, I think, if you will remember the lessons, which for years you have endeavored to impress upon my mind, that all will be explained. When you have endeavored ever since I was able to understand you, to instruct me, not only by precept, but by example, that I was to prefer Freedom to everything else in this world; and that I should not hesitate to sacrifice anything, even life itself, upon the altar of my country when required, you surely should not be surprised that I should, in this hour of extreme peril to my country, offer her my feeble aid."

In another letter to me in answer to the first one I wrote him after I learned of his volunteering, he uses language similar to the above; and then adds:

"When you have endeavored to instruct me from my childhood, not only by precept but by example, that my *first* duty was to my God; my *second,* to my country; and my *third,* to my Parents, you surely can not complain of the legitimate results of such teachings. I have been derelict in all three of these duties, I sorrowfully own; but trust me, My Dear Father, that henceforth it shall be my endeavor to act in a better manner, the part assigned to me in the great Trgedy of life."

His officers all say "he was as bold as a lion; and as gentle as a lamb." Genl. Milroy says "he was brave almost to a fault—generous as the sun, diffusing joy, and life, and animation in every circle in which he moved." But he has closed "the tragedy of life." Few of any age have ever acted their part more nobly. I feel that there is nothing left for me to do; but to build his monument. I had hoped he would have done that for me. But all my hopes are in the grave.

I am solicitous to fix his name in some enduring form in the memory of mankind; for I do not think a nobler sacrifice was every laid upon the altar of *Freedom,* or exacted as an expiation for the crime and curse of human slavery.

But I am a child on this subject—all weakness. Pardon this; and accept my love.

Yours truly.

J. W. Gordon.

RUNNING THE FARM

When husbands left, many women added the men's duties to their own already
considerable work load. Women's letters to husbands at the front were as likely
to focus on finances, once the sole province of the man, as they were on love and
affection. Lydia Peck's husband, thirty-six-year-old Rufus Peck, was a captain
in the Fifty-third Regiment, organized about two months before this letter was
written. In 1860 the Pecks had a farm in Wood Township of Clark County
valued at $2,500, substantial but not as valuable as those of some of their
neighbors.

Newprovidence April 29th 1862

Dear Husband,

Yours of the 17th has just come to hand I was glad to hear from you again
it is strang it takes letters so long to come and go there I thought I had told
you what the sale bill was but if so you have not got it so I will tell you again
it amounte'd to $195.90. Bellows Note $101.35, Croak security, Cooks Note $52
Bellows security[,] Dave Goss Note $16.65, Doubt security[,] Watterman Note
$10, Bellows security Cash $15.90, total $195.90, the Notes are payable in one year
with intrest from date. Bellows said you left no order with him about it and you
wrote to me that I would have to suit my self, and Bellows said the things would
be apt to sell for more at a year credit with intrest than six months without so I
told him to sell with years credit as he would know who to credit, and knowing
him to be your friend when I want advice that I think would take so long to get
from you I ask him but haply I have not troubled him but once that was about
the money Mit Hallet paid I asked him about putting it in the bank as it was
paper and part Kentucky money) his reply was he might put it where the devil
couldent get it I told that was a fact but I asked him only for avice about it as I
did not want to keep it on hands or about the house[.] he said he would take it
himself as he could pay it out and not make his debt more or less I kept the cows
you told me to Jonson and jinny[.] we could not keep one without the other they
was so lost without the other cattle that they got out once and went up to Bailies
as it was, jinny and I get along pretty well but she wont let me milk her any place
but in her stall. It has been so very cold we have not sheard the sheep but it is
warm enough now and I will have it done if I can get any one to do it if not I
will do it myself Ann did not seem to like to give up coming to work at the wool
so I told her if she come and help to wash pick spin and weave up what I wanted
done this fall I would give her two linsy dresses and stocking yarn[.] she said she
would do it but she did not want the dresses as she was not going to wear linsey
unless calico got higher than it is now but that she would make her two blankets.

her parents was here a week or so ago and staid all night I told them if she come
I wanted her to pitchin and work as if she was at home but she need not expect
me to buy her anything[.] they said they wanted her to come and for me to make
her work I told them I did not expect to order her around much[.] as to the boy
you wrote about I don't know who you mean as she has none and as for bringing
Bens boy here I would not alow it for she is as much as I want to board. I let Tom
have 2 and half bushels of potatoes for one gallon of tree molases I had plenty of
them for they sold so low that Bellows only Sold 10 bushels I have 2 or 3 bushel
yet and the children wanted the tree molases I am as saving as I can be and spend
as little money as posable brook doctor bill was 2.50 which is the most I have
spent but that I could not help, my butter has kept us in all the little notions we
want from the store[.] true paid the intrest on his note as usual and I paid jesse as
you told me Hedrick paid $2 of his debt leaving 67 cents behind I saw old baby
Newman last week he said you told him you would not want it till fall I told him
I would need some flour before that and if he would let me have some wheat I
would as soon have it as the money and he said he would let me have some after
harvest. if I see Carnel or can send him word I will have that seen to I had forgot
how much it was till you wrote[.] I was sorry to trouble you about the renting
of the place but I though it was hardly fair to find one horse and only get one
third[.] henry has worked Compry every day except one but he dont push them
much only once in a while he gets a smart fit on him then you would think he
would do it all in a day[.] there is a school started in town bob lucas is teacher
I signed ½ schollar only as I want bub to work some this summer[.] he says he
would like to know if your boys catch any fish down there[.] he dont know what
else to write as I have wrote so much we are well, write as often as convenient,
your Wife

Lydia B. Peck to Capt. R. A. Peck

Peck Family Collection, Indiana Historical Society, Indianapolis.

"I DO NOT KNOW WHAT HE WOULD DO IF IT WAS NOT FOR HIS GIRLS"

*While some farmers who owned their own land volunteered for the Union Army,
many more volunteers worked on someone else's land, either as unpaid workers for
their parents or as hired hands. The drain on farm laborers meant that farmers,
male and female, who remained needed to find new sources of labor to replace the
volunteers. Two key sources were to draw more females into the labor force and to
depend on machinery. Mary Hamilton's father did both to replace the seasonal labor
he probably would have hired before the war.*

Fort Wayne March 20th 1863

Dear Cousin Adelia

I received your letters on the 18 and was very glad to hear from you, but oh how sad it made us all feel when I read the death of your dear father. We are all well at present and hope these few lines may find you and the rest of your folks enjoying good health. For a couple of weeks we had such nice weather that we began to think that we were not going to have any more snow, but lo and behold when we got up this morning the ground was covered with snow about three inches deep and the wind has blowed cold all day, and it is raining this evening. I do not know what it will turn out to be by tomorrow morning.

I have not heard from Uncle Williams folks for a long time: I am going to write a letter to Ester again and jog up her memory and let her know that I have not forgotten her if she has me. I wrote to her the forepart of the winter and have not received an answer yet maby the letter never reached her so I will write another and make shure of it. I had such a good time going to school this winter, but alass school days are gone not to return no more. I am at home now helping Father out of doors all that I can[.] as long as school lasted I did not do him much good for I was away all day and could not do much to help him just in the morning and at night but now I am reddy to answer at any call. I have been out in the barn all day helping him to thrash wheat. he has a machine that he made him self and then he puts all of his grain in the barn and thrashes it just as he wants to use the straw to feed the cattle. When we thrash he has my younger sister drive the horses and my brother to rake the straw from the machine and my oldest sister to pitch the sheaves to me and I have to unbind them and get them up on a table so he can get at them and he feeds the machine him self. I do not know what he would do if it was not for his girls. I tell mother that he could not do any thing if he did not have us girls to wait on him We lost a cow yesterday that was worth 80 dollars to any man. she was the best one out of six of them she was a great favorite with all of us: it always happens so that the best must always go first . . . Oh Adelia how I do wish that you could come out here you would be welcomed by us all. do come if you can. I shall have to bring my letter to a close for it is getting late and my eyes hurt me very much to night. give my love to all the folks and keep a good share for your self excuse all mistake for I am in a hurry.

From your affectionate Cousin
Mary Hamilton

Mary Hamilton Collection, Indiana State Library, Indianapolis.

NO SUPPORT FOR SOLDIERS' FAMILIES

With their husbands off to war, some soldiers' wives struggled to maintain their families in the face of the irregular flow of pay home. Efforts were made to provide relief for such families, but the efforts were limited and locally based. The German-born Rows held real estate valued at only $180 in 1860. D. D. Pratt was a Logansport lawyer and leading figure in the Republican Party; Malisa Row must have believed he would have some pull. There is little information on the Shermans; like the families of many Civil War volunteers, they may have been propertyless and less fixed in place.

Pulaski Pulaski Co
ind Dec the 24 1863

Mr prat

Dear sir I must drop you a few lines and lat you know the sirkimstand I am in My husbend inlestet in 1861 in the 46 Rechment Co H ind vol he inlestet in Pulaski and wen the speches was Made the promes was that his famely shut be taken Care of and he was a Man that lovd his Contry and famely he told them af thay woud see to his famely he woud go thay promest him thay woud be all taken care of and he has bin now in survis better then too years and was alls on dudy wen evar he was Calld one ontill he was wounded in the battle at Champin hill May the 16 last and then was taken to the hosepitel and hase bin thare evar since and he hase Got no pay since he is bin in the hospital he hase bin trying to git his discharge for he is cripeld in his thy and will not be able to March aney More bud thay dit not discharge him thay put his name in the invlid Core and as long as he was with his Rechment and Got his pay I Got along with out aney help but now he hase dra[w]de no pay since he is wounded and I have Com in neede I have sold his teeme since he laft to Git along with and that is all he laft for Me to sell for he was a man that hade to Make aliven with his teeme and hade to Rent and thay hase not bin nothen don for the Soldiers wifs here that I no of at lest thay have nevar bin to see wether we hade aney thing or not and I Cut not Git along aney longer so I went to the township troste and lade in a [complaint] that i hade to have help and he give Me anoder for to Git som few things to Git a long a few days now and they want to put My childern out and have Me take the smalast and Go and work out I have five Childern the oldest is 10 years old next 8 one 6 one 4 and 2 years old these littel childern thay want to put out to save the expence of the Conty this is the way the Butternuts treats the soldiers wifs here I got along too years with out thur c help and now becose My husbend dont Git his pay so I hade to Call one them and Must I now brake up houskeeping to plese these Butternuts for the Most of them that lives here is Butternuts now af you plese write to Me as soon as you git this and lut Me no wether thay can treat soldiers famelys this way I think this woud be Ruther to hard for a man to leve his famely to purtact his Contry and fite for them that is at home as well as for him self and wen he Coms home to find his childern scatert amongs strangers how will he fell thay are Makin op Money for to git the men to inlest now to keep the draft of[f] I think a Man that Gose for the Money will make a poor soldier thay batter lat them be draftet and safe that Money to take care of the famelys and lat them that Gose now have wut our Men Gits that wen too years a Go so no More at present yours in haste

Malisa Row
Wife of George M. Row to Mr prat

D. D. Pratt Papers, Indiana State Library, Indianapolis.

December the 10th 1863

Mr. morton govnore of indiania i take my pen in hand to in form you how us poor Soldiers wifes are treated Some times we have Some thing to eat and Some times we dont and there a[r]nt But four Soldiers wifes in Moors Hill[.] all of our Children are naked for Clothing and they pretend to do [illegible] things and Dont Do any thing and there is a man in this town that Says let the Soldiers wifes go to the poor house where they Belong and i want you to raly up the loyal men if we have got any Among us But Dont say any thing A Bout [w]ho informed you of the fact we are Doged to Death [illegible].

Yours truly
Mrs Mary Sherman
Moors Hill Dearborn Co Ind

Rite Soon and let me [k]now if you get this or not.

Governor Oliver P. Morton Papers, Indiana State Archives, Indianapolis.

WAR AND MADNESS

The anxieties brought about by the war and by the conflicts at home could drive the more mentally fragile into clinical depression or psychosis.

Total no. 2332

No. for the Year, 144

Date of Admission, August 7th 1862

Name of Patient, Amelia A. Lewis

Nativity, Virginia

Post Office, Greencastle

County, Putnam

Age,

Social Condition, Married

No. of Children, 4. 4 dead

Duration of Insanity, 6 weeks   Form of Disease, Mania

Predisposing Cause,

Exciting Cause, Supposed that her Son being in the Army was the Cause, supposed him dead etc.

Propensities, Homicidal and Suicidal

Bodily Disorder,   No. of Attack,

Religion, Baptist   Temperament,

Occupation, Housewifery

Are the Parents of patient blood relations?

Remarks: Made an attempt to destroy herself by using a knife to cut herself

—

Total no. 2441   No. for the Year, 53

Date of Admission, Feb 10, 1863

Name of Patient, Hanah Ellen Duesler

Nativity, New York   Post Office, Lisbon

County, Noble   Age, 29

Social Condition, Married   No. of Children, 6

Duration of Insanity, 6 months   Form of Disease, Melancholia

Predisposing Cause, Unknown

Exciting Cause, War excitement. Fear of draft

Propensities, Suicidal & Homicidal

Bodily Disorder, None   No. of Attack, 1

Religion, None   Temperament,

Occupation, Farmer's wife

Are the Parents of patient blood relations?

Remarks: She left a pair of twins at home 3 mo old.

—

Total no. 2511   No. for the Year, 123

Date of Admission, June 26, 1863

Name of Patient, William Badger

Nativity, Ohio   Post Office, Shelbyville

County, Shelby   Age, 45

Social Condition, Married   No. of Children, 9

Duration of Insanity, 10 days   Form of Disease, Mania

Predisposing Cause, Unknown

Exciting Cause, Scared at soldiers who proffessed that they were going to arrest him

Propensities, Suicidal
Bodily Disorder, Maniacal exhaustion   No. of Attack, 1
Religion, None   Temperament,
Occupation, Farmer
Are the Parents of patient blood relations? Unknown
Remarks:

~

Total no. 2512   No. for the Year, 124
Date of Admission, June 26, 1863
Name of Patient, William M. Wilson
Nativity, Indiana   Post Office, Homer
County, Rush   Age, 33
Social Condition, Widower   No. of Children, 1
Duration of Insanity, 20 days   Form of Disease, Mania
Predisposing Cause, Unknown
Exciting Cause, Excitement. Was enrolling Commission[er] in Company
     with Deputy Provost Marshal Stevens in Rush Co at the time he was fired
     on by the mob and killed.
Propensities, Homicidal, but not decidedly so
Bodily Disorder, None   No. of Attack, 1
Religion, Methodist   Temperament,
Occupation, Farmer
Are the Parents of patient blood relations? No
Remarks: Refer to Inquest papers

~

Total no. 2764   No. for the Year, 178
Date of Admission, Oct 5th, 1864
Name of Patient, William M. Snell
Nativity, Ohio   Post Office, Rockville
County, Parke   Age, 37
Social Condition, Married   No. of Children, 6
Duration of Insanity, 10 days   Form of Disease, Mania
Predisposing Cause, Unknown
Exciting Cause, Fear of Draft. Is drafted.
Propensities, Homicidal & Suicidal
Bodily Disorder, None   No. of Attack, 1
Religion, None   Temperament,

Occupation, Carpenter
Are the Parents of patient blood relations? No
Remarks:

Admission Book number 1, 339, 448, 518, 519, 230, Indiana Hospital for the Insane, Central State Hospital Records, Indiana State Archives, Indianapolis.

THESE TERRIBLE TIMES

For Democrats like Isaac Ireland and Aaron Stryker, the war brought trials on top of the tribulations of daily life. From a family originally from Pennsylvania, Ireland held a Jackson County farm valued at one thousand dollars. New Jersey–born Aaron Stryker was a farmer as well, with real estate valued at only six hundred dollars.

Brownstown July the 21 1861

Dear Brother after delaing to Rite to you I Embrace ths opportoonity to Let you Know that We are all Well at Present and Hope that [t]heas Lines may find you all Injoing the Same Blesing We Lost ower Litle girl Mary Caroline She Died the 6 Day of July this Month with the flu She was 4 years and 3 Months olld[.] She was Sick 5 days[.] the Conexion are all well as Comon at present Mother is Still Very Feeble all the Time Times is very hard heare Crops are all good and Look Promesing I am Farming on nomber one ths year Every Body is Traitors and Torys that Dont Sancton the Ablition wore aganst Slaverey[.] the Chikogo Plat Form Denies the South the Right to the Comon Teritory and Places the Negro on Equality with the Wite man I am sorrey that Thare Ever was a Sectional Man eleted President[.] we are Reping the Reward Now[.] Times is the Dullest I Ever Seen I dont Believe that Wheat Can Bring More than 50 cts Corne wownt Be worth More than 10 or 15 cts this Fall[.] the People are Crazy A Bowt the ware I mean the Fanatics[.] the Same Party that oposed the Mexican Wore are the Same party that are Ergin the Extermination of the South and wanting the Negroes Freed[.] the Republicans Threten to hang Every Body that Dont Believe as tha do god onley Knows the End of ower Troubles Three compnyes has gon From ths County and 5 companyes has organised under the Sate Melitia you Don't know to Day W[h]o is your Frien to Morow I Feel Sad over the Condition of ower Country[.] I Dont K[n]ow What to Right I would Be Glad [to] See you

No more at Present I remain yours

Truley
Isaac Ireland

P.S. I will try and write a few Lines to fill up Isaac's Letter[.] our old Friend Jugde Miller is out hear again this summer and for the Last few days he has been verry

pooreley[.] they think he cannot stand it much Longer[.] we are all in good health
Mother continues to be verry feeble[.] she is Liable to drop of any day so if you
Can Come out this fall you had better try and Come Joseph Miller folks are
all well but I believe he will not build him a house this fall[.] we have plenty to
Eat hear this fall but no money to buye it with[.] write soon and Let me know
wether you will Come out hear this fall and if so how soon we may Look for you
and Mary Ann out and as Many Moore as you Can Bring Give my Love all and a
Kiss to boot yours Respectfully

Aaron Stryker

James Ireland Family Correspondence, Indiana Historical Society, Indianapolis.

"MONEY IS ABUNDANT"

*While the beginning of the war brought fears of economic disaster, by 1863, those
fears had subsided; even Aaron Stryker would celebrate the high prices. The
maintenance of the Union Army provided a ready market for many Hoosiers'
goods, and the fall of Vicksburg led to the opening of the Mississippi River and
access to Indiana's traditional market at New Orleans. As a stepping-off point
for many goods to the army, the Ohio River towns especially prospered, or at
least their middle class did. For the working class, wages rarely kept up with
skyrocketing prices. Here a C. Denby (probably Charles Denby, once colonel
of the Eightieth Indiana and a Democratic politician) adds a postscript to a
business letter to a Captain James L. Orr telling of the prosperity that has overtaken
Evansville.*

PS There will probably be a draft in this Township for 100 men. Some Country
Townships are full up. Considerable efforts have been made to recruit up but
with no great success. There is much sickness here and several ladies have died
lately. Charley Wagner is seldom in town—he said when I saw him he thought of
going back. We are flooded with amusements and this City is rather gay. Dresses
are most extravagant among the fair. Money is abundant and real estate goes off
like hot cakes. There is very little said about the war. People are content to leave
that to the Army and to make money for themselves. Refugees are here by the
hundred and great distress prevails among them. Vast amounts of money are
now given in charity, some compulsory under Mayor Robinson's commercial and
permit dictation, and some voluntary. Combs is pretty low in health. Congress
will probably repeal the $300 clause.

Letter from C. Denby, Evansville, to Captain I. L. Orr, December 15, 1863. James L. Orr Collection, Indiana
Historical Society, Indianapolis.

AIDING THE FREED PEOPLES

The most common volunteer efforts to aid the war came through the U. S. Sanitary Commission and communities' efforts to aid local soldiers. For Quakers and others of humanitarian good will, the refugee crisis of African Americans in the South, escaped to Union lines or abandoned by their masters, prompted them to provide relief. Irish-born Ann C. Thomas headed her household of three boys, aged nine to twelve, together with real estate valued at $1,200. She prospered in the 1860s, with her real estate valued at $3,700 by 1870.

College Corner Jay Co.

Dec 11 1862

My Dear Em

I received yours at least two weeks ago but had not a spare moment to answer your kind letter until just this afternoon. I have been very busy begging for and fitting out a box of clothing to Send to the poor Freed Men women and children I had the pleasure of contributing myself 28 garments Spools Sissors, thimbles, + needles. I had a pushing time to get them made, and to collect that I begged, Mr. Tucker packed the large box, he packed them So hard that his hands pained him for a week after, there was a hundred and Seventy five things in the box besides thread + needles +. We had bed clothes also yarn ++ I had money saved to buy a black Mohair or Silk lustre dress to ware on particular occasions + times, which [the money] I took and laid out for good strong materials to make those things I sent, I thought I could better do without the dress than they, who were robbed of all and especially at this trying time.

I had some thought of going to Ireland when I heard of your City being threatened with shells, but am thankful for the privilege of staying just where I am.

I was afraid you were going to let the Rebels come here and pick me up ++++ so I had a big Mind to part.

Lydia + husband promised me a visit immediately after her Marriage and I expected you and Henry to come with them (I told her to bring you both) as Lydia said you were to be at the wedding, so about the time I expected you all I actually killed the *fatted calf,* prepared all the good things hired help to do so, dressed myself + young ones in our very best, and looked for you all for three or four days; When we sat down to breakfast, we would say, well they will be to dinner actually keeping the goodies waiting hot + cold for a week long and then the visit turned out all fizzle[,] Lydia having skedaddled to Kansas, and you both even not thinking about *your poor relations.*

Blessed are they who expect but little, they shall not be disappointed.

I actually had the Vanity to think that you would judge me worthy of a Visit and have looked for the last three years every fall and summer for you both. True I have no inducements to offer but—but—nevertheless.

You ought to have told us the name of your boy. I am glad to hear of your prosperity in this worlds things, May you be blessed with the realization of *your Eternal Inheritance* purchased for you through the Love of God in, + by, Christ— the Lamb of God that taketh away the Sins of the World!!!

We are all well with the exception of colds.

The boys are at school[.] the[y] are making a little progress in their education. Joseph is as tall as I am. Give my Love to Henry, I should like to see Him.

Yours affectionately,
Ann C. Thomas.

Individual Letters Collection, Earlham College Archives, Earlham College, Richmond, Indiana.

SIX

Race, Slavery, and the Emancipation Proclamation

$\mathscr{S}$LAVERY WAS CENTRAL to the American Civil War. The people at the time of the war—its participants—believed that slavery was the critical issue leading to secession. Moreover, for Americans the issue of slavery was embedded in a complex matrix of race and racial hostility existing since the beginning of European settlement in the New World. The people of Indiana ascribed the source of the war to slavery.

While slavery was understood to be the root cause of the rebellion, in most quarters around the state the issue initially took second place to calls to preserve the integrity of the Union. With the exception of prominent abolitionist voices such as George W. Julian and his family newspaper, pressure to end slavery was muted in Indiana early in the war. Governor Oliver P. Morton, a Republican personally opposed to slavery, worked to mobilize all people in Indiana to back the war effort and aimed to avoid antagonizing state Democrats. However, as the war progressed in 1861 and early 1862, slavery gradually reemerged as the chief issue. Major General John C. Frémont's emancipation edict in Missouri in late 1861 embarrassed President Lincoln and other Republicans in their efforts to recruit Northern Democrats and the border states of Maryland, Kentucky, and Missouri to the Union cause. Indiana Democrats became deeply suspicious of Republican intentions and vowed to protect the institution of slavery as enshrined in the U.S. Constitution. Thomas A. Hendricks, Indiana's Democratic standard-bearer, attacked the abolitionist aims of the Lincoln and Morton administrations in his speech January 8, 1862, at the state Democratic convention, thereby framing the party's opposition stance for the coming year.[1] Democratic politicians and editors focused their attention on the abolitionist designs of the Republicans and predicted that freed African Americans would undercut workers' wages and lead to "amalgamation"—interracial marriage and race mixing. Such race-baiting found receptive ears, as racist attitudes were common among most white people of Indiana, Republicans and Democrats alike.[2]

In 1862 President Lincoln encountered strong pressure from disparate political groups on the issue of slavery. The radical Republican wing of the president's party urged measures to abolish slavery and destroy the Southern slave economy. On the other hand, Democrats favored conciliation of the rebels and counseled against measures aimed at ending slavery. However, events in the continuing war—most notably the flight of thousands of escaping African Americans to the protection of federal lines and the passage of the Confiscation Acts and other legislation[3]—forced Lincoln to act. Guided by his personal antipathy to slavery, he drafted a Preliminary Emancipation Proclamation in the summer of 1862 to free those slaves in areas of the South still in rebellion. Lincoln bided his time until a federal victory in the field would give him a chance to make a public announcement of his plan. The battle of Antietam, in Maryland, in September 1862, though not exactly a resounding Union victory, afforded him his opportunity. The president announced his preliminary proclamation on September 22 and stated that on January 1, 1863, all slaves within the rebellious Southern states would be "thenceforth, and forever free." The inducement that Lincoln held out to Confederate slaveholders was that if their state rejoined the Union, the slaveholders could keep their slaves; by this same reasoning, slaves in the border states and in those areas of the South under occupation by federal forces were not freed under the proclamation. Lincoln's measure was a temporizing one, meant to reflect the changing military situation as well as to appease both the radicals and the Democrats.

Lincoln's preliminary statement was met in the North with jubilation by abolitionists, and with disgust and opprobrium by most Democrats. Confirmed in their fears of abolition, emboldened Democrats turned out in large numbers at the polls, joined by a number who had voted Republican in 1862, and nearly swept the October 1862 elections in Indiana and other states. Moreover, many soldiers, disgusted by the proclamation, voiced their disapproval. Wrote one soldier: "i am out fighting to free the negroes whitch don't set very well on my stomache just now."[4] Some soldiers deserted their units and were sheltered by sympathizing friends and family back home in Indiana.

The proclamation, however, once in force after January 1, 1863, changed the war from a struggle for restoring the Union to an abolitionist endeavor. Free African Americans in the North also rejoiced at a subsequent policy of organizing African American units to fight the rebellion. Indiana's African American men and women joined the war effort. The Twenty-eighth United States Colored Troops Regiment, raised primarily in Indiana, fought in the Army of the Potomac in 1864 and 1865. Approximately 180,000 African American soldiers fought in federal armies—for less pay than white troops received—for the Union, a union without slavery. This group represented a significant number of troops in the latter stages of the war, when war weariness in the North hindered recruiting among whites.[5] White soldiers initially resented the African American presence in the uniformed ranks, although some saw benefit: "I will not grumble a bit if a negro gets killed instead of me, so push them in."[6] By war's end, many white soldiers had recognized the fighting qualities of the African American troops and accepted them as comrades in arms, paralleling their acceptance of the abolition of slavery as a valid goal for the war.[7]

"THE NEW REVOLUTION UPON WHICH WE ARE EMBARKED"

From the beginning of the war, some Indiana abolitionists called for the end of slavery as part of the ultimate resolution.

WHAT IS THE REMEDY!

The fact that slavery is the great source of all our woes as a nation, is now generally, though often reluctantly, conceded. That it has precipitated the present dreadful crisis upon us no sane man doubts. But the irresistible logical sequence is not so generally acknowledged or impressed upon the public mind as it should be—that is, that there can be no *final settlement* of our troubles, no *permanent peace* to the country except through the *extirpation* of its grand *cause,* throughout the length and breadth of the Union, and that NOW is the accepted time for effecting that good work. There is a remarkable silence on this truth, which must be very generally present to the public heart and conscience. The organs of public sentiment are chary of adverting to it. Even the excellent sermon of Mr. Beecher, the conclusion of which we give this week, hints at rather than avows what must have been his conviction in regard to it. We are glad now and then to hail such utterances as the following from that able and influential journal the New York *Evening Post:*

> When we have put down those who seek to substitute a military despotism for the Constitution of our fathers—when we have conquered the treason which is now striving to ruin our commerce and strangle our liberties, then we should be less than sensible men if we did not also put down forever that which has alone supported and strengthened the mutinous aristocrats.
>
> It is impossible not to see that human slavery is the canker-worm which has for so many years gnawed at the heart of our republic.
>
> We should be fatally in error, therefore, as a nation if we did not make an end of this thing, which alone has shackled our progress, and which now has caused the desperate attempt to overthrow the government and the Union.

We have only space this week to touch upon this topic. We shall take early occasion to amplify and enforce the views above indicated. There is great need that it should be done, lest the new Revolution upon which we are embarked, fail of its highest purpose.

Centreville Indiana True Republican, May 16, 1861.

AROUSED TO A SOLEMN DUTY

Lincoln's preliminary Emancipation Proclamation cheered the abolitionists in the Indiana Republican Party.

THE NEWS—LIGHT DAWNING

The rebels are driven out of Maryland, by the hardest and bloodiest fighting of the war. They carried off all their stores and most of their wounded, and were prepared to contest our passage of the Potomac. This escape has disappointed the country, although their repulse is so creditable to our arms. Harper's Ferry has been retaken by our troops. There will probably be but little fighting on the Potomac for some time, both parties being so badly crippled.

The rebels have fallen back from Cincinnati, but Bragg having out-generalled Buell and united with Smith, they are threatening Louisville, where a great panic prevails. Gen. Nelson has ordered the women and children sent away. Bloody times are impending in Kentucky.

At last, the President is arousing himself to a solemn duty. He has issued a proclamation that in all districts of country which shall remain in rebellion on the first day of next January, *the slaves shall be declared free and protected in their freedom by the army and navy of the United States.* He also embodies in his proclamation the late confiscation acts of Congress, and expressly requires their strict enforcement by all our commanders in the field, including the order dismissing from service any officer who shall aid in returning fugitive black men into slavery. We shall publish the proclamation in full next week. The only regret will be that it was not made to take immediate effect. But thank God for it as it is. It will change the entire policy of the war, and gives new hope for our country.

Centreville Indiana True Republican, September 25, 1862.

"THE PENALTY OF THEIR CRIMES"

By contrast, the guarded defense of the proclamation by the organ of the state Republican Party reflected the political difficulties party leaders expected as its result.

THE PRESIDENT'S PROCLAMATION.

The question presented by the President's Proclamation emancipating the slaves in the rebel States is a very simple one. Have those who have thrown off the Constitution, repudiated the laws, and attacked the Government, a right to the protection of the Constitution, the laws or the Government? Must we maintain, to the advantage of those who are destroying us, an institution which they have voluntarily and defiantly withdrawn from our protection? They will have none of our Constitution, and they make their repudiation good in the blood of our bravest and best. Shall we give them still the benefit of that Constitution, when the strength it confers is turned to its destruction? Shall we help ruin ourselves to maintain laws for those who won't have them, and resist their restoration with all their power? The President's proclamation says "No. If the rebels resist the extension over them of the laws which we have made to protect slavery, then slavery shall have no further protection." Upon this [illegible] of the secession: Democratic papers cry out that the President is guilty [of] a "monstrous usurpation," that he has set aside the Constitution, and installed his own will the ruler of the nation. The infinite folly of this clamor almost silences refutation. One feels at a loss how to shape an argument to meet it. Argument is the instinctive effort of the intellect to counteract that which another intellect has misstated, or misused: Its office is lost when it has only the ravings of insanity to oppose. One might as well draw his "syllogisms" against Ophelia's "Pillicock sat on Pillicock Hall," as to make arguments against this monstrous absurdity.—Where in the Constitution is it provided that those who rebel against it shall nevertheless be protected by it? Are they to have all the advantages of disobedience and all the advantages of protection too? "Yes," say these sympathizing gentlemen, "the Constitution protects slavery as well for those who are trying to destroy the Constitution as for those who obey it." When men reach such a pitch of abject drivelling devotion to the institution that has made this war, and now gives it its last convulsive strength, it is time to hand them over to an insane asylum. The proclamation is too sweeping in emancipating the slaves of loyal men in the rebel States, but that is not the cause of the clamor against it. The *Sentinel* and all of its class are not so furiously angry because a half dozen loyal men may lose a half dozen slaves a piece, but because the loss of their slaves by the rebels *weakens the rebellion*. How is it that every white man able to bear arms can be taken from thousands of plantations, as we know they have been, and their families still live in comfort, if not luxury? How is it that while all effective white labor is armed to overthrow the Constitution, there is still labor enough to support them in their desperate scheme? How is it that while half of the white men in the North *must* stay at home, not one-fourth in the South need do so, and that all this enormous difference of strength is turned against us in the war? By the one simple fact that the rebels can use their slaves to do the work which without them they would have to stay at home and do themselves. The slaves are the laboring life-sustaining element of the rebellion. The President's proclamation, as far as it can be made effective, destroys that element of strength, and leaves the rebellion no support at home without weakening its armies in the field. *There* is the secret of the wrath of the whole *Sentinel* tribe. Wherever that proclamation can be made operative, there the rebellion loses its foundation, and its provocation, too. They have no thought of the Constitution except as it furnishes them a pretext to denounce every act that injures the rebellion. Who ever heard the *Sentinel* denounce the Montgomery constitution, which formally destroys the old Constitution of Washington in the rebel states? Nobody. On the contrary, it expressly and earnestly advocated the *abolition of our own Constitution and the adoption of the other.* Whoever heard it censure the rebel States for repudiating the debts due their Northern creditors? Nobody. Was *that* constitutional? Hardly, but it was a good thing for the rebellion. It stole the "sinews of war" from the North, hence the *Sentinel* had not a word to say against it. Whoever heard it condemn the seizure of the government mints and arsenals by the rebels? Nobody. Was that constitutional? Not exactly, but it helped the rebellion, therefore the *Sentinel* kept its "constitutional" objections quiet. Whoever heard it say a word against the exclusion of Northern citizens from the rebel States? Nobody. The Constitution requires the citizens of any State to be given the rights of citizens in every other State, but the *Sentinel* forgot its constitution just then. And it regularly forgot it whenever the rebels violated it. They could repudiate it, spit upon it, kick it out of their States, and the *Sentinel* never dreamed that such proceedings were "unconstitutional." Not a bit of it. But the moment the President orders the arrest of Merryman for burning bridges to keep our troops out of Washington, the *Sentinel* recollects all about the Constitution. So does John C. Breckinridge, and both denounce the President without measure for violating the Constitution! Where was their memory of that document all the time the rebels were kicking it from foot to foot from Texas to South Carolina? Waiting for a chance to weaken the Government and help the rebellion. Breckinridge couldn't wait long, so he went off to the rebel army. The *Sentinel,* more cowardly and more judicious, stays at home to cry out "Constitution" when ever anything appears likely to weaken the rebellion and to forget all about it when its violation occurs south of the Potomac. We commend to it a little impartiality of memory, and a slight equality in the distribution of its abuse. The rebels have certainly not acted in strict conformity to the Constitution all the time, and a little recollection of that fact may do the *Sentinel* good. When it next goes into a hysterical fit over the President's proclamation, let it remember that the protection of the Constitution is a right that can only belong to those who recognize the Constitution, and that rebels have no claim to anything but the penalty of their crimes.

Indianapolis Indiana Daily Journal, September 27, 1862.

"THE PEOPLE OF THIS COUNTY WILL NEVER CONSENT TO RECEIVE SUCH AN IMMIGRATION OF NEGROES"

Democratic Party editorialists resorted to racial fearmongering to attack the Emancipation Proclamation. Democratic rhetoric focused on the revolutionary

*aspects of Lincoln's action, characterizing it as an unconstitutional and temporary
measure, one capable of being overturned in time. The stress, however, was often
on the competition that free black labor posed to white labor, and the hope of
Democratic leaders was that their racist attacks would attract Republicans, many
of whom shared the Democrats' view on race even as they differed on other
measures.*

THE EMANCIPATION PROCLAMATION.

To-morrow the Emancipation Proclamation goes into operation, when, if we
are to believe its promulgator and advocates, the Union is to be restored, peace
will again visit us, our soldiers will return home, our debts will be paid, and
a general political millennium will ensue. But we remember that these same
individuals were full as sanguine, and their predictions equally as broad, about
one year ago, when the confiscation act was passed. We remember they told us
there was nothing the matter, that nobody was hurt; we remember their assurance that the South could be starved out in three months—that the privateers
captured should be hung as pirates; that Mason and Slidell should never be given
up; that upon the fall of Fort Donalson the back-bone of the rebellion was broken;
and that the highways would be filled to overflowing with volunteers, rushing
to sustain "a principle," if the President would only issue his proclamation. To
place much reliance upon their predictions now, we must forget all these things,
and much more—must forget every act of the administration from the inaugural
to the present time; must forget that the men composing it are politicians, and
conceive them to be statesmen.

We do not propose in this article to discuss the constitutionality of the proclamation, or its adaptability as a means of putting down the rebellion. Both of
these questions might be easily disposed of against the measure, by quoting the
words of the President himself. We propose to view it from the stand point of
Abolitionism, and trace its inevitable results upon our social and political systems.
No great nation should enter upon a radical change of its policy of government
without well weighing its probable results, and the utility of its effects; and when
the power of that nation resides not in a few individuals ruling by "divine right,"
but in the great mass of the people, who are sovereigns themselves, and at whose
behest their servants begin and end their official career, no such schemes of radical change should receive their assent until they have been fully discussed.

Assuming then that the proclamation possesses all the vitality and power
claimed for it by its advocates, what will be its effects? first, upon our system of
labor and production, which is of the most vital consequence to the great mass of
our population, the President in his message, says:

"Is it true, then, that colored people can displace any more white labor by being free than remaining slaves? If they stay in their own places they jostle no white laborers. If they leave their old places, they leave them open to white laborers. Logically there is neither more nor less of it."

If the President by this expects to convince the people that the emancipation of the slaves will not seriously interfere with the system of labor now established, he must immensely overrate his own logical powers, or underrate those of his constituents. He virtually says if these "American citizens of African descent," by which euphonious title they are to be hereafter designated, (under penalty of treason, we suppose,) choose to come North, it will not interfere with labor here at all. Oh, no, there is just as much labor to be done upon the continent as ever, the places they left are vacant, and all the white laborer has to do, is to go down and step into his sable lordship's shoes upon the plantation. It may be just possible that this is one of Abraham's jokes, with which he so frequently regales us; if so, the people will be slow to appreciate, not only the joke, but the appropriateness of the time and place in which it was uttered.

What say you, American citizens of Anglo-Saxon descent? Will this jostle your labor or will it not? Are you reduced to the alternative of competing with negro labor, or changing places with him at his own discretion? Or have you the right, the inalienable right, to say that you will do neither? The assertion that a large importation of negroes into the North would not interfere with and degrade the white laborer, is so superlatively ridiculous that it needs no argument to refute. The President admits as much, and thereby stultifies himself by attempting to show that they would not come North, and after all, is compelled to add, if they did, the Northern States could refuse to admit them if they chose. Was he not aware that most of them had already done so by overwhelming majorities? But let us see whether they would come North.

Before the rebellion began there was a large class in the North who believed it would never assume very great proportions, because the great majority of the Southern people were non-slaveholders. They said these non-slaveholders would not fight to protect an institution from which they never expected to derive any benefit, and which was a degradation to themselves. These persons were surprised to find that the non-slaveholders were the first to enter into the rebellion, and are to-day the most ferocious and determined in their hostility to the North. The history of the transactions South show that the slaveholders were, as a general thing, the last to embrace the dire alternative of a resort to arms. Why was it that these non-slaveholders disappointed the Northern people and adopted a course apparently contrary to their own interests? We reply, and no man can gainsay or refute it, it was the fear that a free negro population would be imposed upon them. Whether this fear had foundation in fact, it matters not; it proves conclu-sively what their opinion is, and what their future course will be in regard to this population. It proves that they never will tolerate it in their own midst.

Now we have as yet no official intimation but that the Southern States, after the rebellion shall be crushed, will again stand with all their rights and privileges unimpaired, and granting the abolition of slavery shall have been accomplished, it is as certain as anything in the future can be, that free negroes would be excluded by legislative enactments from them, as a necessary consequence they must come North. The only escape from this dilemma is to compel the Southern people to keep them there. This is precisely what they think we are trying to do now, and it is this supposition which gives them the unity and strength that has defied our utmost efforts for the last eighteen months. The possibility of compelling the South to ac-cept a free negro population depends entirely upon our own ability to exterminate the whole white race there, of which we can have no very sanguine expectations, in view of our past success. Even if we are able to do this, the result would be the overthrow of our whole political system. There is no method short of a complete abandonment of the Constitution, by which the Southern States can be held by military force, as provinces, subject to the arbitrary will of Congress and the admin-istration. Considering then that the proclamation will effect the abolition of slavery, one of two results would follow: we would have to give four millions of negroes an asylum in the North, with all the increased burdens they would bring, in the filling our prisons and poor-houses with criminals and paupers, to say nothing of their degrading presence in our midst, which is no inconsiderable item, in view of the fact that the proportion of Goshen Corporation would be about five hundred, and of Elkhart county over four thousand. We believe the people of this county will never consent to receive such an immigration of negroes, notwithstanding the writers in the *Times* should continue, as they have done heretofore, to assert their equality with themselves, and the desirableness of their presence. The only escape from this is to throw aside our old government, established by our forefathers, make the military superior to the civil power, and concentrate in the hands of Congress and the Presi-dent the sovereignty which now belongs to the people.

People of Elkhart county, how much better and easier will it be to discard all these wild and impracticable schemes, involving at the best a radical change in our whole political and social system, and fall back upon that old constitution which has given us all the prosperity, all the happiness, all the liberty we have ever en-joyed. And in obedience to this principle conduct the war for the sole purpose of overthrowing the military power of the rebellion, leaving the rights of States, the rights of white men, and the rights of negroes, just where Washington, Jefferson, and all the makers of the Constitution left them.

Goshen Democrat, December 31, 1862.

"THE BLACK WAVE OF FREED NEGROES IS SURGING ACROSS THE OHIO"

Nearly a year later, the Goshen Democratic newspaper affirmed that the worst fears of Emancipation were being realized, emphasizing Democrats' twin fears of labor competition and racial mixing.

Indiana Being Africanized

Already the Abolitionists and emancipationists of Indiana have commenced to reap the first fruits of their labors. Already the crest of the black wave of freed negroes is surging across the Ohio, inundating our border counties with the hateful *debris* of Southern slavery, placing the negro side by side and in competition with white labor, forcing the State to assume the support of a horde of black paupers, idlers and thieves, and, as they doubtless fondly hope, paving the way for the attainment of the *Ultima Thule* of the nigger-lovers—the amalgamation of the two races.

Goshen Democrat, November 5, 1863.

"I DON'T LIKE OLD ABE'S PROCLAMATION"

An Indiana soldier voiced his opposition to the Proclamation based on his hatred of African Americans. Andrew Bush was the son of a Maryland-born Owen County farmer; in 1860 he was unmarried and worked his father's substantial acreage.

Feb. 11, 1863
La Grange Hdq. 97. Reg. Ind. Vol.

Dear Mary:

This little bit of a note leaves me in the best of health. James and Samuel are also well. We have not much news here but much anxiety is felt for northern news amongst some of the soldiers in regard to the welfare of old Hoosier. It is reported frequently amongst us that Indiana is about to form a government of her own with some other of the western states. I trust that it ain't so for if it is so, us poor soldiers will have to suffer. Some of our boys are jubilant over the news; they think that if old Indiana should slip out of the Union they would get to go home; but they will find out that they are in mistake for us soldiers don't belong to Indiana, for we are sworn to obey the president of the United States and we are in his service and he can hold us in spite of anything that we and our friends can do.

I don't like old Abe's proclamation but I can't help myself at this time. If I had thought that it was the idea to set the negroes all free they would not have got me to act the part of a soldier in this war. But as it is I am willing to fight for the Union if it will cause the freedom of the last beastly negro in the South for I don't think that they are human. I am in for anything that will cause Union and peace of our once happy government. If peace is ever established they will be one class of men that will know how to enjoy it and that will be the soldiers.

If the big men that made this war would have to do as the common soldier does peace would be made in less than two days. I will just state here in this place what we have had to do, although wrong it may be to write such things though it is the truth. We have had to march forty-five miles in two days and carry all of our accoutrement which weighs eighty pounds with us. When we done that we had no bread or salt. All that we got to eat was hogs that we would get after we come to a halt at night, and sometimes there would be some that would not be lucky enough to get any; this is as true as the rising and setting sun.

When we were on that march I thought that if I was at home I could ask a blessing at the table in good faith; both horrors upon horrors are to be experienced and seen; no one at home can form any idea of how things are. I thought that before I left home that I had drawn a true picture but I was mistaken. A picture can't be drawn; no man can tell all; I have seen men die in the hospital and know no one to lay them straight and they would leave them lay on the cot on which they died on for two and three days before they would be buried. I will not write any more of this at this time. If I will ever get home I will tell it all to you.

I got a letter from you last Sunday which made me feel glad to hear that you were well and all the rest of the folks. But other news that it contained did not please me so well. It was the news of Mother's and Jacob's doings, but I want you to keep still for I think that the day will come that I can come home and then I will straighten things. That lumber that you spoke of in your letter and that gum lumber that is stacked in the big pile is also mine, but if they don't seem disposed to give the lumber up to you you need not dispute with them about it.

The wheat that ain't threshed I will just state how it is. The wheat that growed on the ground that George cleared the half of it belongs to me, and is put in the bottom of the mow. All of the rest of the small grain that ain't threshed I only get the third of. I am sorry that Mother would not give up the bed that belongs to me. She gave me the bed and she can take it in spite of me but don't make a fuss about it. If I get back we can live without it and if I don't get back I hope that you will be well enough off to do without it. I expect that some of the Crag family will need it worse than you and that is the reason that she retained it.

I must close my letter for it is growing late. Jacob Niehart is very sick with the typhoid fever. Excuse bad writing and give my love to all of the friends. I am heartier at this time than I have been for several years. Good-bye for this time. Write soon and direct as before.

This from your ever sincere husband,

Andrew Bush to Mary

~

Fort Grison, Tenn.
March 26th, 1863.

Dear Mary:

This note leaves me in very good health. Hoping that this will find you in the best of health. I received your kind letter and was glad to hear that you was well and I truly hope that this may find your father in a better state of health than he was when you last wrote to me. I have nothing of a strange character to write at this time. Samuel and James are in pretty good health and spirits although we are downhearted at times on the account of the way that our Northern friends are acting, especially some of our Democratic friends in opposing the President's last call of the militia.

I have heard letters read that came from Indiana that had as much Secessionism in them as though they had been written by old Jefferson Davis himself, and from men that professed to be real patriots a year ago when they thought that their patriotism would not be required and they were not needed in the field. But now when the time has come that the government needs their service they begin to make threats and say that they will resist the present call to the last, and if resistance in petty conventions will not do they will resist by taking up arms against our own government. Such language has been written ofttimes to us soldiers time and time again. But I think that they will see their folly when it will be too late to repent. As for my part I will stick to the government as long as I am able to go. At first when old Abe sent forth his proclamation I was awfully down on it. But at the present time I am in for it and I think that it was the best thing that ever was put forth since the administration, for I think it will put an end to the black population, for the Secesh are killing the negroes that are found in our employ as fast as they can get hold of them.

Last week some captured a train of cars about four miles from here and on the train were found four white men and twenty negroes. The negroes they sent to their long homes by shooting them and the white men they gave paroles and let them go. So much for the proclamation. The next proclamation that old Abe puts out I wish he could make it so we could shoot all the negroes we could see for I hate them worse every day, and I intend to shoot one every time that I can get the chance to for I don't think that they are human beings. Therefore every time that I see one close to the picket line I will send them the courtesies of

my old Enfield rifle. I sent ten dollars to John Smaltz in Lancaster you can send
for it when it comes to hand. When you write again tell me how you got along
making the payments on that land. We got that Secesh money that Miller and
Dan sent to us. I have got my likeness taken and will send it right away. Write
soon as this comes to hand. Good-bye and take care of yourself.

Yours truly, Andrew Bush to Mary and Earnest.

Andrew Bush Collection, Indiana State Library, Indianapolis.

"1863 WAS THE YEAR OF JUBILEE FOR TWO AND A HALF MILLIONS OF THE HUMAN FAMILY"

*A Quaker abolitionist woman from Randolph County rejoiced that slavery in the
South was abolished under the Proclamation. The epithet "copperhead" was used by
Republicans to describe Democrats, referring to the snake that struck without warning.*

State of Ind, Randolph County
July the 5th, 1863

Dear brother I again take my pen in hand to write a few lines in answer to thy
letter which I received last 2nd day which gave me satisfaction to hear from thee
and to hear that thy health was improveing we are all well with the exception
of my self. I don't feel well but can be up I am about to day as I was last sabath
when I wrote thee aletter but was so glad to receive aletter from thee I thought I
would write another one I want thee to write oftener.
we are glad to hear that thee is at work in the dineing room where thee can
have plenty to eat thee said it was raining there if it was to rain some here it
would do good for it is very dry and hot and some sickness the small pox is in
the settlement but we havt got it yet and hope we wont. Thee said thee thought
it was a good thing for this state that the relbbes had come into it I don't know
but what it is but I would some rather they would keep out but I don't pitty
the copper heads any we have had visitors to day and they are gone home, So I
will finish my letter. I should be glad to think that the year 1863 was the year of
jubilee for two and a half millions of the human family[8] I am glad to think the
time has come when the slave driver has to drop his whip and run for his life
and the negroes took to fight for their just rights I would rather tho that slavery
could have been abolished on peaceable terms but as it is it never will be. I do
hope that the last darkie will be sot free before the war ends as I always was an
abolishionist, but I reckon I have wrote enought about that I will quit and close
my letter now Nathan I want thee to write oftener than thee has been in the
practice of doing and if thy health is so poor I think the had better try to get

to come home but I must quit and and [sic] remain thy affectionate sister untill death so farewell but don't forget to write

from Sarah M^cnees To Nathan Hiatt

Individual Letters Collection, Earlham College Archives, Earlham College, Richmond, Indiana.

"WE CAN'T WHIP THE SOUTH WITHOUT HER NEGROES"

A Democrat wrote to a Democratic congressman and critiqued the war policies of the Lincoln administration and Republican-dominated Congress, connecting the Emancipation Proclamation to the policy of raising African American troops.

Clark Co. Ind
March 1, 1863

Hon. Jas. A. Cravens
Washington, D.C.

Dr. Sir

After reading the news paper this morning and reflecting some upon the late acts of our congress I thought I would drop you a line, although I have no doubt that you are encumbered by many letters from your friends.

I cant say that a majority of the citizens of this county are pleased with all of the late acts of congress. We did think that the Nineteen free states and Seven territories with a white population of twenty million assisted by Delaware, Maryland, Virginia Kentucky and Missouri were fully able to crush out this rebellion without calling negroes into the our army. If I mistake not the ten slave holding states that have gone wholely into the rebellion have not a white population to exceed Six millions. Lincoln stated in his letter to Greely that he would not interfere with slavery if the rebellion could be put down without it.[9] Now has one to acknowledge that with three men to one and "having all the money means and credit in our hands" we can't whip the south without her negroes. We of the west surely think this most degrading and miserably humiliating on the part of our government. We are firmly of the opinion that there is a very great rong somewhere.

We think that if the war had been conducted on the plan of the Critenden land mark resolutions the rebellion might have been put down long ago.[10] But it seems to be the policy of our congress men to be radical, more radical, most radical. The extreme radical policy that has controled the present session of congress has been the means of runing our own legislature into the opposite extreme. I would not be surprised if there is trouble experienced in parts of this state in enforcing the conscript act. We think the law not just as the whole burden is made to fall on the first class. We would not have complained if we were only to stand the first draft but we don't like the fifty percent added to it. I was expecting a call for more men before the present session of congress adjourned. I am aware the Ultras are afraid of the next session as it will be democratic. I would it were so now.

I heard an ablitionist by the name of W. J. Kirkpatrick say this week that you had been boreing him with your democratic documents untill he was tired of it. If you will send me a share of your favors in the way of public documents I assure you I will not complain but feel very thankful for such favor. If you can send me a copy of the work published by cousin Tom I would be very glad indeed. I have heard nothing from him.

Your friend,
W. W. Rodman

Direct to Charlestown

Cravens mss, Lilly Library, Indiana University, Bloomington.

"THE IDEA OF ADOPTING THE NEGRO INTO THE UNITED STATES SERVICE SEEMS TO BE USELESS"

Many white officers and enlisted men alike discounted the value of enlisting African American men into the Union army. A soldier in the Sixty-third Indiana Volunteer Infantry Regiment voiced his opinion. Andrew J. McGarrah was from Gibson County, where his father was active in the Union Party that fused Republicans and War Democrats.

Shephardsville Bullet Co Ky
Monday Mar 8th '63

Kind Parents

With pleasure I now take the opportunity of answering your kind and welcome letter which I recieved last wednesday. I was glad to hear from you and to hear that you were all well I am in good health and I hope these lines will find you enjoying the same great *blessing.* We have had a very soft and disagreeable winter, a great deal of rain and snow. But the the [*sic*] weather is somewhat *moderating.* To day is a very nice day. It appears as though I could enjoy myself at home working or going *to school.* But it is impossible for me to think of leaving the U. S. Service at the present from the fact that we have men here in the Hospital that is not able for the *service* but cannot be discharged *here.* If we go back to Indianapolis I will meet with an opportunity to get a *discharge* provided they will give me *one.*

Tomorrow is pay day We have 4 months pay Due us but there is some talk of us having to settle our clothing Bill Now and if we do we may not get $52. If I get my pay tomorrow I will send all I can spare *home*. The sutter has kept me in tobacco and such like for some time and I will have to square up with *him*. Our Chaplain visited us yesterday for the first time since the regiment *scattered* and preached us a sermon. his Text was "It is an important saying and worthy of all acceptation that Christ Jesus came in to the world to save sinners.["]

The *Idea* of adopting the negro into the United States service seems to me to be *useless*. I considder they would be of no force at *all*. I believe if the whole black population of the united States were to gether and that one Bomb shell would Disperse the whole of *them*. I may be mistaken.

We will view them in another light Supposing them Brave and ferocious They come in to United States Service and help us to restore our *union* then of course they would consider and justly too that they were entitled to the fellowship of the american *people*, and equalize themselves with *us*, & that *will never do*.—

I wish it was so we could talk together on the subject. You are well aware of what a division it has created in the *North* just talking of *it*. It will create a greater one in the army if it is put into actual force. There is a great many men in the 63rd that would as soon be under the three striped flag as the red white and *Blue*. I want you to let me know if the rebel Simpathisers are doing any thing or proposing any thing in the *north*.

I have not had a letter from Eli since I wrote to you *last*. I got a letter from John and Jos. the other day they are well and still at the same *place*.

I have nothing more of any importance to write at this time So no more

Your Son With Respect
Andrew J. McGarrah
To his Parents Brothers & sisters

P.S. Give my respect to all enquiring friends and do not forget to *write*.

> *These lines are written by a friend*
> *An answer to them you'll please send*
> *Altho' we're very far apart*
> *I wish you well with all My Heart*

A. J. McGarrah

Andrew J. McGarrah Papers, Indiana Historical Society, Indianapolis.

"HERE IS A WIDE FIELD OPENED FOR GOOD"

A letter writer to the abolitionist Indianapolis newspaper praised the soldier-like appearance and behavior of African American troops and praised efforts to help ex-slaves make new lives as free persons. These particular troops, the First Arkansas Volunteers of African Descent, later renamed the Forty-sixth United States Colored Troops Regiment, were commanded by Colonel W. F. Wood, formerly of the

First Indiana Cavalry Regiment. General Asahel Stone was quartermaster general of Indiana during most of the war; Dr. James Thomas Boyd was a homeopathic physician.

From Vicksburg.
On Board Sanitary Steamer Courier, ⎫
Below Cairo, June 6, 1863. ⎭

On our way down we were fired into as I mentioned in my last, but as soon as we came to the mouth of White River we were compelled to lay by for a gunboat, and we waited a whole day—just in the evening we were sent down the river with a convoy (a gunboat) and with another steamboat whose slow movements retarded us greatly, and we had at last to take her in *tow* as the gunboat would not let us go without her, the best we could do was to tow her along as soon as possible.

When we came to Lake Providence we were compelled to wait until our slow consort could unload some suttlers stores; this took all day, and we spent the time in reviewing Colonel Woods' regiment of colored soldiers—they call themselves the Arkansas Hoosiers (as Col. Wood is a Hoosier.)

Col. Wood is quite proud of his men, and well he may be, for they are a fine, robust, determined looking set of men. They were called up and went through the drill, were then formed into a hollow square and we all went into the square when, Col. Wood spoke to his men and introduced us. Gen. Stone and Dr. Boyd of Indianapolis, also addressed the colored soldiers, when they sung "John Brown lies mouldering in the ground," in a manner that would have done credit to any body of men; when we gave three cheers for the "Arkansas Hoosiers" and left fully satisfied that we will hear of their heroic deeds in future; we returned to the boat and just at night we started down the river again. . . .

At Helena we stopped to coal, and several went off the boat to see and talk with Gen. Prentiss, and Rev. Mr. Sawyer, the Superintendent of contrabands. They both speak hopefully of the colored soldiers, but are exceedingly anxious that we should send them school teachers; indeed in every place where we have stopped, where there are camps of contrabands, the cry is, send us teachers, clothing and books! We feel that here is a wide field opened for good. Let us occupy it immediately.

MEDICUS.

Indianapolis Daily Evening Gazette, June 10, 1863.

"FLY TO MY COUNTRYS CALL"

More than 120 Indiana African American men served in the Fifty-fourth Massachusetts Colored Infantry Regiment, which was raised mostly from states other than

Massachusetts. One, a resident of Centreville in Wayne County, expressed both his
patriotic desire to serve his country and a plea for fairness.

Head quarters
Departement of the South
Moris Island N C. Aug 21^{rst} 1864

Govener Morton

Dear Sir

iff you will grant me permision I will explain to you the present Conditions of
my humble self I at first will inform you that I am A. Native of Ind I was Born in
Franklin Co Ind in the town of Brookville / My Residence Now is in Centreville
Wayne Co Ind the 28th of last April one year ago I had what I thought a fair
enducement to fly to my Countrys Call to which Massatusetts sent her Recuting
officers throughout the many Different states to Recruit For this the 54th Regt
mass vol well thinking to my self mass Calles for me she offers me the same pay
as that of the white troops and to enlist as A part of her quoto I Did Not hesitate
But Come as my Country Calls or Called me we left our homes fathers mothers
Brothers and sisters & we arrived at Boston thence we proceeded to our Camp
Called Readville we Remained in Camp Nearely one month we Recieved 50$
Bounty From the state we left Boston when we arived on St Helena Isl we had
the offer of Recieveing our monthly pay how much why ten Dollars per month
to which we Refused of Course Did we enlist for ten No. then I say it was wright
for us to Refuse it Govener Andrews says he was authorized By the Secratary of
war to organize said Regt and gaunteered us we would Recieve the same pay as
that of all other troops. the same treatment Raitions Clothig and Equipt at that
of all soldiers when has there Been any pay offered to us I Can say [None?] Since
last Sept while we have Been fighting and Strugling on the Battle field we have
Never Recieved one Cent of pay No one to Care for the many poor wives and
Children at home think of it Nearely 18 month in the service without one Cent
little Did I think of there Being A Regt Raised in my own state that I Dearely love
so iff you will please inform me I would prefere serving the Remainder of my
Countrys service in my own state Regt I should prefer her having my services

there is many more of the Ind Boys prefers the same so iff it it [sic] is possible
I with the Rest of my Brave Companions Desires you to interceede iff Agreeable
for A Transfer to the first Ind [illegible]

I Remain yours with Respect
Wm E. Edrington
Private
54th Regt Mass vol.
Co [K]

Govener Morton
Dear Sir
you will Confer quite A Faivor in Behalf of the writer iff you will Forward A
letter to me Amediatly iff I Could Be transfered

Governor Oliver P. Morton Papers, Indiana State Archives, Indianapolis.

"WHITE SOLDIERS ARE MORE THAN FRIENDLY"

Schoolteacher Benjamin F. Trail of Knightstown was the highest-ranking African American of the Twenty-eighth United States Colored Troops Regiment, a unit organized in Indiana. He was killed in action in the battle of the Crater near Petersburg, Virginia, on July 30, 1864.[11]

No. 20
Camp Russell WhiteHouse Station Va. June 4 '64

Davey Sande:—

I'm well doing well & well satisfied as any one in the army, of my grade, you will recollect that I wrote 19 and sent it away within 2 hours after setting foot on the shore but as it did not contain much I will write to you again whither you ever get it or not, it will be nothing lost & that is the way I want you all to do too, you must write to me whither you ever think I will get it or not. I will give you some of the particulars of our coming here, as we left Camp Casey Monday morning about 10 , and commenced packing up at 3 then went to Alexandria and laid there till Tuesday; we then about sundown boarded the transport "George Weems" for this place, and traveled down the Potomac about 60 miles, there we anchored right in the middle of the river till morning, about dusk or day break, away we went, & in a short time we were in the great Chesapeak Saltwater where we could look both ways for several hours, and see but very little land, and a great many fish about the size of ordinary logs, or a man; called *porpus* were seen & shot at. Wednesday night we camped, or anchored righ[t] opposite York Town

Next day we arrived at this place about noon and could hear the cannons roaring, *cafloom, caflom* almost every second, & men up on the top of masts of the vessells with their glasses could see the line of battle, 10 miles long, as it was only from 8 to 12 miles distant, and it has been reported that Maj. Gen. Burnsides was shot dead that evening, but we that hear the report dare to tell any one here, but as no one shall know what I write, I will write all that I hear, but I fear my letter will go to Washington & lay there a week or two. At 11 the same night I detailed 100 men to unload the ambulances, & carry the wounded on board the boats which take them away to various hospitals, & every hour since there are more or less dead & wounded brought here, just now there is an ambulance train of more than 500 wagons passing the road about 4 rods in front of my tent, but they were not all wounded to day nor yesterday. We have a nigger rebel here in prison that set in an apple tree in this orchard & killed 5 field officers,—the very ground on which we are camped was occupied 10 days ago by rebs—you have no Idea how many boats are passing two & fro bringing supplies &c, &c—good musiic, by brass band cheer me all day & comfort me all night, on the boats &c—I detailed by order of the Colonel 350 men this morning at 6 to work on fortifications and there are men about 800 men at work with shovels, picks, axes &c, &c, 5 rods south of my tent & onward,—we are expecting an attack at this place I have nothing to do, but order details, & make out Reports, we are only 25 miles from Richmond— wagons are here caperd [caped] and appear like sheep at a distenc, not only by hundreds but by thousands — tents all over the country & at night the lights appear beautiful— you ought to see what kind of different ways people are wounded— if a man comes near where they are unloaded, so as to look at them, he cant get around helping to unload & handle them— eggs are $3.00 a doz. other things in proportion— white soldiers are more than friendly .

I'll write no more, but will aim to write to you all the time 1 or 2 times a week if you will send me *stamps*, (not money) as I guess you would like to hear from me often, or ought to— I don't write many particulars, but I write many more than those who cant write very well & have *but little or no time to write*. Keep writing to me whither I ever get them or not; number all. My love to all—

address
Sergt. Major B.F. Trail 28 U.S.C. Troops
Whitehouse landing Virginia
Via Washington D.C.

Benjamin F. Trail Family Correspondence, Abraham Lincoln Library and Museum, Harrogate, Tennessee.

"KILL ALL, THAT'S MY DOCTRIN"

The Fort Pillow massacre, in which African American troops who had surrendered were killed by their Confederate captors rather than taken prisoner, was one of a series of events that prompted many soldiers to desire destruction and annihilation of the enemy. A soldier from the Tenth Indiana Volunteer Infantry Regiment expressed his views. James Thomas's desire to revenge the death of African American soldiers also highlighted the gradual acceptance by white soldiers of African Americans as comrades fighting in a common cause.

Head quarters 3ᵈ Br 3ᵈ div 14ᵗʰ A.C.
Ringgold, Georga Apr 18/64

Dear Sister

I will write you Afew lines agane Thar is nothing Going on hear worthy of your Attention. helth is good & that is the Main thing in the army Every thing

is quiet hear It is hard to tell when we will Move, but I Dont think we will Move
before the Middle of May if then it May Bee that the rebbals May Make us Move
before that time but if thay Attempt that Thay will have a nice time of it. I See an
account of the Massicree at fort pillow I think we Will remember them for it. I
am Not infavor of taking any more Prisoners Kill all thats My doctrin I am going
to Send you Some More Photographs one is our hospital Steward the other you
will very easley reccognise I am going to Get General Thomas as Soon as I can
& probabley General Rosecrans Then I will have enuff I am glad that the union
party Electid [head] I hope to be at home in good time to give old Morton a vote
for he is the best Man living. he will get allmost All the Soldiers vote in the army
Old Abe is My chois for Presidint I have gist five Month from to day to Serve if
thay Keep Me untill the last day then I am afree Man agane My helth is good
hoping these few lines May find All well I wish you would Send Me afew
Postage Stamps agane I am out & cant get any

Respectfuly James Thomas

Give Oscar My respects & tell him to wright
John Tompkins is at Chattanooga he is a Lieut in the 123 *ind* vollunteers

James. S. Thomas

I received your letter written the 11th inst

James Thomas Papers, Indiana Historical Society, Indianapolis.

SEVEN

The Battle to Control State Government

$\mathcal{A}$LTHOUGH MANY PROMINENT Douglas Democrats, led by Joseph Wright, had joined the Republicans in the "Union Party" fusion, the remaining Democrats retained high hopes for the midterm elections in 1862. Still a strong party, they were aided by the poor progress of the federal war effort through much of 1861 and into 1862. While optimism flourished as federal forces in the west succeeded in occupying parts of Kentucky, Tennessee, Missouri, western Virginia, and Louisiana, the Army of the Potomac stood still in the east. Army casualties everywhere were appalling, caused in no small part by inadequate medical care and horrendous sanitary conditions in military camps. Evidence of bureaucratic mismanagement and corruption by the Lincoln administration bubbled to the surface. The rising threat to civil liberties—arrests of political speakers, attacks on and suppression of Democratic newspapers, and other abuses—caused great concern. On January 8, 1862, Indiana Democrats met and enunciated a party platform and agenda that slammed the abuses and mismanagement of the Lincoln administration and called for a return to "the Union as it was, and the Constitution as it is" under the management of conservative Democrats. Thomas A. Hendricks, Indiana's leading Democrat, addressed the convention to deplore the failures of the Republican government, the rising tide of abolitionism, and the subjugation of the South. He identified the Republican Party as the party of eastern moneyed interests—the bankers, railroad executives, and manufacturers—who were squeezing the west dry with their loan rates, transport fees, and protective tariffs.[1] The drying up of southern markets for Indiana's agricultural production early in the war caused sharp economic hardship initially. Prices rose on nearly all goods and services, and while many Indiana farmers, craftsmen, and business owners profited from higher prices, some—especially those at the bottom of the economic ladder—suffered. Hendricks and his party allies sought to tap the anger that resulted from these economic trends.[2]

Democratic fortunes improved as military setbacks increased in 1862. The shock of Lincoln's preliminary Emancipation Proclamation in September brought many War Democrats back to the party fold, disgusted by the abolitionist turn taken. Democrats won strong majorities in the October elections, taking both houses of the Indiana General Assembly and a majority of the state's congressional seats. The party's success was due to presidential-year turnout among Democrats and a disproportionate number of Republicans absent in the army ranks.[3]

The Democrats strode into the General Assembly confidently on January 8, 1863, intent on curtailing the powers of their nemesis, Governor Oliver P. Morton. With the Emancipation Proclamation now in effect, many Democrats began to voice the demand to end hostilities by an armistice and negotiations with the rebels. They investigated illegal arrests of Democratic speakers by military authorities and denounced abolitionist measures. Republicans accused them of disloyalty and prepared to defend the governor. Republican legislators "bolted"—skipped town—for short periods to deny quorums and prevent the progress of legislative business. The last straw for them was an attempt to give the governor's power to appoint officers of the state militia to a committee controlled by Democratic officeholders. In late February nearly all of the Republican legislators of the State House decamped for Madison, Indiana, leaving the session in limbo. The session adjourned in March without passing a budget bill—a necessary action if state government was to function for the next two years. The Democrats expected that the governor would call them back into session. However, Morton had no intention of recalling the General Assembly. Instead, he obtained promises of funds from the War Department and loans from private New York bankers and Republican county commissioners. Morton stashed these funds in a large steel safe hauled into his State House office, and one of his assistants funded state government from the governor's "Bureau of Finance." Democrats howled at this completely illegal and unconstitutional action but were unable to stop Morton.[4]

Having fought the Democrats and prevailed, at least temporarily, Morton now faced an unexpected challenge to his power from the military. Emanations of disloyalty and dissent echoed loudly throughout the midwestern states. Major General Ambrose E. Burnside, appointed to the command of the Department of the Ohio (encompassing Ohio, Indiana, Michigan, Illinois, and parts of Kentucky), intended to use military power to silence expressions of opposition to the Lincoln administration in his department. The general issued an order warning that military forces would arrest persons and suppress newspapers that criticized the government. Burnside ordered his troops to arrest several prominent Democrats, most notably Clement L. Vallandigham of Ohio, the leading voice of the antiwar wing of the Democratic Party. Burnside's lieutenant in Indiana, Brigadier General Milo S. Hascall, arrested several Democratic newspaper editors and ordered their presses stopped. Democrats, though temporarily cowed by the military action, roared in protest. Morton understood better than the military men that the repressive measures would serve only to energize the Democratic opposition and make controlling his state even more difficult. He endeavored to intervene quietly with Washington leaders to end the military measures and succeeded in removing Hascall and his military order. Morton and Burnside continued to duel as long as the general commanded the department. Subsequent military commanders during the war were more careful not to cross the governor or step on his toes.

"OUR PEOPLE BELIEVE THAT SECESSION MEETINGS SHOULD NOT BE TOLERATED"

Expressions of support for freedom of speech and freedom of the press, often proclaimed in peacetime, sometimes were drowned out by demands to prohibit certain types of speech in wartime. A Republican newspaper editor requested that state military force be used to prevent antiwar Democratic rallies and newspaper utterance. Lambdin P. Milligan, a prominent northern Indiana Democrat, was active in condemning the war and calling for an end to hostilities. He later was a leader in the conspiracies to release Confederate prisoners of war and unite with rebel troops.

Muncie Ind Aug. 3.d 1861.
Mr. Laz. Noble.[5] Adj't of State.

Dear. Sir.

I have been requested to inform you, by citizens of this, and Blackford County, that there is a body of men in the latter county who are open and bold secessionists— In the Blackford *Democrat,* a sheet, which is as traitirous in its tone as any in the Southern Confederacy, has the following call for a meeting.

"The *Genuine* friends of the Union, & the Constitution — those who are *opposed to waging an unjust, and unprofitable crusade* against the Southern people, are requested to meet at the Court House, in Hartford city, on Saturday, Aug 10th 1861, J. R. Coffroth, and L. P. Milligan, of Huntington, will address the people upon the present condition of our national affairs."

When this announcement was made public, there seemed to be a strong disposition on the part of the Union people to put down the meeting by force. When this news reached the ears of those engaged in it, they postponed the meeting till Saturday the 17th inst. This class of men claim to be in favor of Compromise. It is a fact, well authenticated that they exulted over the defeat of the Union forces at Manassas,[6] and some of them hurrah for Jeff. Davis. The meeting is evidently one full of the spirit of treason and secession, and the Union loving people of this region are so incensed that they will not permit it to proceed. The Blackford Democrat will be demolished as sure as fate, unless there is a change in its tone. Our people believe that secession meetings should not be tolerated here, and desire that the militia of the State be called into requisition to disperse the assembly. They prefer this mode to resorting to what might be considered mob violence. Something must be done, or there will be an *unhealthy muss.*

We have thought fit to lay this matter before you, trusting that some such
action as that in Missouri may be taken.[7]

Yours Respctfly
J.F. Duckwall,
Ed. Free Press.

A4017 024596 f11, Adjutant General of Indiana Records, Indiana State Archives, Indianapolis.

"INDIANA WILL LOOSE SIGHT OF PARTY IN THIS HOUR AND RALLY AROUND GOOD MEN"

*Many War Democrats still cherished hopes for an end to partisan conflict in the
North in the early months of 1862. They hoped that all would rally around moderate
principles rather than ideologically driven measures. These hopes were ultimately to
be disappointed, as partisanship born of ideological divide and distrust overwhelmed
commonality. Joseph A. Wright had served as governor of Indiana from 1849 to 1857.
He also served briefly in the U.S. Senate (1862–63) as the replacement for the expelled
Jesse Bright. Allen Hamilton was a prominent Fort Wayne banker.*

Washington City
Mch 8th 1862.

My dear Sir.

Your kind note of the 3d is just at hand. It will give me great pleasure to
serve you. Of the prospects in the case of friend Oakley I know nothing . The
Republican Members will control these matters. Upon·your statement, I shall not
hesitate however to say to the President, Mr Oakley is a worthy man, and urge
his appointment. I concur most fully with your noble sentiments in relation to
this war, and the importance of laying aside party creeds and platforms in this
the hour of our calamity.

We must restore this Government upon the Constitution alone, without
dotting an *i* or crossing a *t*. There is more danger from this Congress doing too
much, than too little: either men and measures are to be feared.

The army will accomplish all in a short time, if we are prudent. I say let
time & movements of the Union men in the South and other developements,
determine our subsequent action. I fear hasty and ultra legislation.

Always happy to hear from you, and to serve you in any way. I cannot doubt
the actions of our beloved State. Indiana will loose sight of party in this hour,
and rally around good men, who look alone to the accomplishment of one great
object.—The integrity and unity of our people and Government, and holding
every inch of our Territory.

Present my regards to your family, and accept assurances of—

Your Friend, faithfully

Joseph A Wright

Hon Allen Hamilton

Fort Wayne

Indiana

Allen Hamilton Papers, Indiana State Library, Indianapolis.

"THE DEMOCRACY OF INDIANA ARE FOR PROSECUTING THE WAR FOR THE MAINTENANCE OF THE CONSTITUTION, AND THE ENFORCEMENT OF THE LAWS"

Some Democrats were confident that their party would restore its dominance both in Indiana and in Congress in the fall elections of 1862. Dr. James Athon, who would run for and win the office of Indiana Secretary of State, banked on the growing distrust of Lincoln and his war aims to rally Indiana Democrats who feared the abolition of slavery, an institution enshrined in the Constitution and protected by federal law.

Indianapolis Ind. March 18th 1862

Hon James A Cravens

My dear Sir,

It has been sometime since I received your letter of the 3^{tho} ult. and had it not been for the late battles, I would long since have replied, but my attention, *and* services have been directed towards taking care of our wounded soldiers. I was at Mound City Hospital for two weeks, during which time I treated over four hundred of the wounded.

I am fully Confirmed, that my proposition for establishing a post hospital at the falls of the Ohio, is not only expedient but demanded by the laws of humanity. The hospitals at Louisville are very much crowded and are not Conducted in that liberal manner, which should characterize our sanitary measures in this terrible hour of the nations history. It is life or death.

Your letter to His Excellency, the President in reference to permitting Abolitionists to desecrate the Smithsonian Institute by their disunion harangues, is gotten up in good taste, and is thrust, in the right direction. I have never had any faith in the professed conservatism of President Lincoln, and I think, the future will develop, the fact, that his real sentiments on the negro question will square, with the views of the most ultra Abolitionists of the present day.

You mention in your letter, that some of our friends were dissatisfied with the proceedings of the late Democratic Convention. This was to be expected, as it is well know—that all parties contain, more or less an element, which is weak in the knees, and can only be brought to stand shoulder to shoulder with us, when there is no lion in the way, but these sun-shine friends, I am happy to say, are being diminished in number, and strength. Our ranks are filling up by acquisitions from the opposition. There is no doubt whatever of the truth of this assertion. The Abolitionists have ceased to charge secession on our Convention, which was Composed of over five hundred men, of the very best Citizens in the State. There was no Bright nor any other influence exercised in that honest, and determined mass of democrats, other than the spontaneous outpourings of patriotism.

Our resolutions speak for themselves, and the man, who can charge in the face of such evidence, that the Convention was governed by anything [other] than love of Country, is so much beneath the dignity of a man, that he should be classed among malicious fools and knaves. But my friend, the charges made by interested parties soon after our Convention, are having a contrary effect, and some gentlemen, whose knees smote together like Belteshazzar for awhile, are coming out, and showing their friends, that they are not inclined to lick the hands, that have not only smitten them, but have ruined the Country.

The democracy of Indiana are for prosecuting the war for the maintenance of the Constitution, and the enforcement of the laws. Who desires more than this? None but Abolitionists.—The very fact that the dominent party ignore their name, is evidence of their weakness—hence, to continue in place they resort to hoodwinking under a new, and spacious name. Already the Union men have selected sore headed democrats to take the field against the regular democratic nominees for Congress, as indeed, for everything else. No Republican dare run for any office, unless he can tie on to the democrats who may go off with the fusion. The Union arrangements are not near so popular now as they were last fall. Ohio and Illinoise have taught the politicians a good, and I hope a wholesome lession—Well my old friend, we have spent many days together—our boyhood; our manhood; on the tented field; in battle; in the lower house; and in the Senate of our State; our sentiments have been the same on all great measures, and my Confidence in you, as a man, as a citizen and true patriot induces me to set you *down,* as a firm supporter of democratic measures.

Your friend
James S. Athon

Cravens mss, Lilly Library, Indiana University, Bloomington.

"OUR ONLY WONDER IS THAT WE WERE NOT BEATEN WORSE"

The heavy defeat at the polls sent Republicans reeling and forced deep soul-searching and fault-finding. Licking its wounds, the main Republican newspaper in the state capital laid blame where it opined that it was due, hoping to rebuild Republican fortunes.

THE RESULT.

We are still without sufficient data to make a just estimate of the majority against us in this State, but we think it will not exceed 8,000, and will probably be less. It is big enough at the least. Of the causes that have produced this most unfortunate result we have not much to say. It is no comfort to see just why we were beaten after we know that is has been soundly done. But one of the causes is so plain, and its influence so direct, that we can't pass it without a word. The terrible inefficiency with which the war has been conducted, has done more than all the President's proclamations to dissatisfy and alienate the people from the Administration. They see their blood spilled, their money wasted, and they see no result at all commensurate with the fearful outlay. They naturally turn away from an administration that takes so much and gives so little. Yet never was anything more grossly unjust than the visitation of this great wrong on the Administration. Every man who has held a guiding place in the management of the war is a Democrat. Democratic generals command our army and a Democrat is commander-in-chief. McClellan is a Democrat, so is Buell, so is Halleck. And to these three men more than all others together is due the worn out patience and wearied heart of this nation. They have controlled this war. It has been in their hands almost from the beginning. The President has abdicated his own judgement and left these officers to have full sway of the army. What have they done with it? Nothing but kill it. And for this failure the Administration is blamed and punished. Nothing could be more outrageously unjust.

Another cause contributed, or rather created this defeat. Without it all other influences would have been feeble. The absence of 70,000 Union voters in the army is the overmastering cause of the catastrophe. If they had been at home the Union ticket would have swept the State by 50,000 majority. In this last levy of 300,000 volunteers there were almost no 8th of January Democrats.[8] A few volunteered, but not one in twenty. In the 70th regiment, which was chiefly raised in this county, there were not fifty 8th of January men altogether. This vast abstraction from the Union strength was enough of itself to defeat us. The Democrats understood this well, and kept their men at home. They boasted that they had abolitionism to whip in Indiana, and it was quite as important to do that as to whip the rebels. Thus it came that five-sixths of the last levy were Union Democrats and Republicans. No party can stand up against such a tremendous loss as this. Our only wonder is that we were not beaten worse.

Indianapolis Indiana Daily Journal, October 17, 1862.

BUELL IS TO BLAME

*Shortly after the stunning Democratic victory in the October 1862 elections, Republicans
assessed the reasons for their electoral failures and called for remedies. Governor
Morton's private secretary (and brother-in-law) wrote to President Lincoln's private
secretary, John G. Nicolay, to give his assessment of the reasons for Republican
failure and to warn of a growing political threat in the Old Northwest.*

Oct 24 1862
J G. Nicholay, Esq
Washington City
D.C.

Sir

Enclosed you will please find two communications which I have just cut
from the Cincinnati Daily Gazette, the ablest of our Western journals, which
I hope you will find time to read. I am satisfied that you have no idea of the
feeling in the West. There is no bright spot. Every one here feels as if our cause
was slowly sinking, and we may as well realize our [3 words illegible]. Despair
is upon every heart; our State was lost by the inactivity of the army. Imbecility
and incompetency reign supreme in this department; Buell has no defenders.
He is a magnificent failure, and no one can understand *why* he is retained. The
command could not [possibly] be put in worse hands. Put in some *General*,
Burnsides, or anybody—and let the Kentucky army do something, while the
roads are yet good. I know how much [easier] it is to find fault than to do better,
but our people are losing confidence in everybody. Gov. Yates was here to-day,
and he represents the same feeling in that State. Illinois should be saved from the
rebels next month, or we will get the first Congress against us, then look [line of
text illegible] humiliation. Our people all have the most implicit confidence in
the President, but they *have not* in our Generals.

Since the recent elections, it is no uncommon thing to hear of prominent
Democrats talking about *"a great Central Government,"* cut off from New-England
and the Cotton States, etc. that is to be the next proposition, and strange as
it may seem, the leading democrats of this State and Kentucky are now
advocating it.

Burnsides is a western man, and and [sic] anxious for a western command.
Let him, or any other [illegible] General who will *fight* be sent here, and I assure
you that the war, so far as the West is concerned, can be brought to a close
before winter.

The following is an extract from a letter from Col. Geo. K. Steele, an aid to
Gov. Morton, now at Louisville. Col. Steele has been a leading citizen of this

State for forty years, and is one of the President's original supporters, and is still an earnest friend of the administration.

"I am sorry to tell you that I find things in a bad shape here. I find many of our men that we counted on as sound union men rejoicing at the result of the Indiana election. I do not wish to create any alarm, but I have my opinion, and think I am not mistaken in saying that the election of the democratic ticket in the North is suicidal to our success for a [illegible]. I have no doubt that the programme is as it is laid down by the democrats of the North, and the secessionists of the South, for the breaking up of the government. I find numbers of men here joining in with Hendricks' plan,[9] men who two weeks ago were for the union as it was but now say we have but one alternative, and that is the restoration of the democratic party, and the making of a north and southwestern Government, to cut loose from the Cotton and New England States, and to show them [illegible] and stand by ourselves. Now sir, my solemn convictions are, that before three months, that the army in Kentucky will be employed to that end, so far as its commander can control it. He had been working with a class of the most damnably filthy politicians that ever infested any community, ever since his appointment in this State. He has given protection, both in this State and Tennessee, to men whom he knew to be disloyal—he has no one else in his counsel but conditional proslavery men and if victory is upon his banner, it is by the Force of public opinion, and the gallant officers under him. You may think I use strong language, but I am every hour more and more convinced that this is the fact. The basis of a settlement will [illegible] and the democracy of the North and South will agree, and many generals are now working with our army to that end. It is almost universally said here now, that it is proven that Lincoln cannot manage the government."

Very Respectfully
Your Obt Servt
W R Holloway
Gov. Private Sec'y

Governor Oliver P. Morton Papers, Letter Press Book, vol. 1 [June 1862–January 1863], Indiana State Archives, Indianapolis.

THE STREETS OF INDIANAPOLIS TO RUN WITH BLOOD

Governor Morton's secretary again wrote to his counterpart in Washington warning of the signs of revolution and strife in Indiana on the eve of the opening of the Indiana General Assembly and after Lincoln's Emancipation Proclamation took effect. Since the Democratic victories in October that gave them control of the Indiana General Assembly, members of that party began to flex their rhetorical muscles in calling for radical change. Suspension of the writ of habeas corpus was, next to race, the issue most often raised by Democrats. President Lincoln on several occasions early in the war suspended the privilege of the writ of habeas corpus, the constitutional right to a trial afforded prisoners. In September 1862, Lincoln promulgated a general suspension of the writ in circumstances where obstruction of recruiting and the draft occurred. The Indiana Supreme Court chief justice mentioned was Samuel E. Perkins, a leading Democrat who used his position to resist the Morton administration.[10]

State of Indiana.
Executive Department.
Indianapolis January 2 1863

Sir:

Enclosed you will please find the closing paragraph of an editorial in Indiana State Sentinel of yesterday It is constantly filled with just such articles, and should be suppressed. We are upon the eve of civil war in Indiana, and you need not be surprised to hear of a collision here at any time. Only yesterday one of our Judges of the Supreme Court (Butternut) declared that the President had no right to issue an order suspending the writ of Habeas Corpus and he should enforce the mandates of his court, if the streets of Indianapolis run with blood. The writ was issued, but he could not enforce it, as he had no troops. He threatened to call upon the Governor to call out the State Militia, but did not do so. The copperheads here, are of the meanest and most detestable character, and are capable of doing anything. Please show the enclosed paragraph to the President

Very Respectfully
W.R. Holloway
Gov. Private Secy
J.G. Nicholay, Esq.
Executive Mansion
Washington
D.C.

[Excerpt from *Sentinel*]:

"Where, then, does ABRAHAM LINCOLN derive his authority to issue a general emancipation proclamation? He has none. If he issues such a document, it is the act of an usurper; it is the exercise of despotic power. It is infamous. It means servile war—the butchery of white men not in arms, of helpless white women and children, by a race of semi barbarians. Are the people willing that the American nation shall become the reproach of the whole civilized world by such acts of infamy? No, never. It cannot be. It must not be If such a proclamation is issued to day, the people should rise in their might and repudiate it and its author. They have the power to do it, and they will be unworthy of the name of men and of Christians, if they do not."

Abraham Lincoln Papers, Library of Congress, Washington, D.C.

"THE LOYAL MEMBERS OF THE LEGISLATURE HAVE *ALL* GONE HOME"

Republicans formed their own secret organizations in preparation for feared Democratic plots and applauded efforts of the Republican legislators in the General Assembly to resist Democratic legislation by bolting. The organizations had various names. "U.C." probably refers to "Union Club." "KGC" refers to the secret Democratic organization called the "Knights of the Golden Circle."

La Fayette Jan 10, 1863,

Dr. Charles M Wetherill

My Dear Friend. Mr Meredith informed me to day that you had not received the package which I sent you containing the Ritual &c of the U.C. We have prepared a new certificate of your Election and appointment as Commissioner, and herewith Enclose it. The UC in La Fayette is not doing anything now. There has not been a Meeting, since Lawrence met with that distressing accident, which resulted in his death, so much deplored, by his immediate circle of friends, and in fact by the whole community. But we did a good work last Autumn, and although not a political organization, it is apparent to any one that we influenced the result of the Election. Probably Mr Colfax owes his Election to the U.C. although he is not a member, to my Knowledge. But the S.U.C. circulated through his district (through our Subordinate Clubs) our 10 000 copies of Gov Wrights Speech, and the testimony from all the C's is that they Effected many changes of votes. In Carroll Co, (Delphi) as you remember they neglected to secure the organization, and now regret it *sorely*. We need it now, if Ever, as the Legislature of Indiana seem bound if possible to precipitate us into revolution, and if possible set us to cutting Each others throats. The peril which now hangs over us may draw us together again. I hope so. The KGC's are thick at Indianapolis, and had a plot to depose Gov. Morton, seize the Arsenal with its 15000 stand of arms, and declare a North-Western Confederacy. But their plots were found out, and prepared for. The Federal victory at Murfreesboro checked them, and as yet no outbreak has occurred. But we are prepared for it, and for one I hope it will come, as there will be *hanging* in Several places.

We Stand upon a Volcano, with a crust so thin, that only a spark will Explode it. We hear this morning that the Loyal members of the Legislature have *all* gone home, thereby preventing a quorum, and also stopping all treasonable Legislation.

I hope they will break up the legislature for the Session. It will prevent Election of traitors to the United States Senate, but I guess we can stand that." I have an addition to my family, a daughter 3 weeks old. Give my kindest regards to your wife & family.

JL Beach

Charles Mayer Wetherill Collection, Indiana State Library, Indianapolis.

"WE WAS ORDERED OUT ONE NIGHT TO TOWN TO BLOW UP THE STATE HOUSE"

With the Democratic Party now firmly in control of the Indiana General Assembly, Democratic leaders sought to clip the wings of Governor Morton, limiting his control of state government as well as his power to appoint officers to Indiana volunteer and Legion (state militia) units. The Republicans fought back, using every weapon they could, fearing the Democrats had revolutionary intentions. Republican and military leaders even deployed troops around the State House in an attempt to intimidate the Democrats. A soldier of the Thirteenth Indiana Light Artillery Battery stationed at Indianapolis described the event.

Jan the 23 1863

Dear brother

I am wel and I hope you ar in the same state of health I resieved your letter this wek and was glad to hear from you and to hear that you got the money I sent you the first guns that we had was sent South and we got other ones in the last battle the guns was all spiked and then thay sent for ourans as they was the nearest we was ordered out one night to town to blow up the state house the representative could not agree and some truble when we got their they agreed and we fired A few rounds of blank catrages and returned to camp it was thwelve oclock when we got to camp at night and three in the morning we had to take our guns to the Depot it is very mudy here it is some thing less than knee deep their is some of the company sick yet and some to the hospital their is lots of talk about freeing the niggers here and lots of the soldiers sayes that they wont fight to free them and I am one amongst them for I dont like the black devils wel enough for that——

if they ar free I would advise you to get A gun and to shoot evry one that comes near that would be my polisy and how is all the folks and how do they get along I know that you cant write very often to me but write as often as you can I have rote 44 letters since I was to home that is almost one evry day the boys ar playing eucher and Edward Miller is playing the fidle

Walles Corbit is back here again and wilkes to but he is gone again A week ago we had good sleigh here and pretty cold [racing?] I will bring my letter to A close for this time:

from your friend and brother
Wm H Ringwalt
to Eli Ringwalt

THE REPUBLICANS BOLT AGAIN

After a brief bolt earlier in the term, the Republican members returned, only for most of them to bolt again and for good when the Democrats attempted to pass a militia bill that divided the authority for the militia between the governor and the other executive officers of the state, most of whom were Democrats elected in the sweep of 1862. Without a quorum, the legislative session came to an end with no significant legislation passed, including appropriations, and Governor Morton refused to call it back into session, running the state from the executive office and leading many Hoosier Democrats to contend that it was one more instance of the failure of Republicans to abide by the law. A Democratic U.S. senator, Thomas Hendricks, was selected before the second bolt.

THE BOLTING MEMBERS.

Mr. KILGORE asked leave of absence for Messs. Griffith and Cass until to morrow noon, that they might visit Madison to see if terms could not be made with the bolting members, who were understood to be in that city.

Mr. HANNA opposed the request. He was for making no terms with those gentlemen. They knew their duty. Let them return and conduct themselves as honorable gentlemen should. The majority would make no compromise with them. For the Republican gentlemen who had remained on this floor, obedient to their oaths, he had the highest respect, but as for the Secessionists, the majority defied them—they defied them.

Mr. PUETT was opposed to adopting a resolution which would authorize any members to go with terms of compromise to men who were standing out in violation of their oaths. Let us remain here, do our duty, and upon the factious minority would rest the responsibility.

Mr. MASON followed in a like argument. Were it not for the revolutionary state of affairs, the sentiment was to bring these men back by force. He entered his protest most emphatically against granting any leave of absence for the purpose of attempting to compromise with them.—The majority should stand upon their rights as representatives of a free people.

Mr. PACKARD said there was a powerful outside pressure brought to bear upon these seceders. Prominent Republicans—Governor Williams among the

number—had told them that these gentlemen would come back. He (Mr. Packard.) wanted to see them come back, but not through any compromise on the part
of the majority. He indorsed the sentiment of Mr. Hanna: if they would come
back and do their duty they would be treated as honorable gentlemen.

Brevier Legislative Reports (1863): 200.

MILITARY PUNISHMENT FOR SPEECH CONSIDERED TREASONOUS

*In an effort to counteract widespread dissent in the Old Northwest and Kentucky,
Major General Ambrose E. Burnside issued General Orders 38 announcing military
punishment for speech and publications deemed to be treasonous by military
commanders in his Department of the Ohio. Brigadier General Milo S. Hascall,
from Goshen in Elkhart County, recently appointed to the command of the District
of Indiana within Burnside's Department, announced his own version for Indiana,
General Orders 9.*[12]

Headquarters District of Indiana
Department of the Ohio.
Indianapolis, Ind. April 25, 1863.

In assuming command of the District of Indiana, the General commanding
deems it advisable and proper to issue the following order, to the end that all may
be advised of the principles which will govern his action:

I. He has no proclamations to issue, nor policy to adopt. That has already been
done, and in his judgment well done, by the Commanding General of this Department. He has no partizan feelings or interests he intends to advance, but desires to
confer freely and fully with the prominent men of all political parties, and invokes
their hearty cooperation in all measures calculated to restore harmony and good
feeling in the State. He neither claims any right to interfere with civil matters in
the State, nor has any desire to do so.

II. The Commanding General is charged with the duty of carrying into effect
the provisions of General Order No. 38, recently issued by Major General Burnside. He purposes doing so. Unmistakable evidence has reached him that the
provisions of this order have been, and are being, violated in various instances by
well meaning men, who are led astray by newspapers and public speakers.—These
latter will therefore be held to the most rigid accountability. There is no use in
trying to dry the stream while its fountains are allowed to flow.

All newspapers or public speakers that counsel or encourage resistance to the
Conscription act, *or any other law of Congress passed as a war measure,* or that endeavor to bring the *war policy* of the Government into disrepute, will be considered
as having violated the order above alluded to and treated accordingly. The country

will have to be saved or lost during the time that this Administration remains in power and therefore he who is factiously and actively opposed to the *war policy of the Administration,* is as much opposed to his Government.

III. The Commanding General indulges the hope that all citizens of the State will see the propriety and necessity of the observance of this Order, and as they regard the interests and welfare of the State and Nation, give him no occasion to take action on account of its violation.

By command of
Brig. Gen. HASCALL.
Ed. R. KERSTETTER,
Capt. and A. A. G.

Indianapolis Indiana Daily Journal, April 27, 1863.

"FOREWARNED IS FOREARMED"

Brigadier General Milo S. Hascall was appointed to the command of the military district of Indiana by Major General Ambrose E. Burnside without the approval of Governor Morton. Morton had preferred that Brigadier General H. B. Carrington be retained in the post. Hascall reported to Burnside a conversation with the governor in which Morton criticized the actions of Burnside for ill-considered and heavy-handed tactics in arresting Democratic newspaper editors and suppressing their newspapers.

Confidential
Head Quarters District of Indiana
DEPARTMENT OF THE OHIO,
Indianapolis, May 16th 1863.

General:—

Certain matters have come to my knowledge recently which I consider it to be by my duty to acquaint you with I would prefer to see you and talk the matter over personally but I cannot well get away and you are as I am aware already overrun with persons seeking a personal interview. I had an interview with Govr Morton yesterday and he told me plainly that he did not consider your order 38 practical, and he thought it could not be carried out—that efforts to enforce it might as well be given up in his opinion, and that it was creating immense difficulty all over the Country. He said also that he thought the manner in which Vallandigham was arrested and subsequently tried entirely unwarranted and could not be justified. He thinks also that no one except attachées of the army or navy can be tried in this manner in Ohio or Indiana. Now after you have taken the position you have, and in accordance with the same I have issued my order and taken my stand, this is very singular ground to occupy. It is admitting away our whole case. I acknowledge that I am not a little embarrassed by this state of things I think all could have been managed very well after the first effervescence was over but for this unexpected "fire in the rear"

I am not discouraged yet, but really I think we had a right to expect different treatment from our friends. I have taken considerable pains to ascertain the cause of this, and had made up my mind that if I could learn that I was the reason of it I would at once ask you to assign me to duty elsewhere as I do not desire to stand in the way of your success in the least From what I can learn this is not the case. The trouble seems to be that you issued order 38 without consulting him and removed Genl Carrington in a similar manner He dont seem to find so much fault with either act as he does with the fact that *he* was not *consulted*. General Buell, incurred his displeasure in a similar manner when he first took command of the Dept and the Govr never ceased in his exertions against him till he was removed and the court organized as it was against him. These facts and surmises I have considered it important to you to know. Forewarned is forearmed. If [I] have done wrong in communicating them to you it is an error of judgment and not of the heart. I have made up my mind to Keep things as quiet as possible till after the Mass meeting here on the 20th and then take hold again. I would like to feel that I am supported somewhere and hope you will answer this as soon as convenient I am taking all precautions in my power to preserve the peace here on the 20th

	I am, General,
	Respectfully
To	Milo S. Hascall
Maj Genl Burnside	Brig Genl Vols
Comdg Dept of Ohio	Comdg

[Endorsement:] This communication being marked confidential is treated as such & respectfully enclosed to the com'g general WHW aag

Burnside Papers, E 159, RG 94, National Archives, Washington, D.C.

"LET ME EXHORT THE PEOPLE TO MODERATION AND SUBMISSION TO THE LAWS"

Amid serious resistance to the draft enrollment in several counties around Indiana, including the murders of draft enrollment officials, Governor Morton reminded the people of the state of the consequences of resistance. Morton also clearly reasserted the primacy of federal and state law over military power as the legitimate authority by which to punish acts of disobedience.

PROCLAMATION BY THE GOVERNOR.

T o the P eople of I ndiana:

Whereas, Resistance has been made in several cases to officers engaged in the execution of the Conscription Law, and to officers and soldiers engaged in arresting deserters from the army, in which blood has been shed and murder committed.

And whereas, These acts of resistance to the Government are high crimes, and fraught with great danger to the public peace, and to the honor of the State; I deem it my duty to *solemnly warn* all persons against resistance to the Government in any form, or hindering, or obstructing any officer thereof in the performance of his duties. And, for the better information of such as have not convenient access to the Penal Statutes, enacted by the Federal and State Governments, and now in force, I herein set forth certain sections contained in said Statutes.

An act of Congress, passed July 31, 1861, reads as follows:

AN ACT TO DEFINE AND PUNISH CERTAIN CONSPIRACIES.

. . .

Any combination, agreement, or understanding forcibly to prevent, hinder or delay the execution of any law of the United States, is by this law made a penal offense, although such combination, agreement, or understanding had not been carried into execution, and clearly covers the case of disloyal societies, which are known to exist in several parts of the State.

The 24th and 25th sections of the Conscription Act, approved March 3d, 1863, read as follows:

. . .

These sections are very broad, and cover every form of opposition to the arrest of deserters and the enforcement of the Conscription law.

By the 25th section it is made a high penal offense to counsel or aid any person to resist the draft; to counsel any person to assault, obstruct, or hinder any officer engaged in making the draft; to counseled any draft man not to appear at the place of rendezvous, or willfully dissuade him from the performance of military duty, as required by law. To bring a case within this section, it is not necessary that there should be a conspiracy or combination.

If one man shall give to another the counsel or advice prohibited in the section, he is subject to the punishment it prescribes. Nor is it material how he shall give this counsel or advice, whether by public speaking, publishing in pamphlets or newspapers, or by private conversation. Nor it is material that such counsel or advice shall be direct and in terms. The law holds a man responsible for the natural and legitimate consequences of his acts; so also for the natural and legitimate effects of what he may say. If what he speaks or publishes is naturally and reasonably calculated to excite the hatred of men against our Government and resistance to the Conscription law, he is within the purview of the section, although in the conclusion he might insert a saving clause, by formally declaring that the laws must be obeyed, and no resistance offered to the Government. In such a case the law will look to the spirit and reasonable effect of what is said, and not to the mere words employed.

It is within my knowledge that public speakers and editors have presented to their hearers and readers every statement, argument and motive that could excite them to hatred of the Government and resistance to the laws, but for their own protection, have interlarded their discourses with set phrases that there must be no violence, or resistance to the laws. Such men are cowardly and treacherous, as they exhort others to do what they are unwilling to do themselves, and seek to put their advice in a form for which they will not be held responsible. The subterfuge will not avail against the provisions of the section I am considering.

. . .

The offenses defined and punished in the statutes I have quoted are below the grade of treason, and the guilt of the accused party may be established by one credible witness, or by circumstantial evidence, as in ordinary criminal prosecutions.

It will be my purpose in the future, as in the past, to do my whole duty to the Government of the United States and the people of Indiana. In the administration of the law, and the performance of official duties, I recognize no parties.

All who obey the laws, keep the peace and discharge their duties as citizens, are alike entitled to and will receive protection in person and property. The alarm which some are attempting to create of the improper interference of the military authorities, may be dismissed as without foundation.

The right of the people peaceably to assemble and petition for a redress of grievances, and speak and publish their opinions touching the policy of the Government, or the conduct of the war, must be respected, and the enjoyment of it protected. But there is a wide difference between the legitimate exercise of this right and that unbridled license of speech which seeks by the assertion of the most atrocious falsehoods, to exasperate the people to madness and drive them into a position of neutrality between their Government and the rebels, if not into the very arms of the rebellion, combine them in dangerous societies, provoke them to resist the laws, and thus contribute directly to weaken our own Government and strengthen the cause of the enemy.

The criticism of one who is friendly to the Government, and who is anxious that it shall succeed and be preserved, and who points out its errors in order that they may be corrected, is wholly different from that denunciation which seeks to bring the Government into contempt and render it odious to the people, thereby withdrawing from it its life, when struggling in battle with a powerful enemy. The one can never be mistaken for the other. It must be borne in mind that the exercise of the plainest rights and privileges may be greatly modified by surrounding circumstances; that what may be proper or innocent and harmless at one time may be dangerous and criminal at another.

To advocate the right of secession and rebellion, or the dissolution of our Government, might be harmless enough in time of profound peace, but when the country is engaged in a desperate civil war, which is consuming the best blood and treasure of the nation, and the misfortune of arms might within a few days bring the enemy upon the soil of our State, will it be contended that the privilege of free speech gives the right to advocate the rebellion, resistance to our own Government, or the abandonment of it to its enemies? That which is idle talk in time of peace may become "aid and comfort to the enemy," and punishable by the laws of the land when that enemy is at our doors.

Let me exhort the people to moderation and submission to the laws, and laying aside their resentments and prejudices, to take counsel only of their duties and the dangers which threaten the nation; and while I assure them that protection shall be extended to life, liberty and property, and that equal and exact justice shall be administered to all, I would impress them with the fact, that if needs be the whole power of the State and Nation will be invoked to execute the laws, preserve the public peace, and bring offenders to punishment.

Given under my hand at the City of Indianapolis, Indiana, this 11th day of June, A.D. 1863.

> Executive Department.
> O. P. MORTON,
> Governor of Indiana.

Indianapolis Indiana Daily Journal, June 12, 1863.

"ARMED FORCES MUST BE EMPLOYED TO CRUSH THE OPPOSITION"

Governor Morton succeeded in having General Hascall removed from command in Indiana (Morton's effort to depose Burnside was unsuccessful) in early June 1863. Hascall's replacement, Brigadier General Orlando B. Willcox, from Michigan, reported to General Burnside on the state of affairs in Indiana soon after his arrival to bolster his request for additional troops.

> Head Quarters District of Indiana, And Michigan
> DEPARTMENT OF THE OHIO.
> Indianapolis, June 17th 1863.

General

I telegraphed you last night that I would write. When I relieved Genl Hascall, I found in this state a highly angry and excited condition of feeling. So far as the newspapers show this state of things appears to have subsided, but outrages, violences, and disorders of various Kinds have broken out in Rush, Johnson, Fulton, Putnam, Boone, and Montgomery Counties, of which I have telegraphed you as they arose. The worst case occured in Sullivan County, while Genl Hascall was in command. There a Provost Guard of fifty men sent to make arrests for opposition to the enrollment, was met by an armed force estimated at 200, before which the guard retreated and returned without performing the duty on which they were sent. And the insurgents openly defy the laws and the authority of the Government.

I found the case in the hands of Gov. Morton and the Asst. Prov. Marshal Genl Col. Conrad Baker. The Governor sent down to have testimony taken on which to make arrests. But it seems now that the people are so intimidated by threats that they fear to give testimony against the criminals. In this County about 1000 men are reported armed and drilling. In the other counties conciliatory measures are being employed, for the most part, by Gov. Morton which may succeed in part, but sooner or later, before the enrollment is completed, armed forces must be employed to crush the opposition.

In some of the Counties the enrollment is being done secretly, so far as it can be, the worst cases being reserved for armed assistance. The Law of Congress requires that the draft shall be made from the enrollment which shall be made before the 1st of July. You can therefore appreciate the importance of having an efficient force at hand.

Besides, the Com. Genl. of Prisoners says that he cannot dispence with Camp Morton for Rebel prisoners, and he notifies me that I may expect a lot at any time. Col. Baker is daily calling for troops for the different counties to protect the Enrolling officers.

I have thus briefly stated the necessity for troops in Indiana, and remain

Genl. Your *Obdt Servt,*

O B Willcox

Brig. Genl. Comd'g.

Burnside Papers, E 159, RG 94, National Archives, Washington, D.C.

"OUR DIFFICULTIES CAN SOON BE SETTLED"

While Democrats had won majorities in the Indiana General Assembly, the extralegal methods of the governor and the Republican minority thwarted their ambitions to change their outsider status. Republicans controlled the presidency and Congress, and Morton had effectively throttled Democratic power. Democrats in the spring and early summer of 1863 felt aggrieved by federal measures and gubernatorial fiat that rode roughshod over their concerns. In June, the Paoli American Eagle *issued a feeble call for compromise and cooperation.*

PARTY PERSECUTIONS.

Our opponents have a great deal to say about laying aside party until the war is over, &c.—But what kind of an example do they set towards bringing about such a state of things?—Have they relaxed any of their party schemes? Have they held out the olive branch of peace to the Democratic party, and said to them that they would bury the hatched, and unite with them and counsel together as to the best ways and means of putting down the rebellion? No, they have done nothing of the kind. They have contented themselves with demanding that the Democratic party should quietly give up all their principles, and aid them in carrying out their doctrines. Is this right—is this the way to harmonize the people?

In days past, when our country was in trouble did our leading statesman pursue such a course? Certainly not. Jackson, Clay, Adams and Webster and all our leading men come together, and acted in concert for the preservation of the country. No one party then set itself up to dictate the terms upon which their opponents should join them—they all come together and consulted as to the best policy to be pursued, and then united. Such should be the case now.

The Democratic party constitutes at least half the people in the North, and our rulers should show them some courtesy in the affairs of the country—they have to help do the fighting, and sound policy would say that they should be consulted as to the management of the war. Let our leading men of all parties get together and agree upon a plan that all can work to, by each party yielding a part of their notions, and our difficulties can soon be settled.

Our opponents will yet find out that the miserable course of persecution pursued towards us; will not pay in the end. They will find that persecution of Democrats will not make them love their persecutors. The continual cry of secessionist against every Democrat, by *half brainless fools,* will not be quietly submitted to much longer.

Paoli American Eagle, June 18, 1863.

EIGHT

~

The Morgan Raid

*T*HE OHIO RIVER offered little protection to the people of Indiana during the Civil War. Relatively narrow and often fordable in numerous places during summer and periods of drought, the river was a porous barrier to chaos, mayhem, and murder. From the earliest days of the rebellion, southern Indiana residents feared that Southern armies would sweep northward across the Ohio to pillage and kill. Federal and state authorities received countless pleas for protection. Amid the political confusion in Kentucky in the early months of hostilities in 1861, Governor Oliver P. Morton of Indiana did all he could to lend aid to southern Indiana. The reorganized state militia, the Indiana Legion, achieved its highest state of readiness in the Ohio River counties. Morton scrounged together some artillery pieces from federal arsenals and his Legion commanders placed them on the heights overlooking and commanding the river's fords and shallow places. Federal muskets reached the hands of the Legion's river border regiments as quickly as Morton could pry them from the U.S. Army's quartermasters. Navy gunboats patrolled the river's length.[1]

Still, the Ohio River border was too long to be guarded along its entirety. Guerrillas operating in Kentucky had little problem crossing the river when they wished, often to escape federal pursuers. Sometimes they did more than hide in the hills. In July 1862, a Confederate guerrilla force under Adam Johnson posted several logs painted black to resemble artillery pieces on the Kentucky shore opposite Newburgh in Warrick County, Indiana. Johnson demanded the surrender of the town, on threat of shelling and destroying it. The town's leaders surrendered, and the guerrillas crossed, looted the town of its military stores and food (an army hospital with convalescent troops was located there), and recrossed to Kentucky and escaped. State authorities and Indiana's citizens were indignant at this violation of state soil, and Morton organized a relentless chase after the guerrilla band, with federal troops scouring western Kentucky for months. Indiana authorities continued to be vigilant about cross-river raids during the rest of the Civil War.

Brigadier General John Hunt Morgan, a Confederate cavalry commander from Kentucky, in 1862 had achieved renown or infamy (depending on one's viewpoint) as a dashing and effective cavalry raider, plaguing federal troops and garrisons throughout Union-occupied Kentucky and Tennessee. Morgan's success in 1862 forced federal commanders to place thousands of troops behind the front lines to guard vulnerable places: railroad lines, supply depots, and other military locations. By his daring and lightning raids, Morgan also rallied pro-rebel sentiments throughout the South and, it must be said, the North.[2]

On June 17, 1863, a company-sized force of Morgan's cavalry crossed the Ohio River under Captain Thomas Henry Hines (who later in the war became an important operative for Confederate secret services in the Northern states and Canada), entering Perry County and riding north toward Orange County. Their plan ostensibly was to steal horses. They traveled through Indiana disguised as federal cavalry. However, their identities were discovered, and the local Legion quickly mobilized to catch them. Most of Hines's force were killed or captured near Leavenworth in Crawford County on June 20, but Hines himself escaped and rejoined his commander. This raid again pointed to the vulnerability of the river border, and Governor Morton increased his efforts to strengthen the state's defenses.

In early July 1863, Morgan, commanding a force of about 2,500 cavalry, rode north from Tennessee into Kentucky on a diversionary raid. Engaging federal garrisons in Kentucky, he continued north to the Ohio River. Though apparently under orders from Confederate General Braxton Bragg not to cross the river, on July 7 Morgan and his troopers captured two steamboats at Brandenburg, Kentucky, and converged on that town to cross the river. News of the capture of the boats reached federal commanders, but on July 8 gunboats failed to stop the crossing. Legion commanders called out their troops and prepared to resist the rebels and halt their landing on the Indiana side. However, the rebel cavalry outnumbered the Legion forces and after a skirmish forced the Legion to withdraw to Corydon, the county seat of Harrison County. There Legion forces numbering about four hundred men converged and prepared to resist Morgan's troopers. In a small battle fought near the town on the morning of July 9, the militiamen were overwhelmed by the veteran rebel cavalrymen and artillerists. The Legion force surrendered to Morgan, who promptly released them, plundered the town, and rode off in the afternoon northward.

News of the crossing and battle galvanized the state's leaders, and Governor Morton and military commanders organized the Legion and available federal troops to resist Morgan. Morton, his staff, and federal officials organized thousands of men who quickly collected in Indianapolis—Legion companies, volunteers, and others—into makeshift regiments and sent them to southern Indiana to resist the invaders. Morton also successfully resisted the efforts of Major General Ambrose E. Burnside to place Indiana under martial law during the crisis; the governor deemed it unwise to give injudicious military authorities too much power over state matters.

Morgan's intentions were not known, and all parts of the southern half of the state were ordered to prepare to resist his advance. However, Morgan sent detachments of his force north and east, through Floyd, Orange, and Washington counties. The town of Salem was plundered, bridges were burned, and railroad tracks were torn up. The raiders spread out toward Brownstown, in Jackson County, keeping pursuers guessing, but veered east through Scott County toward Madison in Jefferson County. They by-passed Madison to the north and rode to Vernon, in Jennings County, pillaging all the way. At several points Indiana's makeshift regiments and Legion companies blocked Morgan's path, skirmishing with the raiders, but Morgan eluded them. Federal cavalry who followed Morgan from Kentucky pursued the rebels doggedly, keeping them from lingering long anywhere. Gunboats also shadowed the raiders along the Ohio River should they try to recross the river back to Kentucky. Morgan's force rode—pushed—into Ohio on July 13, pursued by federal cavalry and Indiana volunteers. Most of the Legion ended their pursuit at the state line, disbanded, and went home.

Morgan's raiders continued through southern Ohio, constantly harried by federal pursuers. An attempt to recross the Ohio River failed when federal cavalry caught them on July 18; Morgan lost much of his command as prisoners. He escaped but was forced to surrender near the Pennsylvania border in northeastern Ohio on July 26. The raid caused the destruction of his effective fighting force.

As in previous raids into Indiana, the state's people were shocked and indignant at the war being brought into their homes. Republicans and Democrats alike turned out to resist the raiders. However, evidence suggests that some in Indiana saw Morgan as a Southern hero and assisted him along his route. The suggestion that simple disobedience to Bragg's orders was the reason for the raid is hardly sufficient to explain Morgan's motives. The reasons for the raid—and Hines's foray in the previous month—remain unclear.

"REBELS HAVE INVADED INDIANA IN CONSIDERABLE FORCE"

With the appearance of Morgan and his cavalry, Hoosiers organized. Governor Oliver P. Morton called on every able-bodied white man in the southern half of the state to resist the invaders.

> Executive Department of Indiana
> Adjutant General's Office
> Indianapolis July 9. 1863.
> General Military Orders.

Satisfactory evidence having been received that the Rebels have invaded Indiana in considerable force, it is hereby ordered and required that all able-bodied white male citizens in the several counties South of the National road[3] forthwith form themselves into companies of at least sixty persons, elect officers and arm themselves with such arms as they may be able to procure. Said companies will perfect themselves in military drill as rapidly as possible, and hold themselves subject to further orders from this Department. It is desired that they should be mounted, in all cases where it is possible.

The people in all other parts of the State are earnestly requested to form military companies and hold themselves subject to orders.

Prompt reports of the formation of companies should be forwarded by telegraph.

All officers of the Indiana Legion are charged with the execution of this order, and all United States officers are requested to render such assistance as may be in their power.

(Signed:) O. P. Morton
Governor and
Commander-in-Chief

Governor Oliver P. Morton Papers, Indiana State Archives, Indianapolis.

"WAKE UP OLD HOOSIER"

Among Morgan's troops were some Hoosiers, including Greencastle resident Henry Stone, who had been born in Kentucky and considered himself a native Kentuckian. His father was a substantial farmer, and Henry himself was an eighteen-year-old law student in 1860. A nephew of the Republican U.S. senator Henry Lane, Stone joined Morgan in September 1862 to avoid the Northern draft. Stone was apparently most exercised about the issue of slavery. In a February 13, 1863, letter, he wrote: "All I have to say is, the man that endorses [the Emancipation] Proclamation is a demon, is a fit disciple of Satan, and I hope he may be 'handled very roughly' in the 'Day of Judgment,' and I think he will."

On the Ohio River.
30 Miles below Louisville.
Wednesday 8th July, 1863.

Dear Father:

I am here with Gen Morgan's Command which is now crossing the Ohio into Hoosier We crossed the Cumberland on the 2nd. The River was twenty feet above fording. We turned our horses in, and, the men came over in canoes with their saddles. The wagons were put on canoes, piece at a time and brought over. We had a small fight at Burksville killing & capturing 30 Yanks At Green River Bridge we had a pretty hard fight, in which we gained nothing. At Lebanon we fought Col Chas Hanson (brother of the lamented Roger) who had a force of 500 strongly stationed in the R.R. Depot, which our artillery couldn't bear on, only at the roof. After six hours we caused them to surrender. A portion of the town was burnt. Any amount of stores (Government) were burnt. On the 6th we took the train 20 miles south of Louisville, capturing the mail and 20 Yankee officers, one a Col. Last night we took two transports and the regular packet, and have them now transporting the command over the River. When we got here this morning, two hundred Yanks with a piece of artillery attacked us from the Ind side. These we drove away; and then a gunboat fought us an hour or two, when it was driven away up the river. At this moment all is quiet and the regiments are crossing as rapidly as possible.

Wake up old Hoosier now We intend [to] live off the Yanks hereafter, and let the North feel like the South has felt some of the horrors of war. Horses we expect to take whenever needed, forage and provisions also. In fact it is concluded that living is cheaper in Indiana and Ohio than Tenn. If the Democrats want to put down despotism let them turn out now. I hope I'll get close enough to pay you a visit. My health is good and my spirits buoyant at this time. I guess citizen Yanks are somewhat alarmed up North. Well they may be. This will be the first opportunity of the Northern people seeing Morgan, and they'll see enough. I just imagine now how the women will bug their eyes out at seeing a rebel army. Will Thomas, Henry and Jim How Jones, & Hiram & Tom, Butter Bowen & Henry. Andy English, Everman Barnes, Capt Coleman & myself will probably take a "square meal" with you soon. Love to all the boys & mother and yourself. Your son, Henry

Stone Family Papers, Kentucky Historical Society, Frankfort, Kentucky.

THE RAIDERS IN SALEM

After the battle at Corydon, Morgan and his troops passed through Salem.

Morgan's Raiders pillaged Salem, Indiana more extensively than the other communities through which they traveled.

MORTON FIGHTS MARTIAL LAW

Governor Morton skirmished with the generals who commanded military forces in Indiana over the best means to combat dissent, resistance to the government, and lawlessness. Three days into the Morgan raid, General Burnside requested the imposition of martial law in Indiana, the better to organize against the rebel invaders. Morton refused, but Governor David Tod of Ohio acceded to Burnside's request for martial law during Morgan's raid.[4] Edwin M. Stanton was secretary of war.

1863
E.M. Stanton
Washington
July 11
Sent

I send you copy of a dispatch received from Gen Burnside, and my answer to it
Cincinnati, July 11, 1863

To Gov. O.P. Morton

I am decidedly of the opinion that martial law should be declared in this Department, with the condition that it is not to interfere with any civil matter either public or private except in instances to be enumerated. It should be done with a view of more readily controlling the militia force in the Department Neither official nor private business need be interfered with. I am not willing to take this step however, without consultation with the Governors of the different States, and therefore request your acquiescence Please answer as soon as possible
A.E. Burnside Maj. Gen

∼

To Maj. Gen. Burnside
Comd'g Dept. Ohio Cincinnati.

If I understand the purpose to be accomplished by declaring martial law in your department, I am opposed to it, as I am unable to see any good to grow out of it, but much possible harm. So far as the present invasion of Indiana is concerned it can certainly do no good, and so far as calling out and organizing the militia either to repel invasion or maintain order, I am satisfied it can be better done by State than Federal authority. I say to you frankly that so far as Indiana is concerned it would be highly inexpedient in my judgment
O. P. Morton

"I NEVER EXPECTED TO SEE SUCH TIMES AS THESE HERE"

A southeastern Indiana woman reported on the raid to her husband away in the army.

New Pennington July the 15/63

My dear Husband

it is with pleasure that I take my pen in hand to write you a few lines to let you know how I am getting along I came down to Pennington last Saturday and have been here ever since there has been quite exciting times since I came here. the Rebbles have been through here and have played smash with every thing they captured Versailles Osgood & Vernon. they destroyed a great deal at Vernon two bridges the rail-road and some buildings. they were also at Sunmansville and all the towns down that way. there was some few through here but they did not do any mischief they were saw prowling around through the woods in small squads but I supose they thought Pennington not worth bothering with. their chief aim was to destroy the RR they tore up this RR some but did not do much damage for our men came up on them and they had to skedaddle. the Home guards have been all called away. and they few men that are here have armed themselves and are as well prepared as they can be in case of an emergency. we have had pickets out on all the roads until yesterday. but I guess as they thought the danger was about over they called them in yesterday. they say there was about 5000 of the Rebbels at Sunmansville they stole a great many horses they took two from Joe Osborn they stripped John Clarks store & took him prisoner they took him with them about 5 mile and when they found out he was a butternut they give him an old horse and told him to go home for they did not want any such cowardly villians that was a traitor to their country with them for they had no use of them. oh I think that is so good for the butternuts. but I never expected to see such times as these here. but I am afraid they will be more than this before this war is over. I will not tell you any more about this raid for I expect you know more about [it] than I do. they tried to take Napoleon but Bernard Mullen was there with a whole Regiment of cavalry & defended the place. oh you never did see such a time as there was here & at Newpoint the women & children went about town screaming & holoring fit to kill themselves & when the news came that they were fighting at Sunmansville & Napoleon and that there was more of their men than there was of ours some of the women like to have went crazy but they were drove back and did not get to come any further it apears that they had separated and were going in diferent companies but the one that was on this RR was the largest band of them & it was suposed that their intention was to go on to Indianapolis

July the 17 1863

Dear Husband since writing the above I have received your letter dated the 14th You say you mailed one the day before for me but I did not receive it it may have came to the Office and some of our folks may have taken it out for me: uncle Asahel was a Greensburg yesterday and brought out this one. I am having a very pleasant visit. thanks to my little baby carriage if it was not for that I could not go any where at all. I walked down here and brought it with me so that I could run around when I got here. I do not know when I will go home it may not be for a week. our boarders left the day before I came down here so there is not much to do there it apears that you did not receive my letter written July the third in which I told you how your Mother came up to our house and acused me of writing mischief to you to keep you from writing to them she was very angry and said it was not the only time I had caused a disturbance in the family. if I have been the cause of any ill feeling between you I am sorry for it for I am sure that it was not my intention to be that is the dificulty which I spoke to you about which you said you did not understand in my first page I have told you all the particulars that I was acquainted with concerning the Morgan raid. the report here this morning is that the Rebbs are at Brookville, but I do not beleive that is so. I supose you have saw all the particular of the Indiana Raid in the papers it is in the 15

Newton Robbertson told me he saw you in Laurencburg on the 14 I believe it was but he must have been mistaken he said that you was going on double quick and that he could not get to speak to you. you must excuse this poor scribble for I have had to write it with one baby in my arms and my foot on *the cradle* of the other

Zora was still very poorly when I came down here but the change and the fresh air have done wonders for her she is so much better. the baby has got the sore mouth very bad and it is going through him and I am afraid it will nearly kill him for it is very dangerous. Milo Robbertson was wounded in the battle of Gettsyburg the report was at first that he was killed but since then we heard that he was only wounded

Randolph and Ad was out with the ballance in pursuit of Morgan but I supose he will be home today well I can not write any more for it is about mail time and the children bother me so that I can scarcely write at all. I am sorry that you did not get my letter which I wrote the 2d but it was like the ballance of my letter not of much consequence please write as soon as you recieve this and let me know [w]here you are and what you are doing

Ever your loving
& afectionate wife
Kate

Please excuse this scribling and acept this card as a token of my love—and keep it to remember me by. I have not time to look over this letter but if you find any mistakes please look over them

Kate Starks Letters, Indiana State Library, Indianapolis.

NINE

⁓

Dissent, Violence, and Conspiracy

$\mathscr{T}$HE CIVIL WAR was fought all over Indiana—in courthouses, city and town streets, saloons, churches, schoolhouses and playgrounds; in fields, forests, and swamps—wherever people met, congregated, argued, and disputed. Beyond being merely a military struggle fought in the South between warring armies, the Civil War was first and foremost a political struggle between two competing ideologies, one espousing slavery as a part of the political, social, and economic fabric of the nation, and the other rejecting it. Just as the people of the South rebelled against the Union to protect slavery, so too did people in Indiana fight about slavery and its role in society.

After warfare began between the United States and the Confederate States, several measures undertaken by the federal government under President Abraham Lincoln and a Republican-controlled Congress to aid the war effort exacerbated internal political and ideological tensions. Such measures as an income tax, the Confiscation Acts to seize rebel-owned property in the North, the Emancipation Proclamation to free slaves in the states in rebellion, the Enrollment Act of 1863 establishing a federal draft, and military arrests of civilians enraged conservative Democrats, who saw the measures as so many blows struck against the United States Constitution, specifically, the right of assembly and the freedoms of speech and the press. Further, they saw the use of military tribunals to try civilians from Indiana and other Northern states as a violation of constitutional rights.

As political conflict at the national level boiled over into warfare, politics in Indiana likewise produced violence and bloodshed. Numerous politically motivated shootings, knifings, and fistfights occurred throughout the state, involving men, women, and children. Political passions could not be restrained, and many politically related murders resulted. Fights were frequent at political rallies and meetings; members of the opposing party would linger on the fringes of open-air rallies, heckling and abusing speakers, and the resulting fights would escalate into riots. Alcohol frequently contributed to such brawls, as event organizers supplied drinks to participants as inducements for attendance, and their opponents often partook as well. In other cases, armed men interrupted political meetings to threaten and intimidate speakers and audiences into quiescence. Speakers traveled with armed bodyguards to ward off violence; however, the presence of such armed men often precipitated violent reactions.

The presence of armed troops in Indiana played a significant role in much of the violence committed. To paraphrase the military theorist Carl von Clausewitz, war is political action using other means. Soldiers, especially volunteers, accepted violence as a political tool. In Indiana, federal troops and state militia—the Indiana Legion—clashed with Democrats who opposed the war against the rebellious South. They employed the means at their disposal—armed force and intimidation—to attack and punish those whom they viewed as sympathetic to the rebellion. Military authorities used their power to arrest Democratic political speakers and newspaper editors who criticized the Lincoln administration and its handling of the war effort. Violence against newspapers in Indiana was widespread and frequent. Troops ransacked newspaper offices and destroyed presses, often without any official or legal repercussions. Troops also were often present at polling places, usually as voters themselves, but in some cases positioned to intimidate Democratic voters and dissuade them from voting.

Conservative Democrats resisted government measures such as the federal draft in 1863 and 1864. Even Governor Morton feared that measures like the substitute clause of the Enrollment Act—whereby drafted men could pay to avoid military service—would drive dissent and should be ignored: "I can assure you that this feature in the Bill is creating much excitement and ill feeling towards the Government among the poorer classes generally, without regard to party and may if it is not subdued lead, to a popular storm under cover of which the execution of the Conscription Act may be greatly hindered or even defeated in some portions of our Country."' Draft violence was rampant throughout Indiana. In the summer of 1863, several draft enrollment officials were shot dead and others assaulted. In addition, shootings and death resulted when draft dodgers and deserters, often aided by family and friends, resisted arrest by troops and government officials.

Conservative Democrats adopted certain symbols to identify themselves and their opposition to government tyranny. Republicans often called backwoods country dwellers "butternuts," a disparaging reflection on their poor, subsistence-level agricultural ways, such as wearing homespun clothing dyed with the nuts of the butternut hickory, a common tree in Indiana. By 1863 Democrats embraced the image by wearing butternut pins on their dresses, bonnets, watch chains, and lapels. Similarly, Democrats employed the "copperhead" epithet, wearing a penny in a show of defiance. Enraged Republicans often insisted on removing these symbols of resistance, and Democrats often dared them to try: "We learn that a religious meeting at Henkin's school house was broken up on last Sunday night by four individuals, who entered the house while divine services were being held, with arms in their hands, and their guns cocked, demanding in Hascallian manner that all those having butternuts upon their persons should immediately take them off."[2] Thus, wherever the two partisan groups met—in churches, schoolhouses, markets, and saloons—many fights resulted.

Early in the armed struggle, amid partisan conflict and violence, prowar political leaders and federal officials in Indiana began to believe that antiwar opponents of the Lincoln administration were secretly organizing and acting to subvert the war effort. The idea that groups would meet in secret to discuss politics and political action was far from foreign to mid-nineteenth-century American society: numerous fraternal organizations existed to cater to the social, spiritual, and intellectual needs of Victorian male society, and political clubs formed an important part of political life. Clubs, party activities, family, and other social forces played a large role in forming party allegiances, transmitting political ideology, and mobilizing party workers for political action.[3] Both the Democratic and Republican parties supported and were supported by adjunct political and social organizations, which were part of a broader culture of organizations that included groups like the Masons, Knights Templar, Oddfellows, and many others—some of which maintained secrecy and secret rituals. These networks enabled men to join with others to socialize, develop friendships, and advance their economic well-being as well as social or political causes with other like-minded men. This "joiner" culture played an important role in masculine culture of the period.[4]

When Republicans in Indiana began to suspect that groups met secretly to discuss politics and ways to oppose the war policies of the Lincoln administration, they relied on informants to provide them with details about the groups and their aims that distinguished them from the conventional organizations and showed them to be of a different character. Based on the information supplied to them, Republican leaders in Indiana believed in the existence of secret conspiracies to subvert the Northern war effort. This conviction grew in intensity during the course of the war, as the evidence mounted regarding the aims and activities of the secret organizers. Governor Oliver P. Morton was the key figure in collecting information and mobilizing state and federal government efforts to combat what he saw as a significant threat. In 1862 Morton worked to collect information on secret groups throughout Indiana. In the early summer party leaders publicized their suspicions, as well as communicating their fears to the Lincoln administration in Washington. Concerted efforts to expose the secret groups by employing state and federal grand juries in Indiana failed. Democrats denied the existence of secret organizations and accused Republicans of organizing their own. (Indeed, Republicans organized several secret organizations, such as the Union Leagues and others, and sought arms for them in order to combat the Democrats.)

The U.S. Army emerged as the chief means by which to collect information and combat the effects of the secret groups. Widespread desertion in the army prompted this action. Colonel (later Brigadier General) Henry B. Carrington worked closely with Governor Morton and other officials to collect information on the groups, collectively identified during much of the war as the Knights of the Golden Circle (an organization that existed prior to the Civil War to support the spread of slavery throughout the Caribbean and Gulf region). Subsequent names for the groups were the Order of American Knights and the Sons of Liberty. As the war progressed, army intelligence in Indiana and neighboring states pointed to the arming of these groups for self-defense, for resistance to the draft, or for what were seen as even more sinister purposes. At the end of 1862 and into 1863, after Democrats had won significant electoral victories in the Indiana and Illinois legislatures, federal and state officials in Indiana and neighboring states became aware of talk among Democratic politicians of a plan to separate the Old Northwest from New England and other eastern states. The purpose of this plan was to become independent of the financial and manufacturing interests of the East that had the effect, in some Democrats' view, of oppressing the agrarian interests of the northwestern states. Morton and others communicated this perceived threat to President Lincoln and other Washington officials with great urgency.

Intelligence detected communication between secret groups in the North and the Confederate government. In the summer of 1864, U.S. Army spies successfully infiltrated the organizations and fed reliable information to Union army and political leadership on their aims and activities. Morton, Carrington, and others were convinced that the secret groups were working in coordination with Confederate agents operating out of Canada to arm themselves to carry out a number of actions, including raids on prisoner-of-war camps in the Midwest holding thousands of Confederate prisoners, such as Camp Morton in Indianapolis. Once released, the Confederate soldiers would seize federal arsenals and armories, arm themselves, and unite with Confederate cavalry operating in Kentucky. Confederate officials hoped that this force of several thousand freed prisoners and cavalry, along with a general uprising of Northerners sympathetic to the Southern war effort, would pressure federal troops to withdraw from the outskirts of Atlanta so as to secure federal railroad and other supply routes, as well as to put down the insurrection. However, the plots failed, primarily because the conspirators lost courage at the last moment.[5]

In late summer and early autumn of 1864 federal troops in Indiana arrested a number of leading Indiana Democrats and accused them of leadership in secret organizations and conspiring in league with Southern rebels against the U.S. government. These political figures, including Lambdin P. Milligan, Harrison H. Dodd, and others, went before a military commission tribunal organized by the U.S. Army and were tried for treason. The trials proved a sensation, and succeeded (as Morton and other Republicans hoped) in turning many against the Democratic

Party in the state and federal elections of October and November 1864. Republican candidates won in landslides.

"BURNED BY AN INCENDIARY"

Many acts of arson were committed in Indiana during the Civil War. Barns, haystacks, schoolhouses, houses, and other property owned by persons on all sides of the partisan divide were burned, often as revenge for acts of support for or opposition to the war effort. Below is a small sampling of newspaper notices mentioning arson.

☞ Bently Mendenhall, who has been engaged in watching the bridge over Blue river, at Knightstown, for sometime past, discovered a man in the act of setting fire to the bridge on Wednesday night last. He welcomed the incendiary by a "fire in the rear," which caused him to turn an involuntary somersault. He was carried away by a couple of accomplices. From the quantity of blood found near the spot, it is thought that Bently "settled the hash" of one scoundrel.

Richmond Broad Axe of Freedom, October 5, 1861.

∼

We are informed that the barn of Geo. FLORA, of Union township, in this County, was burned one night last week, together with about 800 bushels of wheat. It is charged as the work of an incindiary, on what grounds we have not learned.—Rumor says Mr. FLORA was recently engaged in the arrest of a deserter, and that the barn was burned in revenge for this.—We do not know what grounds there are for the charge. If the charge is true, the occurrence will occasion but little surprise. Society is fast degenerating into perfect lawlessness, and from the President down to the humblest citizen the doctrine of force, reprisals and barbarism is fast obtaining. The olden times of "law and order" were too tame. Republican times better suit the age.

Plymouth Weekly Democrat, August 13, 1863.

∼

On Sunday night the store of 'Squire Parr, on the Michigan road, two miles south of Northfield [Boone County], was burned by an incendiary, and the contents consumed in it. The loss was about $4,000. About two weeks ago Squire Parr received an anonymous note warning him to leave in two days or he would be burned out. His offense was that he voted the Democratic ticket

How long will these outrages be endured?

Indianapolis Daily State Sentinel, August 19, 1863.

~

We have received intelligence of another demonstration on the part of the traitors in Putnam county. A mill, belonging to a Union man, living in Monroe township, was burnt by them. This is but one of the thousands of their base acts, and the perpetrators should be feretted out and punished to the full extent of the law, if we have any severe enough for such acts.

We understand that Putnam county can muster one thousand Home Guards, and Monroe township, where their act was committed, about one hundred. They drill regularly, and use the Governments arms while the sympathizers muster as regularly but a short distance from them. The two rebels, Stone and Allen, who were captured with Morgan, are from this neighborhood, and have no delicacy in telling that such is the case. We would like to know what the Home Guards amount to, if they cant protect the property of Union men in the neighborhood. They probably like to muster and have *reviews* like the one on last Friday, at Greencastle.

Indianapolis Daily Evening Gazette, October 9, 1863.

~

INCENDIARIES.—

An attempt was made a few evenings since to burn the warehouses of Messrs. Bynum & Moris and G. W. Cones at Thorntown. Combustibles were carried & placed under each and the matsh applied, but watchers were about, and the fires extinguished before they could do any damage. The perpetrators were seen and shot at, but not identified. The supposed cause is political animosity, as threats have been whispered about of late that Thorntown should be burnt up because of its Unionism.

In Jackson township a few days ago, a wheat stack on the farm of Mr. Cragin was set on fire and burned up by some fiend, supposed to be instigated by political hostility.

Lebanon Patriot, August 19, 1864.

"THESE ABOLITIONISTS ARE INDEED A PRETTY SET OF PIMPS"

Newspaper editors commonly used epithets such as "abolitionist," "negro lovers," "copperhead," and "butternut" to describe their opposition counterparts. A Democratic newspaper vituperatively recounted an attack on a worship service held in a rural schoolhouse.

DISGRACEFUL CONDUCT

A party of abolition cut-throats numbered something like forty or fifty, assembled at Morgan's school house in Lancaster township, last Sabbath, for the purpose of disturbing a meeting at which Rev. George Hubbert was to preach.— They had threatened for weeks that Hubbert, who loves the Union better than ten thousand such abolition vagabonds as were there congregated, should preach under the Stars and Stripes raised by *them,* or not at all. Mr Hubbert went to fill his appointment, and found these violators of the peace and disturbers of religious assemblages ready to carry out their threats. He declined to preach under any flag raised by abolitionists. He had no objections to preaching under the Stars and Stripes; but it was a bitter mockery for such base hypocrites, and outlaws to God and man, who never breathed a Union sentiment in their lives, to place the flag over any person. The meeting was then removed from the school-house to Mr. Henry Brombaugh's barn, whither the cowardly dogs of abolitionism had not the courage to follow. We learn that close by the school-house were concealed twenty negro lovers armed with shot-guns ready to emerge should any difficulty occur. We apprehend they would have met as warm a reception as hell itself is able to give if they had come out.

These abolitionists are indeed a pretty set of pimps to carry the Stars and Stripes. Their whole lives have been devoted to denouncing the objects it symbolizes, and the flag itself. They have cheered those who have assailed it as a "flaunting lie," "hate's polluted rag," and every other dirty epithet their foul tongues could utter, and blackened hearts conceive, in times gone by, and their respect for it now, is about the same as a murderer entertains for his victim. The God-forsaken wretches who defiled the Sabbath by disturbing a religious meeting should be prosecuted, and taught to know that the Stars and Stripes furnish no protection to such gallows-birds as they who carried it on that day, and whose conduct was unbecoming a civilized community.

Huntington Democrat, July 3, 1862.

"ARBITRARY ARRESTS FOR DIFFERENCES OF OPINION"

In the run-up to the fall 1862 elections, Democratic speakers unleashed a torrent of denunciation of the Lincoln administration and other Republican leaders. The Lincoln administration responded by arresting many speakers who criticized its management of the war on the grounds that their criticism retarded volunteering and recruiting for the army.[6] Many Republicans and pro-Union partisans seized this opportunity to put their rivals in prison by sending reports to state and federal officials denouncing Democratic speakers. Several prominent Indiana Democrats were arrested for giving speeches critical of the war effort.

ARRESTS OF SEDITIOUS PERSONS.

Many communications are addressed to Governor Morton in regard to the arrest of seditious persons. Business of that nature is specially confided to the United States Marshal, by the order of the Secretary of War, to whom all communications should be addressed.

We would suggest to the well-meaning and patriotic citizens of our State that arrests of any one should not be advised unless he be guilty of some grave and unwarranted offence against the laws. Arbitrary arrests for differences of opinion do the country and the Union cause more harm than good. Such as are guilty of overt acts of treason, or of discouraging enlistments, or of resisting the draft, ought to be punished; but the proof should be certain before the party is placed in custody.

Again, there are some small minded people in every neighborhood who, though they may talk treason all day long, exert no influence whatever in community, and the arrest of such serves no good purpose. The effect is otherwise, as the insidious and influential secessionists make the occurrence a text for prating treason.

Indianapolis Indiana Daily Journal, September 8, 1862.

VIOLENCE AGAINST THE PRESS

Soldiers and civilians committed dozens of violent attacks on Indiana newspapers and editors in an effort to punish them for the sentiments they printed. Soldiers attacked newspapers more often than civilians did, and at other times official military policies were enacted to restrict newspaper political speech. Most violence was directed at Democratic newspapers. Such attacks often energized Democrats to oppose what they viewed as attacks on civil liberties protected under the federal Constitution.

For the True Republican.
From the Fifth Cavalry.
Camp Leeson, near Rockport, Ind.,
February 2, 1863.

In my last I left you in anticipation of a promised dinner on the 8th of January and I am happy to state the promise was wholly fulfilled, and more too. Instead of a dinner for a company, we had one for a regiment; for after the boys had stuffed away all they could in their capacious stomachs, they had two or three days rations left for those who took care of it.

There is quite a marked difference in the citizens of this and your portion of the State. Here the loyal, true government-loving portion are more decided and firm—more outspoken and zealous in its cause than there, and the butternut class more bitter, if possible, and outspoken in favor of Jeff's kingdom. The loyal portion is largely in the ascendent, and more zealous, warm-hearted people do not exist than they are.

We have had some excitement here in the last few days. There was published in Rockport a small paper called the Rockport *Democrat*, whose highest ambition was to malign and vilify the administration and government, and to extol to the skies the present Butternut Legislature. (The last copy of the paper I enclose.) On the night of the 29th ult. some persons, who had stood the nuisance as long as they could, took it into their heads to abate it, and entered the office and knocked it into 'pi.'[7] This, I presume, you printers understand, but your correspondent does not, having never witnessed any thing of the kind.

Well, as a matter of course it was done by soldiers, as they are the only persons presumed to do any wrong, and Co. B being the nearest camp, it was saddled upon them.

At this dire catastrophe the Butternuts became very much exasperated.—Poor company B must be annihilated, and so one company, principally of the Butternut stamp, and that portion who had surrendered their arms after the Owensboro fight,[8] drew their arms and 600 rounds of ammunition, and another Butternut company north of us drew 1200 rounds, and made some very significant hints that company B would go up, sure.

At Rockport there was rifled cannon placed by Gov. Morton for the protection of the place, and there being some hints dropped that the Butternuts would turn the cannon upon our camp, the captain sent a squad to town and quietly brought the cannon to camp, and we still hold it, and are still numbered among the U. S. army, and have night and morning roll call as usual.

Miles Stalings, of Dublin, chanced upon a Butternut of Kentucky, who happened to get over to Rockport, and was howling for king Jeff and his government, and promptly arrested and brought him to camp, and we held him for a few days until he could furnish security for two thousand dollars to keep the peace in general, and take a pretty stringent oath to be a good Union man hereafter. More anon.

Respectfully,

D.

Centreville Indiana True Republican, February 12, 1863.

"IF I SHOULD HAPPEN TO BE SHOT"

Political conflict involved all members of communities. In this northern Indiana example, a young man recounted to his sweetheart his experience as a Union League bodyguard for a violently abolitionist preacher, soldier, and politician, William Copp. Copp, formerly chaplain and captain of the Ninth Indiana Volunteer Infantry Regiment, gave a speech that provoked violence from the antiwar, anti-emancipation Democrats of Lake County. Women and children as well as men participated in the violence that ensued.

LaPorte March 3 1863

Dear Mary

I once more have the pleasure of addressing you mary scince I wrote to you last I have Been in what you may call Battle Last Friday we got a telagraph that mr Copp was to speak at Calumet and that the seccessaners said that if he came there to speak that they would mob and Kill him he also stated that he wanted men. Remember Copp knew nothing about this despach well as a member of the union Club by our Oath we are bound to protect a brother, of which he is amember well I will go on and state the particulars our band was notified that we were to go to calumet on an extra train at ¼ past 6 O clock well I was armed with a heavy colt Revolver and a small 7 shooting cartrige pistol makeing 13 shoots in all there were 75 of us Enlisted Copp Body we were divided into 7 squads of 10 in each squad I Belong to squad 1 well we got there, Mary it is heart rendering that things have come to such a pitch we got there and there set old men 50 & 60 years old with there rifles & shot guns and the [women?] with revolvers in their hands. Directly after after [sic] we got there one irishman commenced and he was put out pell mell with a sore head so that ended him then a young fellow said out side dont strike a Drunken man but strike a sober one well he blowed around considerable until he said that he would like to put a ball through that (dan son of a Bitch) meaning copp no sooner had he sayed it than he was brought to the ground with a butt end of a rifle so that that ended his carear well he layed there a bout 10 minutes and got up then he said that he was a seccessanist and a young Boy about 13 years old and he sayed did you say you are a seccessanist and he sayed yes and the boy said take this and drew his gun and put it against his Brest and pulled the triger the cap snapped and the gun did not go the little boy cried and said my father the Rebles shot and I will shoot him that saved his life so that ended that scrape then copp was speaking about the sessanist about calumet and mentioned some names then up jumps a young fellow and said it was a dam Lie and that he was not afraid of copp or any other man now see the audicity of the samps to get right up and say that in the face [of] about 80 mene all armed with revolvers and about 20 with rifles that he was not afraid of any of them well copp told him if he did not shut up he [would] shoot him he jumped on top of the seat and threw back his head and said shoot & be damned copp starded after him and got half way down the isle when father and uncle Charley caught him and he coaxed them to let him go that he wanted to make an example of him the women cried out shoot him shoot him well they

put him out a doors and his friends had to carry him home he got hurt so bad
so that ended him then another fellow commenced and he got pommeled Bad
to that they took him home in a wagon that was all the fuss then the meeting
passed off quietly then George Roberts sung By Request the following songs
after Which the oath of alleigance was taken one man did not take the women
hollored make him take it and they marched him forward and made him take it

> Song
>
> We follow Gen Rosancras if he leads us to Hell
>   We follow Gen Rosancras if he leads us to Hell
> we follow Gen Rosancras if he leads us to Hell
> and plant the old flag there
> 2
> we are all going down to Chatanooga
> we are all going down to Chatanooga
> we are all going down to Chatanooga
> and plant the old flag there
>
> we follow Gen Hooker if he leads us to heaven
> we follow Gen Hooker if he leads us to heaven
> we follow Gen Hooker if he leads us to heaven
> and we plant the old flag there

also sing old aunt Rhody
thene 3 Cheers for copp 3 cheers for the union 3 Cheers for Rosancras and 3
cheers Lincoln and 3 grones for traitors. then the meeting Broke up we escorted
the captin down to the place where he stopped then we went down to the cars
and started home we had not got over one mile when they began a row and
hurrah for Jeff Davis and the southren Confedracy the old men told them that if
they done it again they shoot them they done it and they shoot one man thru the
Breast with a rifle he died in 2 hours

then a nother sayed he was a traitor and he did not care a dam who knew
it they toll him thay would shoot him if he did not be still he sayed shoot and
be dam the consequense was that he got 5 Rifle ball through him then they
conmence fireing on both sides their was 5 wounded on theirs side and none on
ours 3 of then have since died and gone to Hell the place they belong I tell you
what then old men some of them walked 15 miles with their Rifles did not come
for fun they came to shoot Rebles if the undertook to carry their threat into
execution and they hurrah for Davis and glory be to god that they did shoot and
killd 3 and wounded 2 if the dirty Low Lifed s[c]amps O Mary I wish our laport
boy had haved been there we would haved a Killed then all and burnt the houses

mary they say if he comes there to preash on sunday the irish will Kill him therefore I may not be with you I am going to calumet and if they undertake it the devile will be to pay we are a going to protect him and that we do if they commence a fuss then on sunday the town of calumet will be laid in ashes Mary if I should happen to be shot I hope to go [to] heaven and if I never meet you on earth I meet you there if I should get my wind stopped look out for another good union boy never say a word to a seccessionist. Remembering that through them I came to death My Love to all

Your

Albert

LaPorte County Historical Society, LaPorte, Indiana.

"IT HAINT THE INION THEY ARE AFTER IT IS TO BRAK DOWN THE CONSTITUTION"

The Enrollment Act passed by Congress in March 1863 provoked widespread anger among Democrats, who saw it as but another assault on the U.S. Constitution. Here, a twenty-six-year-old blacksmith from Bluffton, Wells County, in northern Indiana, voiced his opposition to the draft and vowed armed resistance to the government if it intended to enforce the draft.

Bluffton March 23rd 1863

Dear Brother I take my pen to answer your letter and let you know that we are all well and hoping you the same and I am glad you have Parm's likness and futher about this draft I know how it will work in this place it wont work at all you need not be a bit a fraid of it it [*sic*] the People will rice and say we will not give an other man or an other Dollar and if a solger runs of the sitison protects him there is 800 hundred [*sic*] men meet in the town of Fort Wayne and took an oath that they would fight as long as they could before they would go they all have six Shooters and a bowe knife and they are arming a round Bluffton like every thing most every body has a revolver, and we wont stant it. it haint the inion they are after it is to brak down the Constitution and there is nothing left of the Constitution now but a shadow and ther is a going to be a big meeting Democratic meeting in Fort Wayne the seckant Week in April and then you will see the dust fly And futher I pitty Billy Brine but tell him the first of April is coming soon he must be care full or he will get fooled a gin, Billy out to told her to kiss his when she aked him the seckont time then the joke would be on her so Billy has to carry it all

We sent our Best respect to you all and write soon this is all from your beloved Broth.

Edwin Santee

Write soon about the Conscript Bill and how the draft is going own I am ancious to here.

Wells County Historical Society, Bluffton, Indiana.

"SOMETHING SHOULD BE DONE TO SHOW TRAITORS IN THIS LOCALITY THAT THE LAW MUST BE SUSTAINED"

This eyewitness account recalled the shooting death in Brown County of a soldier by a Democratic state legislator, Lewis Prosser, during a Democratic rally. Prosser himself was shot by an army officer and died of his wounds several days later.

Morgantown April 28th 1863

A't. Gen Noble

Dear Sir

I trust you will pardon me for communicating to you at this time, upon the Subject of the condition of this locality you doubtless have been advised in reference to the foul murder of a U.S. Soldier by the Deparado Prosser of Brown County, a leader of the KGCs I was present as one of the invited speakers and am frank to say the act was unmitigated & without cause immediately some 500 KGCs were called together to protect Prosser, all of them being armed thus defying the law & the Government Mr Hester was present I am correctly informed and made them a speesh and drilled them in the manuel of Arms According to my understanding this is a violation of Order No 38 of Gen Burnside⁹ now sir if Hester could be arrested and punished or confined— I feel sure this part of Indiana would would [sic] not present such a factious opposition to the Law & Government he weilds a great influence over the K.G.Cs in Brown, Jackson, Monroe and Morgan Counties. indeed—Something—should be done to show traitors in this locality that the law must be sustained and Union men protected. Men through fear are adhearing & joining the K.G.Cs from the fact they have no assurance or Security of their lives as these traitors are allowed to talk & do as they please without an effort upon the Authorities of the Government to vindicate its Supemacy. Hopeing something may be done speedily. I remain your

Obedient Servant

J. J. Johnson

A4017 024596 f13, Adjutant General of Indiana Records, Indiana State Archives, Indianapolis.

"YOU CANNOT BE AWARE OF THE FULL EXTENT OF THE DANGER"

Democratic state legislator James Hester was present at the Brown County shootings of a soldier and Democratic state legislator a few days previous. He darkly warned

Governor Morton of the danger ahead should Democrats continue to be targeted for
violence and persecution.

(Copy)

Nashville Ind. April 23. 1863.

His Excy, Gov. O.P. Morton,
Indianapolis
Ind.

Sir,

In what I write believe I am actuated by no other motive than a sincere desire
to prevent civil war in this State. You cannot be aware of the full extent of the
danger; and as I believe you sincerely desire peace at home, I shall venture to
write you which I trust you will take in no offensive light. I have said the danger
is imminent. The first collision between the military and the citizens of any
magnitude, will be the signal for a general uprising not only in this State but
throughout the Northern States. I assure you on the honor of a man, that by
severe exertions I have prevented an outbreak on several occasions. This feeling is
not the result of secret political organizations, tho' these have been auxilliary to
it. It owes its origin to a wide spread feeling that there is one law for a Democrat
and another for a Republican, that Democrats are to be handed over to the
tender mercies of irresponsible military tribunals, without law and without right;
that you, as Gov. of the State will not interfere to prevent a violation of the State
Laws by the military and that in the forthcoming draft none but Democrats are
to be conscripted, that to be effected thro' the Republican secret organization

Assured by your Excellency that you will protect all alike that the laws and
civil authority of the State will be maintained & the State Courts will not be
stripped of their usual jurisdiction I can vouch for peace as I verily believe.

Can you not consistently do this by public communication,?

Very Resptl'y
(Signed) James S. Hester

Burnside Papers, E 159, RG 94, National Archives, Washington, D.C.

DRAFT RESISTANCE

Since the passage of the Enrollment Act in March 1863, opposition to the draft
swelled, with resistance of all sorts occurring in many Indiana counties. Military
authorities sent troops to quell riot and bloodshed in several counties.

AN ENROLLING OFFICER ASSAULTED By A WOMAN.—

A Terre Haute virago attacked Mr. B. M. Harrison, who was making the enrollment, and forced him to beat a hasty retreat by scalding him with boiling oil and

water, so that his life is in danger. An attempt was made by the City Marshal to arrest her for assault with intent to kill, but she resisted the arrest, and struck the Marshal twice with a hot iron from the stove, injuring him severely.

Weekly Vincennes Western Sun, June 13, 1863.

∽

☞ An imaginative young friend of ours, has just finished enrolling his part of Franklin township, without any remarkable incident, except that a big Irish woman, who did not want her husband's name put down, struck him plump in the forehead with a goose egg. He says the sudden bursting of such a golden prospect before him made a very vivial impression at the time.

New Castle Courier, June 18, 1863.

∽

Rush County Tragedy—Death of Hon. John F. Stevens.

. . . The Enrolling officer for Walker township, in Rush county, had been fired upon while taking the enrollment, and sent word to Capt. McQuiston, Provost Marshal for this District, for assistance. Mr. Stevens (being Deputy Provost Marshal) and Mr. Dick Craycraft were sent up a week ago last Tuesday evening to assist in completing the enrollment On the following day, in the neighborhood of Slabtown [Homer], while quietly and inoffensively performing their duties as officers of the Government, they were, in open day, fired upon by two or more cowardly traitors and assassins concealed in a wheat field along the side of the road. Stevens was shot dead and Craycraft very seriously, if not mortally, wounded. The news reached here about three o'clock the same day, and soon spread over the city. We never before witnessed such excitement and indignation. A prominent and highly respected citizen, stricken down so suddenly and shockingly, it could not be otherwise.

. . .

We unhesitatingly say that the anti-war Democracy are responsible for this murder. Some of them may condemn this particular act, we have heard them do it and we will honestly say, we believe sincerely that the effect of their teachings is clearly seen in the terrible deed.

Greensburg Decatur Republican, June 18, 1863.

"ASSEMBLED AND ARMED, FOR THE PURPOSE OF INAUGURATING CIVIL WAR IN THIS COMMUNITY"

In the spring of 1863, several violent incidents that threatened to swell into larger uprisings prompted Governor Oliver P. Morton to dispatch a mediator to sort out the matter and conciliate partisan feelings. Morton sent Indiana Legion (state militia) commander Brigadier General John L. Mansfield to several communities where violence flared. Mansfield often managed to calm partisan rancor and hold down violent outbreaks in the communities he visited. In Warren County, Mansfield asked two local leaders—one Democrat, one Republican—to compile the following report on a recent upheaval.

Hon O.P. Morton Governer of the State of Indiana

Governer — The undersigned commission appointed by Brig Gen Mansfield to take the evidence of witnesses touching the conduct of Lieut H.C. Johnson in the troubles at Williamsport on the 1st and 2nd days of June 1862 [sic 1863], and report to your Excellency, have the honor to respectfully Submit the following report along with the evidence in the case

A number of the Soldiers belonging to Co K 33^d Ind Voluntere Infantry, were in this (Warren) County on a visit to their relations and friends. . . . While the soldiers ball was progressing. some members of Co K went to the Canon Hotel kept in Williamsport, and desired to get something to drink. (There being a bar or liquor Saloon connected with the Hotel) They found the Hotel closed and the outside doors bolted. Being unable by noise and knocks upon the door to arrouse the proprietor they concluded to break or knock the entrance door open. The evidence is conflicting whether the soldiers forced an entrance or whether the proprietor finally unbolted the door and let them in; at all events they gained an entrance. About this time Lieut Johnson made his appearance at the Hotel door and walked in, Mr John Canon the proprietor imediately drew a revolver and threatened to shoot Lieut Johnson. A very sharp altercation of words passed between ~~them~~ the parties which very nearly resulted in personal violence. This however was prevented by the interference of other parties Mr. Canon was warmly identified in interest with what is known as the Democratic (or (Butternut), party. While Lieut Johnson and the soldiers remained in the Hotel and on the side walk in front of the Hotel, some of the witnesses testified to an unusual ringing of the hotel bell, which they afterwards understood was a signal for *something.* Whether it was or not, in a few minutes thereafter a procession of men from Forty to Sixty in number suddenly made their appearance armed with clubs rocks pistols and revolvers, and marched in front of and opposite to the hotel, a portion of them standing in the street. A soldier by the name of John Graham approached one of this company and asked him to lay dow his club, which he refused to do. Graham then took hold of the club and endeavored to wrench it out of his hands, a scuffle ensued between them, which was the occasion for others of the company of citizens and the soldiers present to use violence Several pistols shots were fired by the citizens Some threw stones

and some used clubs This demonstration imediately attracted the attention of
the soldiers on the ground The alarm was sounded and the soldiers in the ball
room came on "double quick" to "the scene of strife" They all rallied under the
command of Leut Johnson, most of them were destitute of arms, but they threw
rocks clubs or brick bats as was most convenient at the company of citizens.
When the soldiers got fairly into "Line of battle" the citizens commenced a
retreat, which according to the best military authority present was "tolerably
"fast and irregular."

. . . The citizens were identified as those belonging to the democratic party.
The soldiers were up all night looking after the citizens, on the morning
following about daylight the soldiers went into the saloon connected with
the Canon hotel and unheaded the whiskey barrels and spilt the whiskey and
broke some of the glassware about the bar. they also entered the bakery on the
opposite side of the street and arrested George Mahn one of the proprietors and
held him in custody for a while Pusued and Hunted for his father Peter Mahn,
on suspicion that he was also connected with the disturbances of the evening
before. He however escaped their search and went to Covington Fountain
County in company with other citizen of this county The soldiers through the
day visited several citizens and demanded their arms, also some houses and
demanded arms if any about the premises. . . .

Through the day parties from town and near town went into the country
notifying the democracy of what had taken place and that their party friends
in town were in danger, the result of which was that a large number of the
Democracy of this and adjoining counties estimated at from five hundred to
Eight Hundred collected on the following evening in squads on the different
roads leading into to town with the view of attacting the soldiers and of
arresting some of the prominent union citizens and holding them as hostages
for the damage done by the soldiers and also to compel certain union citizens
to repair the damages done to Canon and others, and if they would not then to
burn and destroy their property. The soldiers were on the allert and had armed
themselves as well as the scarcity of firearms in town would permit. About 1
oclock A.M. of the 3^d of June the union citizens in Town were arroused and
notified that a large number of Butternutts were only a short distance from town
and were about to attack the place. in a short time many of the men assembled
at the public square for the purpose of defending the town, after waiting until
near morning and no signs of the enemys approach it was concluded that the
attack had been abandoned. The citizens and soldiers began quietly to leave
"Their *entrenchments* and disperse The reason afterwards assigned, why the
democrats did not execute their purpose of attacking the soldiers and the town
was that Peter Mahn and others who went to Covington after consulting there

concluded to send Mr Trullinger the Sheriff of Fountain County to Indianapolis to see your Excellency and to implore protection to persons and property

Mr Trullinger it is said returned in the night and stated to the army of democratic citizens that the Governor had given him assurances that a man would be sent the next day to investigate the matter

Upon receiving this inteligence they concluded to not make the attack

Brigadier General Mansfield did arrive by the train June 3^d charged with the duty of investigating the cause of the troubles.

He heard the complaints of the different parties in the afternoon, and in the evening addressed a large congregation of citizens, of both parties, in the court room. The remarks of the General were conciliatory in spirit, giving excellent advice to all. Thorough in patriotic devotion to the country and for the overthrow of the rebellion.

By his advice and assistance an arrangement was made which was satisfactory to the parties concerned. This commission was appointed, money was contributed by the citizens to pay for the whiskey spilled. The angry feelings subsided and quiett and order again prevailed in the whole community

To persons not acquainted with the facts and circumstances this may appear to be but a trifling matter. But when it is remembered that a large number of People were already assembled and armed, for the purpose of inaugerating civil war in this community and that it was only averted by the timely and judicious management of your Excellency, which was solicited and accepted by your political opponents, and that from this community it would certainly have extended to others, then the importance of the mission of Brig Gen Mansfield will be more fully appreciated.

All of which is respectfully submitted

Joseph H. Brown
Alvin High

33rd Indiana Volunteer Infantry Regimental Correspondence, Indiana State Archives, Indianapolis.

"LET NO ARMS COME TO THIS COUNTY"

Governor Morton's staff received many reports from around the state of groups hostile to the Lincoln administration that were attempting to arm themselves. A method used to obtain arms was to organize companies under the Militia Law passed by the Indiana General Assembly in 1861 creating the Indiana Legion. State Republican officials endeavored to keep arms out the hands of Democrats, and to arm only those Legion companies deemed loyal to the federal government. Crawfordsville lawyer M. D. White suggested a more equitable solution to reduce violence.

Private

Crawfordsville
June 23^d 1863.

Gen'l Noble
Indianapolis.

Dear Sir.

George Lamb of this place who was formerly a Captain in the 15th Ind Vols but was discharged on account ill health desires me to ask your permission to raise an artillery company. Mr. Lamb is sound in the Union Faith—and I presume would make a good officer.

General, there is another matter I wish to speak to you about. The Copperheads in this County are some what troublesome and in several Townships have organized to resist the enrollment; these organizations are however giving away somewhat. But they are now engaged in organizing Military companies under the "Militia law" with a view of drawing arms. They say, they intend to see whether the state will arm republicans and refuse democrats arms. Now, my suggestion is this, as companies are being organized composed exclusively of partisans, and each hostile to the other, that you let no arms come to this county, to any company.

Of course I do not wish to dictate, but this seems to me to be prudent.

Our Brown Township insurgents have sent for me to make them a speech tomorrow, I hope to see the mob disperse.

Yours M. D. White

Civil War General Correspondence, Indiana State Archives, Indianapolis.

SECRET ORGANIZATION UNCOVERED

In the early months of the rebellion, information collected by federal officials pointed to secret organizations being formed in Indiana with the avowed purpose of opposing the war. In this instance, John P. Usher, a Terre Haute attorney and Republican politician, and assistant secretary of the interior in the Lincoln administration, shared with Republican U.S. Senator Henry S. Lane intelligence he had gained of a secret antiwar organization in Terre Haute. The membership listed in this memorandum is a "who's who" of Democratic political leadership in Terre Haute and western Indiana.

The[re] is an organization in the city of Terre Haute Indiana, known as the M.P.s or Mutual Protection.

The officers of this society are
>   President
> Vice   "
> Past Worthy
>   Chaplin.

The objects of the order.

1st opposition to the Administration

2   "   " paying the War Tax

3   Not to take up arms against the Southern Confederacy and only in self defence or the order.

4   Swear to protect each other.

Places of Meeting.

Mayor Stewart's office	W.S. Cooper's residence
S. Hannegan	Vorhees + Risley's office

Signals for calling Meetings.

One separate tap accompanied with four others on Court House bell.

Signals for calling a Meeting of emergency.

Same taps on No. 2 Engine House bell and assemble near Universalist Church.

Mode of Initiating candidate.

After the candidate enters the room the following interrogatories are propounded to him.

Question	Are you a democrat or a Republican?
Ans.	I am not a Rep.
Ques.	Are you in favor of supporting the war?
Ans.	No.
Ques.	Are you opposed to the war tax
Ans.	I am.
Ques.	Will you pledge yourself at the risk of life and property not to raise arms except to protect this organization and yourself?
Ans.	I will.

The candidate then takes the following oath.

The candidate raising right hand says:

I _____ do solemnly swear that I will not divulge any secrets nor let be known any business or transaction that shall be done in this order—that I will oppose the present Administration—that I will not pay the war tax or take up arms to fight against the Southern Confederacy and only in self defense or this organization which I pledge myself to do at the risk of life and property and whenever I receive the sign from a brother I will answer.

After taking the oath the candidate signs his name to the oath.

Manner of entering a Lodge.

Go to the door and give three raps and put your mouth to key hole and give the initials M P. or Mutual Protection.

You enter the room and salute the Past Worthy by drawing the four and second finger of right hand on each corner of the mouth drawing them down to the chin keeping the thumb under the chin.

Manner of recognition on street.

Rub the right eye with the four finger of the right hand.

The person challenged Answers—by rubbing the left eye with 2^d finger of left hand

The person challenged

If in the morning says How is it this morning?

" " " afternoon " " " " to day?

" " " evening " " " " " night?

The challenged person says "All is up."

A list of names belonging to the order so far as known.

W.H Stewert Mayor.	Danl. Cren Dep. Marshal
W.S. Cooper	J.T. Hoffman " "
S. Hannegan Dep. Clerk	C H Bailey Recorder Vigo Co.
John Risley Lawyer	B W Hannah Lawyer
J H Blake Clerk	John Sayer
G.F Cookerly Editor Journal	Fred. Beardsdorf
T.B. Snapp	James Tolbert
Thos. Maddigan Marshal	Dr Warner
Thos. Martin	John Ellison
John Beauchamp	Robt. Thomas
Isaac Beauchamp	Patrick Shannon Banker
Ch^s Kern	P. Tally
Jacob Kern	J Gale
John E Wilkinson	J B Edmunds Editor of Journal
N Earnhart	H M Pratt
John Bruns	*N.F. Cunningham*
John D Bell	Ed. Gailrett
Mike Griffen Dep. Marshall	B.F. Kuppenheimer
A Joyce	
Chs Cochran Depot Agt E&CRR	
Saml Wigley	
Geo Purdy Constable	

Cam Lee
D W. Vorhees
H B. Cornwell former Post Master
John G. Davis Belongs in Rockville Ia
Jack Rawlston Supt Gas Works
John Wasson
John O'Connell
John Katzenbach
Fred. Lerner
William Maloney
John Burget
Joseph Reevey Depot Agt. Alton RR
Lem Wood
Ed. Price Treas Sullivan Co. belongs in Sullivan Co
R. Garvin   "   "   "   "   "   "   "
Alex. Manning.
H.S. Tillotson
R.H. Simpson
Wm Standeford
H K Wilson State Senator belongs in Sullivan Co.
Joshua B. Otey
Worthington
J Haggerty.

Memorandum.

On Friday evening last, November 22d 1861, a meeting was held at which there were about sixteen present among them Joshua B. Otey, H. K Wilson of Sullivan, P. Shannon & G.F. Cookerly.

Otey said he had lately been south as far as Memphis—that he had since he returned received three letters from the south and if any of them wished to send letters he could do so for them—said that some of the confederate Army officers and our officers, in Kentucky, had lately had a private conference and that our officers had agreed not to attack them—that it was known in the south that Genl Hunter was with the south in sympathy and that he prevented Fremont from reinforcing Col. Mulligan—and said they were satisfied in the south that Genl. McClellan would never attack the army on the Potomac as he was in feeling, and sympathy with the Southern Confederacy—that the secession of 45 Counties in N. Carolinia from the S. Confederacy was a *sham* and was done to make the Admr—believe they wanted to compromise and come back into the Union when in fact they did it to gain time better prepare by spring.

H K. Wilson said there was a company of over 200 raised to tare up the RR track when the 43d Reg. went south they reconsidered the matter and concluded not to do it—he said a plan was fixed to kill Capt. Darnell and the 1st Lieut. if they ever returned to Sullivan—that Thomas (who is Orderly Sargt) would have been killed if he had not left Sullivan so soon.

It was remarked that Vorhees was in the habit of getting drunk and talking about the order and if he did not quit drinking and talking they would be compelled to turn him out, but he was all right when sober.

After the meeting adjourned, Cookerly said to *one* of the members, it was a *good thing* in some respects but he did not like an order that was against the Constitution and the laws.

[Endorsed on back] Memorandum handed me by J.P. Usher on the 26th Nov 1861. H. S. Lane (Opposition to the war and Lincoln's Administration.)

Lane-Elston Papers, Indiana Historical Society, Indianapolis.

"THE FACT IS WELL ESTABLISHED"

In the spring and early summer of 1862, Indiana Republican officials worked to gather information on Democratic antiwar groups. Governor Morton shared his concerns about secret antiwar organizations and internal dissent with Secretary of War Edwin M. Stanton, and urged federal action to suppress Democratic newspapers as well as requesting arms to equip the Indiana Legion.

CONFIDENTIAL]   STATE OF INDIANA, EXECUTIVE DEPT.,

Indianapolis, June 25 [186]2

Hon. Edwin M. Stanton,
Secretary of War, Washington, D. C.:
Dear Sir: I desire to call your especial attention to certain matters existing in this State which, in my judgment, deeply concern the welfare and interest of both the State and General Governments.

The fact is well established that there is a secret political organization in Indiana, estimated and claimed to be 10,000 strong, the leading objects of which are to embarrass all effort to recruit men for the military service of the United States, to embitter public sentiment and manufacture public opinion against the levying and collection of taxes to defray the expenses of the present war, and, generally to create distrust in and bad feeling toward the Government and its recognized and legally constituted authorities. Another object is to circulate and foster newspapers of extremely doubtful loyalty—papers that sympathize with the rebellion and oppose and disparage continually and persistently the

efforts of the Government to put down traitors and crush out treason. The
sheets particularly favored in this way I believe to be the Indiana State Sentinel,
published in this city; the Cincinnati Enquirer, the Dayton Empire, and the
Chicago Times. They are doing incalculable injury to the Union cause, not, it
is true, openly and in plain terms, but by invidious, malignant, and vituperative
attacks upon Union men, by their continued apologies for the crimes committed
by the leaders of the rebellion, and by their failure to condemn their cause and
conduct. By means of these presses bad feeling, discontent, and a disposition to
resist the laws are engendered in the minds of many citizens, not only in Indiana,
but in many of the neighboring counties in Kentucky, who have become insolent
and abusive toward those engaged in the military service and those who are
endeavoring to raise additional troops for our armies. In regard to the course
of the Sentinel I can positively state that in its sympathies it is as thoroughly
opposed to our Government as the Charlestown Mercury or Richmond
Enquirer, even where its disguise is but transparent and does not even serve
as a cloak for its real opinion and sentiments. The rebel prisoners confined in
Camp Morton, in the city, regard and esteem it as their defender, ally, and friend.
Recently it has published a series of articles with the intent and for the purpose
of creating a distrust in the minds of the people as to the constitutionality
and validity of the act of Congress making the Treasury notes issued by the
Government a legal tender. I mention this particular matter only to show the
general character of this sheet. Its general tone and tenor is to oppose whatever
the Government favors, to show that, whatever our resources and ability may
be, we cannot carry the war to a successful termination without violating and
breaking down the Constitution which we profess to be fighting to preserve,
asserting that the responsibility of the war rests wholly upon the North, without
a single word in condemnation of the traitors of the South, charging repeatedly
and boldly that the sole aim and object is to interfere with their rights by
securing the abolition of slavery.

The organization alluded to is confined to no particular locality, but evidently
is in operation in every county in the State. Its members are bound by oaths and
their meetings are guarded by armed men.

These facts have been coming to me for some weeks past from all parts
of the State, substantiated by evidence which leaves no doubt in my mind of
their truth.

I am forced to believe that the present is the most critical period in our history
since the commencement of the present war.

. . .

As an important and necessary measure, allow me to recommend that at least
ten thousand stand of good arms be furnished as early as possible for the use of

our loyal citizens to be organized as militia throughout the State, under the law creating the "Indiana Legion."

I cannot undertake the organization of this force until I know certainly that the arms will be supplied, and when. The "Legion" has already been efficiently organized in most of the counties bordering on the Ohio River. It has been very valuable as a means for raising three years' troops, several regiments having been almost entirely made up from it. I am confident similar results will follow after its organization in other parts of the State.

. . .

I respectfully submit these matters for your early consideration, and trust my suggestions in regard to arms may meet with your approbation, and that some plan to correct the evils complained of may be speedily devised.

Very truly, your obedient servant,

O. P. Morton

Governor Oliver P. Morton Papers, Letter Press Book vol. 1, 9–17, Indiana State Archives; also in *The War of the Rebellion: A Compilation of the Official Records of the Union and Confederate Armies* (Washington, D.C.: GPO, 1899), ser. 3, vol. 2, 176–77.

AN UNVEILED THREAT

Harrison H. Dodd, an Indianapolis printer and leading local Democrat, was one of the leaders of the secret organizations in Indiana that planned an uprising in the summer of 1864. Dodd's oblique acknowledgment of the existence of the Knights of the Golden Circle organization in his speech to the Indianapolis Democratic Club suggested the ideological basis for its existence. The Mr. Brown who also addressed the meeting was a State Representative, Jason Brown, who had been arrested by military authority in 1862 for making a political speech.

THE DEEOCRATIC [SIC] CLUB—ADDRESS OF H H. DODD.—

The regular weekly meeting of the Club last night was largely attended, as usual. After the meeting was called to order, Wm. H. Talbott, Esq, the President, in a neat speech tendered his resignation of the office. He gave a brief history of the rise of the Club and its present condition, and trusted that some one would be elected to succeed him who could devote more time to the duties of the office than he could do now.

H. H. Dodd, Esq., was nominated by Mr. Vandegriff, and elected by acclamation.

Mr. Dodd, on taking the chair, returned thanks for the honor conferred upon him. He said, as the speaker announced for the evening was not present, he would, with the permission of the meeting, read an address which he had prepared for a[n]other occasion but as it expressed his views on the subjects agitating the public mind, would be appropriate now. They were his undivided views, and he alone was responsible for them.

Mr. Dodd then read an address, which, for beauty of language and clearness of expression, we have seldom heard equaled. The reading was also excellent, and it was listened to by the large audience of ladies and gentlemen with marked attention. The style was elevated, and the expression of sentiment was clear and bold, so that all could understand. The point we shall notice hereafter.

Mr. Dodd frankly expressed his belief that the old Union was gone forever—a thing of the past. He hoped that he was wrong in this conviction, for if anything was dear to him it was the glories that clustered around our whole country. If its reconstruction were possible, war would only defer and defeat all hope. It would add to the already embittered feeling. The cause of the war he ascribed to the officious intermeddling of the Abolitionists of the North, and if there ever was a reunion, or a reconstruction, these people must give up their isms for the sake of their country.

He spoke of the charge against the Democratic party of scheming for the establishment of a Northwestern Confederacy, leaving New England out There was nothing of the kind contemplated so far as he knew, but the great West knew her interest, and would never consent to be the hewers of wood and drawers of water for any section. The Yankee States were said to have all the brains, and it was for them to say by their acts whether or no they would continue the bond of Union. They must discard their Sumners and Wilsons, and elevate their Curtises and Winthrops, if they valued the alliance.

He spoke of the Knights of the Golden Circle, and said that although he did not desire to injure the sale of the book on that subject, he did not believe any such order existed.[10] There might be an order, not for any treasonable purposes, but to keep the powers that be within their constitutional limits, a true and devoted Union order in existence, and if some men wished to find out its objects and aims further than this, they have only to do as they have done before, place arms in the hands of their sons and send them to the polls in company with hired ruffians to intimidate and overawe peaceable citizens in the exercise of a constitutional right. Let them try this again, and they might find out what the secret order meant.

But we cannot notice this able address further to night. There were some happy local hits that brought down the house.

Mr. Brown, of Jackson county, addressed the meeting in an eloquent and stirring speech, in which he handled the editor of the Journal without gloves.

"THE CONDITION OF AFFAIRS IN INDIANA"

Governor Morton attempted to confer personally with President Lincoln regarding the growing threat of insurrection in the states of the Old Northwest, and particularly Indiana. Failing to secure a timely meeting, Morton sent a trusted confidante, Robert Dale Owen, with this letter outlining his intelligence of the conspiracy and his plan to combat it. Owen, the son of New Harmony founder Robert Owen, had been a long-time Democrat and had the trust of Secretary of War Edwin M. Stanton as well.

Strictly confidential.
State of Indiana.
Executive Department.
Indianapolis February 9th, 1863.

His Excellency
Abraham Lincoln,
Pres^t of the United States,

Sir,

I trust you will pardon me for briefly calling your attention to the condition of affairs in Indiana and the North West generally.

The Democratic scheme may be briefly stated thus: End the war by any means whatever at the earliest moment.

This of course lets the Rebel States go, and acknowledges the Southern Confederacy. They will then propose to the Rebels a re-union and re-construction upon the condition of leaving out the New England States; this they believe the Rebel leaders will accept and so do I. It would withdraw twelve votes from the Senate, and leave the Slave States in a permanent majority in that body, which they would take care to retain by admitting no more Free States into the new Union.

[New York] Govr. Seymour and the leading Democratic politicians of New York and Pennsylvania are in the scheme and hope to be able to Carry their States for it.

Every democratic paper in Indiana is teeming with abuse of New England and it is the theme of every speech. *First;* they allege that New England has brought upon us the War by a fanatical crusade against Slavery. *Second;* that the people of the North West are burdened with a heavy tariff, levied for the benefit of New England manufacturers. *Third;* that western produce is heavily taxed by exorbitant rates of transportation charged by the Rail Roads connecting the West with the Eastern cities; (and this last is true,) from which they argue that the free navigation of the Mississippi is indispensable to our prosperity, and that we can never consent to be separated from the people who control the mouth of that River. *Fourth;* that our market is in the South, that our commercial and social relations are chiefly with the people of that section, and not with the people of New England.   These views are already entertained by the mass of the Democratic party, and there is great danger of their spreading until they are embraced by a large majority of our people, unless means are promptly used to counteract them. They are using every means in their power to corrupt and debauch the public mind.

Secret societies, which are but another type of the Knights of the Golden Circle, are being established in every County and Township in the State of Indiana. Speeches, Pamphlets and Newspapers are distributed in vast numbers and at great expense, and every man who can or will read is bountifully supplied, with the most treasonable and poisonous literature.

If New York and Pennsylvania will not embark in this scheme, it is determined to go on without them; and if the people of the North West should not readily consent to an immediate union with the Rebel States, the scheme of a North Western Confederacy will be first tried as an incipient and preparatory measure.   What is the remedy for these impending evils?   *First;* a rigorous and successful prosecution of the War, unto the final suppression of the Rebellion.   *Second;* if the Rebellion cannot be wholly suppressed then the opening of the Mississippi, the occupation of that river by our Gunboats and the thorough conquest and subjugation of the West bank must be had. This cuts the Rebellion in two; the river forms an impassable gulf to the rebel arms, and guarantees the loyalty of the North Western States by securing their commercial and material interests.   In that event, we should secure the mighty West from the Mississippi to the Pacific; the Rebellion would be confined to a few old Slave States without hope of expansion and must speedily perish. *Third;* the people must be aroused and educated to understand their true interests by the publication and distribution of documents adapted to the common understanding, discussing the financial commercial and social relations between the Eastern and Western States. In this matter, there is not an hour to lose. Documents should at once be prepared, showing where is the great market for the productions of the North West, what proportion of these productions are consumed in the New England States, and what in the Slave States.   Upon this subject there is great ignorance and misrepresentation, and documents discussing it and many other topics should be placed in the hands of every man and woman in the North West.

I hope you will confer freely with the bearer of this letter, the Hon. Robert Dale Owen. He understands well the situation of affairs here, and his suggestions will be entitled to your immediate and earliest consideration.

I desired to meet you at Harrisburg, for the purpose of explaining to you more fully than I can write, the Condition of Affairs in Indiana and the North West generally.

I have the honor to be

Very Resp'y Yours

O.P. Morton

STARTLING INTELLIGENCE

In the summer of 1864 antigovernment dissenters conspired to organize forces to foment unrest and rebellion in Indiana and elsewhere. Harrison H. Dodd, a leading conspirator, traveled the state organizing cells of the Sons of Liberty, the secret organization that planned an uprising in Indiana. General Carrington superintended the government effort to collect intelligence on and counteract the conspiracy.

Brownstown Ind

Aug. 6th 1864.

Gen Carrington &

OP Morton Gov of Ind. }

Gents,

We were started by the intelligence, this morning, of the robery and shooting of one of the best citizens of this county (Jackson) by an unknown party of men supposed to be from the County of Washington. There is an organised band of butternuts and thieves in Washington County who have made a raid into this County on Sunday last disturbed a church, and hallooed for Jeff. Davis &c &c and retired. There have been several roberies in Washington Co. within the last ten days: this side of Salem. The Sons of Liberty, alias KGCs alias OAK's were organised in this place within the last 10 days. S.W Holmes Co Auditor is chairman of their Lodge and all the prominent butternuts of this Tp (Brownstown) belong to them. They were organised by two men from Indianapolis one of whom was Mr Dodd.

The young man shot & robbed was Ashur W Elliott—step son of Wm Graham late of Driftwood Tp. We are at a loss what to do but know that something must be done to counteract these villains or we are gone up.

Many loyal men are anxiously awaiting your reply to this—expecting advice as to what should be done.

Your Obedt Servt

Saml W Tanner

"THESE FACTS WILL OPEN THE EYES OF THE PEOPLE"

Acting on intelligence, military authorities in Indianapolis raided the printing warehouse of Harrison H. Dodd, and found a large number of boxes filled with revolvers and ammunition. Papers and printed materials were also discovered in Dodd's office. Dodd and others were arrested shortly thereafter. The Republican press trumpeted the news.

WHAT SAY YOU NOW!

PREPARATIONS FOR A REVOLUTION IN INDIANA

LARGE QUANTITIES OF ARMS AND AMMUNITION SENT HERE.

If any one doubts that we have traitors in Indiana, let such an one read our dispatches this morning. Twenty-six boxes of arms and ammunition have been sent from the East to the Grand Commander of the Sons of Liberty, H. H. Dodd. A book was found in his safe containing the names of the members of that treasonable order, among which are the names of the Democratic Secretary and Auditor of State, and Attorney-General, JOSEPH E. MCDONALD, who is now the Democratic candidate for Governor, and last, but not least, J. J. BINGHAM, editor of the State *Sentinel*. The latter is the Chairman of the Committee which recently issued the address to the Democracy, counseling that party to arm. Who is this body of Democratic office-holders connected with? Who have they introduced into this treasonable order called "Sons of Liberty?" Four Hundred Rebel Prisoners! Thus stands the treason unmasked. *Rebel prisoners, Democratic office-holders and a Democratic candidate for Governor* of this State, *all joined together* to inaugurate bloody rebellion here in Indiana, All Arming!!

We think these facts will open the eyes of the people of this State somewhat. Why are the rebel prisoners taken into this treasonable order? Why are the leading Democrats in it? Why is the order arming? Answer these questions you quiet and loyal Democrats who refused to believe. Are we to transfer the rebellion from the South to the North; and are we to behold bloody treason in Indiana?

Talk no more as to that address of the State Central Committee, above alluded to, which talked of the right to bear arms, and the duty of Democrats to arm. The right of the citizen, on all proper occasions to bear arms, is undisputed. This is not the exercise of that right. It is the first bloody step towards treason. It means rebellion. It means arson, robbery, murder, and every other crime known among men. They are all comprised in the single word: Treason. These arms were purchased for the "Sons of Liberty" in Indiana, among whom are four hundred rebel prisoners. That these prisoners were to be armed if they could be released, there can be no doubt.

Loyal Democrats! What is your duty? It is plain. Come out from among the traitors.

Indianapolis Indiana Daily Journal, August 22, 1864.

THE CONSPIRACY TRIALS

The military commission trial of H. H. Dodd for treason commenced in late September 1864, two weeks prior to state elections. The star witness for the army prosecution was Felix G. Stidger, a former federal soldier from Kentucky who, acting under orders from his Kentucky and Indiana army spymasters, infiltrated the Kentucky and Indiana organizations of the Sons of Liberty. Stidger testified for four days. The following excerpt from the first day of his testimony lays bare the secret plans of the Sons of Liberty to lead an uprising in Indiana and other states. Stidger's and others' testimony, published in Republican newspapers throughout Indiana and the North, contributed to the Republican landslide victories of October and November.

Official Report

of the

Trial of Harrison H. Dodd,

Charged With

Conspiracy Against the Government—Affording
Aid and Comfort to the Rebels—Inciting Insurrection—
Disloyal Practices, and Violation of the Laws of War.

—

FOURTH DAY.
COURT ROOM, INDIANAPOLIS, INDIANA.
September 27, 1864, 2 o'clock P. M.

. . .

Q. [by Major Horace L. Burnett, Judge Advocate of the commission and prosecutor] You may State what Dodd said to you was the plan agreed on at Chicago.

A. Dodd said they had agreed to seize the camps here of rebel prisoners—Camp Morton, Camp Chase, in Ohio, Camp Douglas, at Chicago, and the depot of prisoners at Johnson's Island. They were going to seize the arsenals here, at Springfield, Ohio, or Illinois, I do not know which—the arsenals at Springfield and Chicago, Illinois. They were going to arm these prisoners with the arms thus seized, raise all the members of the Order they could and arm them, and as many men as they could organize on the 15th or 16th of August, and that was fixed as the day of the uprising. Each

Commander was to move all his men toward, and concentrate them in Louisville. They were to ask the co-operation of Colonel Syphert and Colonel Jesse, of the rebel army, who were then in Kentucky, to seize Louisville and hold it until their forces could co-operate. They were to seize Louisville and Jeffersonville and New Albany, and the rebels were to hold them until these forces could come to Louisville and hold these places.

Q. Was there any difference of opinion at Chicago as to the course to be taken?

A. At Chicago there was a difference about whether they were to wait until after they were sure of the co-operation of rebel forces, or go ahead without waiting for the rebels.

Q. How was the thing finally fixed?

A. Dodd sent Harrison to see Milligan, Humphreys, and Walker and get them here before that day. They did not come. Dodd read me letters from them, which were not signed, and which he said was from them. They said they were to go ahead at the time designated to release and arm the prisoners and members of the Order, and eventually to unite at Louisville. Harrison was a messenger who went to see those men and have them come here. I left on Saturday. He did not send to Walker for he was in New York, and expected to be here that week. He also sent a messenger to Dr. Bowles.

Q. From whom did Dodd read letters to you?

A. He read letters purporting to come from Milligan and Humphreys, but I am not sure whether there was one from Dr. Bowles or not.

Q. Did you see the signatures or hand-writing?

A. I saw the hand-writing.

Q. Did you recognize it?

A. I did not.

Q. If Dodd told you who were at Chicago, state who they were.

A. I did not learn of any one being there but Judge Bullitt, Dr. Bowles, Dick Barrett, Dodd, and Walker.

Q. How did you learn that they were there.

A. From Dodd. He told me they were there. He arranged this plan. There were other persons there from Illinois and from this State.

Q. What day did they meet at Chicago?

A. The meeting was to have been on the 20th of July, and was called about that time.

Q. Was it first arranged to have a meeting earlier than that?

A. It was first arranged to have a meeting of the Supreme Council of the Order on the first day of July.

Q. Why did that meeting not take place?

A. It was postponed on account of the postponement of the National Democratic Convention.

Q. Did it take place on the 20th of July?

A. Yes sir.

Q. Did you learn from Dodd what rank these men had in the Order?

A. Yes sir.

Q. What rank did Dodd hold in the order?

A. He was Grand Commander of the State of Indiana.

Q. What rank did Bowles have in the Order?

A. Major-General of the Order, commanding one of the districts of the State.

Q. What rank did David T. Yeagle [Yeakle] hold?

A. He had held the same rank as Bowles, but was thrown out on the 14th day of June, and Walker elected in his place.

Q. What rank did Milligan hold?

A. The same rank as Bowles.

Q. What rank did Walker hold?

A. The same as Bowles.

Q. What was the rank of J. F. Bullitt?

A. Grand Commander of the State of Kentucky.

Q. How do the Grand Commanders rank in the Order, compared with Major Generals?

A. Grand Commanders rank over Major Generals.

Q. Who composed the meeting at Chicago?

A. They were Major Generals and Grand Commanders of the Order.

Q. What day was set for the uprising to take place?

A. The first time was set in Illinois, which was to be the 3d or 17th of August. Dodd told me at the last meeting, the 15th or 16th was the day set.

Q. Why do you say it was on the 3d or the 17th of August?

A. That was the day given me, by Piper of Springfield. The day was to be as Vallandigham chose. That is what Piper told me.

Q. Who is Piper?

A. He said he was appointed on Vallandigham's staff.

Q. What is Vallandigham's rank in the Order of the Sons of Liberty?

A. Supreme Commander of the United States.

Q. Did you learn whether his orders were to be supreme orders above all other orders or laws?

A. I learned from members of the Order, that his orders were to be obeyed above all other orders, and the books of the Order taught as much.

The counsel for the accused objected—that unless Piper was a member of the Order, evidence as to him was not admissible, but the objection was withdrawn.

Q. Did you meet Piper as a member of the Order?

A. I met him in the Grand Council of the State of Kentucky.

Q. Was the time of this uprising to be as Vallandigham, who claimed to be a leader in the Order, should determine?

A. That was the first programme. The day had been set from the 3d to the 17th, and if they were sufficiently ready, he was to decide on which day they should rise.

Q. Where was this uprising to be?

A. It was to be general in Ohio, Indiana, Illinois, Missouri, and as much of Kentucky as could be worked.

Q. Did you know of Dodd, or any member of the Order, taking steps to communicate to rebels anything about the Order?

A. I know of members of the Order doing so. A rebel Colonel was given the secrets of the Order, and requested to disseminate them [at?] the South. Judge Bullitt admitted to me that he had tried to have a conference with Colonel Jesse.

Q. Who else did he communicate with?

A. He also sent a man to have a conference with Colonel Syphert, of the rebel army, to ascertain when he could best co-operate with him on Louisville, or use his forces in the capture of Louisville. . . .

Indianapolis Daily Journal, September 30, 1864.

DEMOCRATS IN TROUBLE

The exposure of the Northwest Conspiracy left the Democratic Party in disarray. A series of arrests of prominent Democrats occurred by military order; all were charged with treason. Harrison H. Dodd was put on trial first, in the trial above in which Stidger testifed, but escaped custody in early October and fled to Canada. By late October, a second trial before a military tribunal, of William Bowles, Lambdin Milligan, Stephen Horsey, and Andrew Humphreys, began. J. J. Bingham, the editor of the party organ, the Indianapolis Daily Sentinel, *and Horace Heffren, two leading Democrats who had also been arrested by military authority, both turned state's evidence, testifying against the four. This trial would result in the conviction of all four, with all but Humphreys sentenced to die. The second trial coincided with the run-up to the presidential election, and Democrats tried desperately to turn the election toward a question of equality for African Americans and the unpopular draft.*

The argument in a nut shell.

Look at this picture.	Then on this.
Elect	Elect
Lincoln	Mcclellan
and the	and the whole
Black Republican Ticket	*Democratic Ticket*
You will bring on NEGRO EQUALITY,	You will defeat NEGRO EQUALITY,
more DEBT, HARDER TIMES, another	restore Prosperity, re-establish the
DRAFT	UNION!!
Universal anarchy, and ultimate	In an honorable, permanent and happy
RUIN!	PEACE!

Indianapolis Daily Sentinel, October 25, 1864.

THE PRESIDENTIAL BALLOT

Thanks to concerns about Democratic loyalty, the good news of Sherman's successes in Georgia, and the furlough of a sizeable number of Indiana troops, the Republicans roared back from their 1862 defeats to retake the Indiana House, retain the governor's seat, and reelect Abraham Lincoln with 5,700 more votes than Lincoln and Bell combined had received in 1860, versus an increase of less than 2,900 for the Democrats.

Walter Dean Burnham, *Presidential Ballots, 1836–1892* (Baltimore: Johns Hopkins University Press, 1955), 249.

Voting Republican, 1864

- 16%- 40%
- 40.01% - 50%
- 50.01% - 60%
- 60.01% - 81%

TEN

⁓

War's End

*T*HE REPUBLICAN TRIUMPH in the fall elections of 1864 was followed by triumph on the battlefield. Marginalized by revelations of conspiracies in their ranks, Democrats retained little voice in the political realm. The conspiracy trials also dampened dissent within the state, and the late 1864 and 1865 drafts came off without much conflict, despite Governor Morton's fear of serious resistance.[1]

When news of Lee's surrender to Grant at Appomattox Court House reached Indiana, the cheering began. While Hoosiers recognized that the Confederacy still had other active armies, they understood that Lee's defeat portended the end of the war. But even before the other Confederate armies could all surrender, the assassination of Abraham Lincoln drained the moment of its joy: "It was mixing the bitter with the sweet, victory with death."[2] Even the Democrats' party organ, the *Indianapolis State Sentinel,* conceded: "Mr. Lincoln was pre-eminently a good man and no one came in contact with him without being impressed with the kindness of his heart and the honesty of his purposes." The article continued: "Four years ago, but few thought that the nation could survive the shock of civil war; but with that fixedness of purpose, and that independence of judgment, which were stiriking [*sic*] characteristics of the man, he pursued the policy which he had marked out at the beginning of his administration, varied in its execution however, by changing circumstances, until success appeared to be within his grasp."[3] Lincoln's funeral train wound its way through Indiana, passing through Richmond and stopping in Indianapolis, where his body lay in state in the Indiana State House, then continuing north to Chicago.

More than 24,000 Hoosiers had died in the war. The children, wives, and parents of the war dead would be denied the support that these men would have provided. The federal government, by establishing a military pension for such children, wives, and aged parents, attempted to step in. But many other Hoosier families would still be affected by the war, even if their soldiers returned alive. Many soldiers' health would never fully recover from battle wounds and disease, reducing the survivors' ability to provide for their families. Finally, the mental strain of the war, with its intense horrors, would haunt some for the rest of their lives.[4]

The expanded federal pension system reveals a dimension of the post–Civil War nation not immediately evident to many at the time: the expanded role of the federal government in the lives of its citizens. To successfully prosecute the war, the federal government took onto itself powers it had previously left to the states—the draft, for instance. Moreover, four years without the South's participation in the federal government had weakened the Democratic Party to the extent that the Republicans were able to carve out a variety of economic policies long sought by the Whigs before them to encourage the development of the nation: the land-grant colleges, a national banking system, and a stronger tariff, to name just three. Most of the Republican policies worked to make the federal government more important to the daily lives of Americans.[5]

With the war's end, Indiana Republicans quickly lost interest in executing the convicted conspirators, sending letters to Andrew Johnson asking for commutation. Senator Henry Lane wrote that "their execution under the circumstances might have the effect to take away their character as great criminals and make their misguided and deluded followers to regard them rather in the light of Martyrs than traitors."[6] Johnson commuted the three death sentences to life in prison. For many sympathetic to the conspirators, that commutation spoke of the illegitimate political impulses behind the original conviction. Lambdin P. Milligan's appeal of the conviction eventually reached the U.S. Supreme Court, which ruled in *Ex parte Milligan* that the trial by military commission was unconstitutional. Although the government had already indicted the conspirators in civilian court, those charges were eventually dropped.[7]

What did not change with the war's end was the vitriolic racism of the Democratic Party. For about a decade longer, the party's primary message remained the equality of all white men. Concerns were often raised about the influx of former slaves into the state. Hostility to African Americans sometimes erupted into violence, especially in the southern third of the state. The Republican majority included many who agreed with the racism espoused by the Democrats. Reflecting that racism, the Republican state platform, like the national one, reserved the decision on African American suffrage to the states, at least the "loyal" ones. Indiana Republicans could ratify the Fourteenth Amendment and remain consistent with that platform. Not long after winning the 1868 election with an implicit promise to prevent African American suffrage in the state, the Republican national leadership, including newly elected senator Oliver P. Morton, reversed course. In the U.S. Senate, Morton helped lead the passage of the Fifteenth Amendment, giving to African Americans the right to vote nationwide. When the amendment was presented to the Indiana legislature, the Democratic minority unsuccessfully attempted to prevent its ratification by resigning en masse twice. In going against its state platform, the state's Republican leadership signaled a willingness to transcend the racial politics of the past and move toward the position of equality, though that stance cost the Republicans control of the legislature in 1870.[8]

The conflict over race was not the only difference rooted in the Civil War that continued to divide Hoosier communities. Some Hoosier Republicans viewed their Democratic neighbors as traitors; Hoosier Democrats resented that Republicans had changed the whole nature of society. The impact of this division reached far beyond the realm of politics, into the social fabric of family, church, and community, and made the operation of a civil society much more difficult in the postbellum years.

The impact of the war would be felt in Indiana for a generation, and the changes it brought could not always be reversed. Once the war was over, Hoosiers again focused on the rhythms of daily life, and their concerns became more individualized: they went off in their own directions.

FORT WAYNE "SURRENDERS"

Northern Indiana, and in particular the counties surrounding Fort Wayne, were a bastion of antiwar strength during the Civil War. Fort Wayne itself was strongly Democratic and had been the scene of riots and violence. But the joy of the moment was clear, as is evident in N. B. Tower's letter to his cousin Alfred J. Riley in Hartford, Connecticut.

The Rebel City of Fort Wayne this morning surrendered to the Union the American flag for the first time in four + years now floating from the top of the Court House The Copperhead funeral largely attended.

[Telegram] "Union Citizens," Fort Wayne, to Morton, April 10, 1865, Governor Oliver P. Morton Papers, Morton Telegraphic Correspondence, Indiana State Archives, Indianapolis.

~

Fort Wayne Apr 10th / 65

Dear Cousin Alfred

I should have answered your letter before, I write home every week and I suppose you have heard from us, so your turn has come. I can hardly sit still long enough to write this for we are all rejoicing over the surrender of Lee's Army. The stores are all shut business jenerally suspended. Cannons firing, bells ringing, boys shouting, and this afternoon there is to be a general jolification. (how, we all ought to rejoice.) rumours (of peace terms agreed upon.) almost too good to be true. I suppose this will have a tendency to bring things down still more. they have not fallen much every one is holding of[f] not purchasing till they are lower. how do you all do. I suppose you are at Mr. Hudson's. yet.

the Eastern people will feel like going crazy over. the good news. Mr Tower hired a rebel deserter from Lee's army to help him work. for a week, he is from Alabama. has been in Virginia most of the time I think he has been an Oficer. was in that raid into Pensylvania.. he seems as glad as any of us over the news. we asked him if he felt as good as we did, said he ought to feel better. now he could go home sooner, has not heard from his home for a long time. he says they thought when the war first began they wer going to have a big frolic. did not expect it was going to amount to much. how does old Hartford flourish now Connecticut is all right. Buckingham another term for governer. there has been a draft here. and so many exempt they ar to draft 100 more to morrow. these men will not see much service they ought not to feel very bad about going now I have received some newspapers the Hartford Press I suppose they were from you for which I am very thankfull. they give me a good deal of information that I am interested in. Mr Tower takes two dailys but they do not interest me much.. we are all going down town to see the parade. how is aunt Margaret. remember me to her, and Aunt Lydia and Martha, Charly, & Father & Mother Mr Tower say's he must write to your Father & Mother has been very busy. of late I am quite well also are the rest of the family. I have not been home-sick yet. but you are not forgotten by me I assure you for I visit you in my dreams as well as in waking hours write and tell me all the news, tell Charley to write. accept much love.

From Your Affectionate
Cousin. N. B Tower.

N. B. Tower Papers, Indiana Historical Society, Indianapolis.

A SOLDIER ON THE DEATH OF LINCOLN

Alexander Starbuck was a young Randolph County enlistee in the Indiana Ninth Cavalry, only about eighteen when this letter was written.

Camp 4 Miles from Vicksburg Miss Aprill 19th/65 Dear father[,] it is with great pleasure that I Seat my Self [to] answer your kind letter of the 9th of Apr I was glad to hear from you I was Sorry to hear of the death of Somany folks but I Suppose we cannot live Allways I do not See how Elihue wil get along with Such A large family of Children I got that money you Sent me and was glad to get it[.] you may Send me 2$ dollars more and then I can get along Father I Suppose you have herd the Solemn news of the death of our good old President A Lincoln[.] that beet any thing I ever herd Father evry thing both in town and out is wrapt in mourning. Even the Soldiers wears A black ribbin around ther arms[.] there was a rebble oficer here Commanding the Exchange and when he herd it got up and packed up his things and left about midnight and went Across the lines and I

her that he Actualy Cried al the way to Black River that is the line I heard that he
Said it would be as bad on them as it would on us for he Said they would have to
Come under Andy Johnson but I am in hopes that the war [is] over and I think it
is for we have heard that Reruting and they going mustering out the men I Shall
Send down to town to morrow and Se if that box is there I am going to Send you
A Magnolia leaf for they grow thick around here[.] the trees grow about the Size
of the beech and look Some like the hickory[.] the land is good here but it is So
hilly they can hardly tend it

    I gess I have wrote all I can think of So I will Close by Asking you to write Soon

write Soon

A S Starbuck

to his Father

W. R Starbuck

I must tell you how much I Weigh. I weigh 169 pounds heavier than I ever
weighed in my life

Alexander S. Starbuck letters, Earlham College Archives, Earlham College, Richmond, Indiana.

"REBEL LEADERS WILL GET THEIR DUES"

*Lincoln's death brought cries of vengeance from some. Caleb Mills was one of the
leading education advocates in the state. His son was a lieutenant of the Forty-
ninth U.S. Colored Infantry, Louisiana volunteers; African American regiments had
white officers.*

Crawfordsville,

April 17, 1865.

Lieut. B. M. Mills,

My Dear Son.

    We were overwhelmed on Saturday forenoon, about 9 o'clock, with the
intelligence that Pres. Lincoln had been assassinated & was dead. Such a shock
can neither be conceived nor described. After recovering from the first stunning
effect produced by the terrible announcement, the first thought was, "the Lord
reigns" & can make the wrath of wicked men & devils to praise him, bring good
out of evil, light out of darkness; & the second was that this horrible tragedy will
prove a vial of wrath on the rebellion more dire than any that has preceeded it.
It will turn mercy into vengeance & fire the heart of the nation to such a degree
that the rebel leaders will get their dues & that justice will not be cheated out
of its victims. The approach of peace has blinded many people to the atrocities
of the rebellion, & they began to talk about pardoning the *rebel rascals,* & their
miserable sympathizers were whinning in with the senseless talk about pardon.

It would seem but nothing but some such astounding event as the assassination could break up the delusion, & open the eyes of the public to the folly, & madness of such a feeling just taking hold of an unreflecting multitude. Thank God, the delusion is dissapated, the spell is broken, & we can begin to see light already. Moses has been called to die Nebo (see Deut 34 Chap) in sight of the promised land of peace & Joshua is commissioned to leave Israel to the conquest of the land, the measure of whose wickedness was now full, Gen. 15:16. The Agags of rebellion will now be hewed in pieces (1 Sam 15:32 & 33). God's ways are wonderful, his hand in our deliverance from the power of the rebellion & from our own folly is so striking & manifest, that none can fail to see it & ascribe our salvation to Infinite Love & wisdom. I rejoice & bless God for his love & mercy toward us as a nation.

This mornings Gasette contains some stiring editorials which you will read with a responsive amen *"imo pertare."*

I expect to start on my agency tomorrow & you will have to depend on home correspondents. Julia got her letter a day or two ago, & she & mother will write you perhaps at the close of the week. I will write you occasionally. We have just heard of the capture of Mobile. The work of squelching the rebellion is in the process of rapid accomplishment. I wrote you immediately on receipt of your letter, requesting the documents about your box, & gave you advice in the premises. I can see no reason why you may not, with propriety & honor, resign within a month or six weeks. Your country will not need your services after Canby's expedition has crushed Alabama & the balance of Mississippi, & I wish you to come home as soon as your resignation is accepted. It will hardly be worth while for you have clothing sent you for so short a time, or indeed to purchase it at V. You will not wish wear military clothes when you get home, you will find some improvements about the house lot & garden. I leave the details to Julia to describe. I will send you the last package of the Gasettes tomorrow with this. I say last, as I shall be away & shall not continue during my absence. The Herald & Evangelist will be sent till you leave for home.

Your Aff Father.

P.S.

It is about 12 midnight. I have been writing to Webster. Enquire in the Parole camp for Capt. Elliot of the 44 Reg. U.S. C.I. as he was taken prisoner at Franklin, & show him all the kindness in your power. [?] Hadley has been promoted to Capt. of his company. Remember me to Capt. Hall & Chaplain Merrill.

"Letters of Caleb Mills Written to his Son, Lieutenant Benjamin Marshall Mills, 49th U.S. Colored Infantry, 1864–1865: Letters of the Son to his Parents during that Period," 72–73, bound typescript, Indiana Historical Society, Indianapolis.

A POEM ON LINCOLN'S DEATH

In typical nineteenth-century fashion, some lamented Lincoln's death in the form of poetry, but even this sentimental form could not obscure the political beliefs of its female creator.

[For the Courier.]

On the Death of the President.

BY PENELOPE.

The patriot prince has fallen!
   Snatched from the nation's head,
The saviour of his country, sleeps
   Among the voiceless dead.

Now draped in deepest mourning,
   We hear, from shore to shore,
Our land through all her coasts, lament
   That, Lincoln is no more.

Long had he firmly held the helm,
   Through tempests thick and sore,
Till, o'er the billowy sea of blood,
   The ship had neared the shore.

He hailed the port of peace, and strove
   The wounds of strife to close,
And to a fault, it may be said,
   Forgave his country's foes.

Where has the vile assassin skulked
   That drew the fatal bead?
Earth has no corner that does not
   Detest this fiendish deed

Dupe of the monster Treason, who
   Has paid the price in gold;—
Hired, like the other traitor,
   By whom our Lord was sold.

Oh writhing, dying Rebeldom!
  Thou'st stretched thy stiffening hand
Against the best of Presidents
  That ever blessed a land.

For what! Ye "Southern Chivalry"
  And Golden Circle Knight,
Thou Secesh serpant, Legion,
  Didst bring thy self to light?

To gain thy clan a deeper curse,
  Thy name a' darker stain?—
Thou'st slain the friend of Freedom,
  But Freedom, is not slain.

And though the mortal form of him
  We love, returns to dust
The *cause* that he espoused, will live
  As long as *God is just.*

New Castle Courier, May 4, 1865.

JOY AT LINCOLN'S DEATH

One target of Penelope's poem was undoubtedly those in her community and elsewhere who cheered Lincoln's death.

REJOICING.—Five soldiers were hung by their comrades 'til almost dead, at Indianapolis, for rejoicing over the assassination of the President.

Some of the citizens of Middletown expressed their disgust for a "refugee" who expressed his gratification at the crime, by tarring and feathering him, and other delicate attentions.

In Prairie township we learn some of the "Sons" openly rejoiced as might have been expected over the National calamity.

In our own place it is reported that one Bearly, on receipt of the news exclaimed, Bully! Bully!! Bully!!!

New Castle Courier, April 27, 1865.

POSTWAR MENTAL ILLNESS IN VETERANS

War took a psychological toll on thousands of soldiers. Many suffered from what today we would call post-traumatic stress disorder. Brigadier General Newell Gleason,

the former commander of the Eighty-seventh Indiana, eventually killed himself after
suffering years of mental torment. A personal physician provided a case history of
his patient. The letter highlights the medical profession's inability to understand
and deal with mental illness at the time.

Dr. George L. Andrew, LaPorte, to Dr. O. Everts, Superintendent of the
hospital, 11/30/1874:
LaPorte Ind Nov 30th 1874
Dr O. Everts Supt Asylum for Insane

Dear Doctor,

In filling up the Blank to accompany Genl Gleason I have as the supposed
cause of his insanity "Malarial poisoning" & gave "about ten days" as the period
of its [inration ?]. It was my intention to write you a history of the case to be
appended, if you saw fit, to the certificate, and this I do all the more willingly
since Mrs. Gleason requests, etc.

Two years ago last summer, if I remember correctly, Genl Gleason
was some months engaged in locating & surveying the route of a Rail Road
from upper Michigan to Ohio running through a highly malarious region. He
came home affected with quite a complication of disorders for which he was
treated by Dr. Rose. Some of his symptoms were relieved but there remained
a state of great depression which gave himself & his friends much anxiety. His
"will power" as he expressed it—seemed gone, his physical system seemed to
partake of the same character; he was weak, easily exhausted, his bowels were
sluggish and his skin inactive. He slept tolerably well the early part of the night
sometimes, but usually even this sleep was very "laborious," filled with dreams
that seemed to make sleep exhaustive rather than refreshing. From 3 o'clock &
sometimes earlier was the hardest part of the day for him. He would sometimes
talk a little with Mrs. G & then fall asleep again, but more frequently would
rise & walk about the house sometimes in great distress—chiefly mental. In
March last he placed himself under my care & has been under my observation
at intervals ever since.—Thinking that the original cause, as already described,
might be still operative I commenced, besides the occasional use of laxatives, to
ply him with Fowler's Solution & [flext Gels ?] equal parts (quinine had already
been given freely enough as I thought) pushing the arsenic as far as I thought
prudent. This was followed by various preparations of [?] of strychnine. One of
these I have by one now

Rx [Strychnia [g?]]
Ferris Pyrophos
Quin Sulph

Acid Phosph. Dil
Syrup Zinziberis]

S.—One teaspoonful before each meal. he seemed to me to be improving under this last but so slowly if at all that I enclosed his own written statement in my history of the case at his request to Dr. W.A. Hammond of N.Y. who advised the use of the following Rx

Pepsia Saccharat
Calcii Bromidi
Ergota fluidi
Hyd. Chlor. Phosph. Cal.

The S. dose a teaspoonful in water before each meal.

Dr. H. predicted immediate & favorable results from the use of this medicine, & Genl G. commenced its use with a good deal of hope. Just before this however he had at my urgent request accepted a commission to examine some lands in N. Mich. which involved "roughing it" for about three weeks, & he returned in improved spirits from that trip. Soon after commensing the use of Dr. H's pres[criptio]n he said that he felt that the disease was giving way—that he could feel it tingling at the back of his head & neck. He did seem to be improving, his energy returned, from feeling able to do nothing he came after a while to believe that he could do everything Fearing that the medicine was unduly exciting him, it was partially discontinued on the 14th & entirely on the 18th His exuberance continued however to increase to such a degree that it became necessary to watch and finally to restrain him.

You will have ascertained ere this reaches you that his word may be relied upon as when sane. When he "surrendered" & gave his parole here I felt certain that he could be implicitly trusted. I need not particularize as to the special delusions which afflict him. They lie on the surface.

Please let me know if there be anything you wish to know about him not mentioned here & if you think he would like to hear from me at any time.

Hoping for the speedy restoration of my friend & for your prosperity I remain

Very Truly Yours
Geo. L. Andrew

Inquest and Admission Records, Central State Hospital Records, Indiana State Archives, Indianapolis.

EX PARTE MILLIGAN

Soon after the conviction of Lambdin P. Milligan and others for conspiracy, the war ended, and President Johnson commuted the death sentences to life in prison.

*The larger legal issue of the legitimacy of the military tribunal remained and was
appealed to the Supreme Court, which in* Ex parte Milligan *roundly condemned
the use of military courts while the civilian ones remained open.*

U.S. Supreme Court
EX PARTE MILLIGAN, 71 U.U. 2 (1866)
71 U.S. 2 (Wall.)
EX PARTE MILLIGAN,
December Term, 1866

. . .

Mr. Justice DAVIS delivered the opinion of the court.
On the 10th day of May, 1865, Lambdin P. Milligan presented a petition to the
Circuit Court of the United States for the District of Indiana, to be discharged
from an alleged unlawful imprisonment. . . .

. . .

Milligan insists that said military commission had no jurisdiction to try him upon
the charges preferred, or upon any charges whatever; because he was a citizen of
the United States and the State of Indiana, and had not been, since the commencement of the late Rebellion, a resident of any of the States whose citizens were
arrayed against the government, and that the right of trial by jury was guaranteed
to him by the Constitution of the United States.

. . .

The importance of the main question presented by this record cannot be over-
stated; for it involves the very framework of the government and the fundamental
principles of American liberty.

During the late wicked Rebellion, the temper of the times did not allow that calm-
ness in deliberation and discussion so necessary to a correct conclusion of a purely
judicial question. Then, considerations of safety were mingled with the exercise
of power; and feelings and interests prevailed which are happily terminated. Now
that the public safety is assured, this question, as well as all others, can be discussed
and decided without passion or the admixture of any element not required to
form a legal judgment. We approach the investigation of this case, fully sensible of
the magnitude of the inquiry and the necessity of full and cautious deliberation.

. . .

The controlling question in the case is this: Upon the facts stated in Milligan's petition, and the exhibits filed, had the military commission mentioned in it jurisdiction,
legally, to try and sentence him? Milligan, not a resident of one of the rebellious
states, or a prisoner of war, but a citizen of Indiana for twenty years past, and never
in the military or naval service, is, while at his home, arrested by the military power

of the United States, imprisoned, and, on certain criminal charges preferred against him, tried, convicted, and sentenced to be hanged by a military commission, organized under the direction of the military commander of the military district of Indiana. Had this tribunal the legal power and authority to try and punish this man?

No graver question was ever considered by this court, nor one which more nearly concerns the rights of the whole people; for it is the birthright of every American citizen when charged with crime, to be tried and punished according to law. The power of punishment is, alone through the means which the laws have provided for that purpose, and if they are ineffectual, there is an immunity from punishment, no matter how great an offender the individual may be, or how much his crimes may have shocked the sense of justice of the country, or endangered its safety. By the protection of the law human rights are secured; withdraw that protection, and they are at the mercy of wicked rulers. or the clamor of an excited people. If there was law to justify this military trial, it is not our province to interfere; if there was not, it is our duty to declare the nullity of the whole proceedings. The decision of this question does not depend on argument or judicial precedents, numerous and highly illustrative as they are. These precedents inform us of the extent of the struggle to preserve liberty and to relieve those in civil life from military trials. The founders of our government were familiar with the history of that struggle; and secured in a written constitution every right which the people had wrested from power during a contest of ages. By that Constitution and the laws authorized by it this question must be determined. The provisions of that instrument on the administration of criminal justice are too plain and direct, to leave room for misconstruction or doubt of their true meaning. Those applicable to this case are found in that clause of the original Constitution which says, "That the trial of all crimes, except in case of impeachment, shall be by jury;" and in the fourth, fifth, and sixth articles of the amendments. . . .
. . .

Have any of the rights guaranteed by the Constitution been violated in the case of Milligan? and if so, what are they?

Every trial involves the exercise of judicial power; and from what source did not the military commission that tried him derive their authority? Certainly no part of the judicial power of the country was conferred on them; because the Constitution expressly vests it 'in one supreme court and such inferior courts as the Congress may from time to time ordain and establish,' and it is not pretended that the commission was a court ordained and established by Congress. They cannot justify on the mandate of the President; because he is controlled by law, and has his appropriate sphere of duty, which is to execute, not to make, the laws; and there is 'no unwritten criminal code to which resort can be had as a source of jurisdiction.'

But it is said that the jurisdiction is complete under the 'laws and usages of war.' It can serve no useful purpose to inquire what those laws and usages are, whence they originated, where found, and on whom they operate; they can never be applied to citizens in states which have upheld the authority of the government, and where the courts are open and their process unobstructed. This court has judicial knowledge that in Indiana the Federal authority was always unopposed, and its courts always open to hear criminal accusations and redress grievances; and no usage of war could sanction a military trial there for any offence whatever of a citizen in civil life, in nowise connected with the military service. Congress could grant no such power; and to the honor of our national legislature be it said, it has never been provoked by the state of the country even to attempt its exercise. One of the plainest constitutional provisions was, therefore, infringed when Milligan was tried by a court not ordained and established by Congress, and not composed of judges appointed during good behavior.

. . .

Another guarantee of freedom was broken when Milligan was denied a trial by jury. The great minds of the country have differed on the correct interpretation to be given to various provisions of the Federal Constitution; and judicial decision has been often invoked to settle their true meaning; but until recently no one ever doubted that the right of trial by jury was fortified in the organic law against the power of attack. . . .

. . .

It is claimed that martial law covers with its broad mantle the proceedings of this military commission. The proposition is this: that in a time of war the commander of an armed force (if in his opinion the exigencies of the country demand it, and of which he is to judge), has the power, within the lines of his military district, to suspend all civil rights and their remedies, and subject citizens as well as soldiers to the rule of his will; and in the exercise of his lawful authority cannot be restrained, except by his superior officer or the President of the United States.

If this position is sound to the extent claimed, then when war exists, foreign or domestic, and the country is subdivided into military departments for mere convenience, the commander of one of them can, if he chooses, within his limits, on the plea of necessity, with the approval of the Executive, substitute military force for and to the exclusion of the laws, and punish all persons, as he thinks right and proper, without fixed or certain rules.

The statement of this proposition shows its importance; for, if true, republican government is a failure, and there is an end of liberty regulated by law. Martial law, established on such a basis, destroys every guarantee of the Constitution, and effectually renders the 'military independent of and superior to the civil power.' . . . Civil liberty and this kind of martial law cannot endure together; the antagonism is irreconcilable; and, in the conflict, one or the other must perish.

This nation, as experience has proved, cannot always remain at peace, and has no right to expect that it will always have wise and humane rulers, sincerely attached to the principles of the Constitution. Wicked men, ambitious of power, with hatred of liberty and contempt of law, may fill the place once occupied by Washington and Lincoln; and if this right is conceded, and the calamities of war again befall us, the dangers to human liberty are frightful to contemplate. If our fathers had failed to provide for just such a contingency, they would have been false to the trust reposed in them. They knew—the history of the world told them—the nation they were founding, be its existence short or long, would be involved in war; how often or how long continued, human foresight could not tell; and that unlimited power, wherever lodged at such a time, was especially hazardous to freemen. For this, and other equally weighty reasons, they secured the inheritance they had fought to maintain, by incorporating in a written constitution the safeguards which time had proved were essential to its preservation. Not one of these safeguards can the President, or Congress, or the Judiciary disturb, except the one concerning the writ of habeas corpus.

It is essential to the safety of every government that, in a great crisis, like the one we have just passed through, there should be a power somewhere of suspending the writ of habeas corpus. . . . Unquestionably, there is then an exigency which demands that the government, if it should see fit in the exercise of a proper discretion to make arrests, should not be required to produce the persons arrested in answer to a writ of habeas corpus. The Constitution goes no further. It does not say after a writ of habeas corpus is denied a citizen, that he shall be tried otherwise than by the course of the common law; if it had intended this result, it was easy by the use of direct words to have accomplished it. The illustrious men who framed that instrument were guarding the foundations of civil liberty against the abuses of unlimited power; they were full of wisdom, and the lessons of history informed them that a trial by an established court, assisted by an impartial jury, was the only sure way of protecting the citizen against oppression and wrong. Knowing this, they limited the suspension to one great right, and left the rest to remain forever inviolable. But, it is insisted that the safety of the country in time of war demands that this broad claim for martial law shall be sustained. If this were true, it could be well said that a country, preserved at the sacrifice of all the cardinal principles of liberty, is not worth the cost of preservation. Happily, it is not so.

. . .

Ex parte Milligan, 71 U.S. 2 (1866), 107–9, 118–26.

CHANGE IN THE ECONOMY AND SOCIETY

The war had a clear impact on some aspects of Indiana's economy and society. Tracing the changes over the long period makes the unique elements of the 1860s more evident.

	1850	1860	1870	1880
Males	506,178	699,260	857,994	1,010,361
Females	470,976	651,168	822,643	967,940
African Americans	11,262	11,428	24,560	39,228
Improved acres	5,046,543	8,242,183	10,104,279	13,933,738
Farm value	$136,385,173	$356,712,175	$634,804,189	$635,236,111
Value of farm machinery	$6,704,444	$10,457,897	$17,676,591	$20,476,988
Value livestock	$22,478,555	$41,855,539	$83,776,782	$71,068,758
Corn, bushels of	52,964,363	71,558,919	51,094,538	115,482,300
Wheat, bushels of	6,214,458	16,848,267	27,747,222	47,284,853
Persons employed in manufacturing	15,242	20,753	58,852	65,687
Value of manufacturing	$18,922,651	$41,840,434	$108,617,278	$148,006,011

U.S. Census Bureau, published U.S. census, 1850–80.

EVANSVILLE RACE RIOT

During the war, several Indiana communities saw race riots, as aggrieved Democrats took out their frustrations with the war on the race they increasingly saw as responsible for causing it. After the war, a terrible race riot in Evansville began a pattern of lynching and expelling of African Americans from communities in Indiana that persisted for over half a century. James G. Jones, an Evansville Republican leader, asked the governor for assistance.

Evansville, Aug 2nd 1865

Gov. O. P. Morton

We had here on Monday last an outrageous riot resulting forcibly taking from the Jail and Murdering two negro prisoners who were confined on a charge of rape and an attempt to murder the woman who was ravished who was a german Catholic and on her way to church at the time of the offense. Whatever they may say there is no doubt that a large majority of the Catholics who are numerous as well as a large portion of the Butternuts of every class & nation, Justify the mob and indeed were instrumental in cultivating and encouraging the mob spirit.

Papers for this purpose were openly circulated and numerously signed before any violence was committed The same parties are determined to exterminate or banish all the negroes and threaten to kill them and burn the houses they occupy. Tuesday night the[y] burnt the house of an honest industrious old negro who has lived here for twenty years without giving offense to any one and last night they set fire to another house which was vacant but had been occupied by negroes. they threaten to destroy by fire two large tobacco Steweries in which negroes are employed unless the proprietors cease to employ the negroes who are preferred because they have been accustomed to the kind of work to be done and are therefore more skilful and expert The prospect is that this state of things will continue until the offenders or some of them are punished. It is the opinion of the Civil officers as well as intelligent citizens generally that an attemp to arrest & punish any of the rioters at this time without the presence and aid of a Military force would result in a more extensive and destructive riot than the one mentioned, in which the citizens engaged in bringing the offenders to justice, and their property, would be made the objects of vengeance

The men who broke the jail and those who actually murdered the prisoners walk the streets night and day and pursue their business just as if they had committed no offense. They know that they can be identified by dozens of witnesses but they feel so well assured of protection by the mob that by their conduct they seem to dare the civil authorities to arrest them

A large number of Kentuckians live among us who came here since the war commenced It is not necessary to suggest to you the party who have their sympathies—the good citizens or the mob.   At the time the prisoners were taken from the jail & murdered a number of citizens of Henderson [Kentucky] were in the crowd & had been for hours and by their talk encouraged the mob and after the deed was done the[y] went home and reported and the result was a general rejoicing and an extensive drunk   Mayor Baker is absent and the council is without a recognized head

What I want to suggest is this—that two companies of Militia—picked men—be called into actual service—without letting it be known what the object is, and when they are organized equipped and sufficiently drilled let i[t] commence to arrest and confine those offenders who are not entitled to give bail and recognize those who are

Until the authorities make it manifest that they have the power and are determined to punish all such offenders our lives and property will not be safe and the longer we delay the more bold and impudent the mobocrats will become and their number will increase daily

I have not made any suggestion to the Council except that they should increase the polise force and I dont want to if it can be avoided for some of them would be certain to make every measure and suggestion public and thus enable every felon to escape. I would be glad if Lt Gov Baker could come down and see and hear and report to you the state of things It is impossible to write all the reasons why we should have a regular Military force subject to strict Military law and discipline Gov Baker could in a day or two fully inform himself

Respectfully &

Jas. G. Jones

Conrad Baker Papers, Indiana Historical Society, Indianapolis.

DEMOCRATIC OPPOSITION TO AFRICAN AMERICAN EQUALITY

For the Paoli American Eagle, *Democratic principles could be reduced to opposition to anything extending rights and privileges to African Americans.*

THE AMERICAN EAGLE.

To day we recommence the publication of the Eagle. . .

The Eagle, in politics, will be what it has always been, a straight out advocate of Democratic principles.

Our opponents are now making a strong effort to extend to the negro population the same rights and privileges enjoyed by the white citizens. We shall oppose this move to the last. We are satisfied no worse calamity could befall our people and country than that of placing the negro upon an equality with the whites.

We shall oppose negroes coming into Indiana and settling; for such a policy will destroy the wages of the laboring white man—compelling him to become worse than a slave. And every man that has to do day-labor for a living, and votes the Republican ticket, is aiding to destroy his own wages. We shall, in our humble way, do all we can to prevent any change in our State Constitution or laws, on this subject.

The latest news of the day will be given, and every effort need to make the paper interesting to its readers.

Paoli American Eagle, August 3, 1865.

ASSISTING THE FREED PEOPLES

Some Hoosiers, most notably among the Friends, went South after the war to assist the freed peoples in their transition from slavery to freedom. Support efforts included construction of schools, churches, and hospitals. Education was foremost, and both men and women taught in these new schools. Mary Jane Edwards of Raysville was one such teacher, and these are the first entries from her diary recording her experience.

1866. Monday January 1.

This morning ushered in the new year a glad and joyous day it has been to thousands who have celebrated it with feasting and merriment. Around the bier of the dying year few mourners were gathered, but many listened closely for the knell of the departing year that they might join in the first shout of welcome to the New Year. A happy new year to *all* the world over, may it really be, and may all drink more deeply of the water of life, may all learn wisdom, that their joy may be a deep pure joy, which the world cannot give, neither take away; And may they turn to Him who is able to help when disappointment comes, and clouds overspread the sky.

~

1866. Tuesday, January 2.

Today opened school for the first time, in the new schoolhouse designed for me, with about 45 scholars of both sexes, and ages from 6 year to 25, most of them in the very first principles of education. A very small number, if any of them are of pure African descent and many of them show that they have a large proportion of white blood in their veins.

Education has been withheld from this people as faithfully as if it was poison, by those who presumed to rule over them, but the days of their cruel reign are past and the oppressed, now free may go forth, in the enjoyment of privileges hitherto denied them.

~

1866. Wednesday, January 3.

School again and more pupils, too. Today we tried to grade our schools by Transferring to sister Lizzie the more advanced pupils, to Beulah C Ellyson the intermediate, and to myself the juvenile classes.

We went home at dinner time and found Henry B Hill of Carthage and Dillon Hayworth of Plainfield direct from the north. They visited our school in the afternoon, and Henry talked to the children considerably, his words were very kind and sympathizing, he seemed to feel very deeply for the people [whose] wrongs we are trying in some [manner] to redress. He is on his way to Lauderdale to purchase land in behalf of the Ex Com of Indiana Y. Meeting

~

1866. Thursday, January 4.

Henry B. Hill went to Vicksburg to day to see Elkahah Beard and if possible get him to accompany him to Lauderdale, he said he would pass here on his way to that point and offered to bear letters from us to our friends in the north if we will send them to the train on seventh day morning next. We yesterday received a letter from home, the first word that we have heard since leaving there on the fourth of twelfth month last. News mostly satisfactory.

The arrangements in our schools are pretty much completed so that we can begin to labor to some advantage therein.

$\sim$

1866. Friday, January 5.

The fourth day of school & the last for the week I have over eighty scholars enrolled, my school has been quite full during the week just passed but I suppose many of the present enrollment will drop off; so that some of those who have not yet obtained places in school may get in by vacant places being thus made. We have sent quite a number away who seemed very anxious to come to school with the hope that there will be an opportunity at some future time. Many of them manifest a great interest in learning, and I think this class will make very good progress.

$\sim$

1866. Saturday, January 6.

To the teacher a day of rest from the duties of the schoolroom but often a very busy day in other duties. Finished a letter to be sent by Henry B. Hill to Timothy Harrison of Richmond giving an account of our expenses and the manner in which we have been employed since coming south, sent it to the train, but the bearer [Hill] was not there. Received a dispatch stating that he had deferred going to Lauderdale until second day, when he would pass here.

We are so far from home that any one whom we have ever seen before seems like a friend from home almost. It is cheering to see the face of a true Yankee.

$\sim$

1866. Sunday, January 7.

Went up to my schoolhouse for the purpose of holding Sabbath school, among the pupils of my day school, and such others as may wish to attend. Twenty four were present, somewhat encouraging for a beginning.

Many of the people seem thirsty for instruction and are glad tracts to read, or to listen to reading. While we were engaged in our Sabbath schools John Watson went to the stockade to read to the prisoners, and at the close of our schools he and a number of colored people, some soldiers and others came into my school house, and we held a meeting, John Watson spoke.

$\sim$

1866. Monday, January 8.

Sent our letter to the train. H. B. Hill was there and Dr. Hood from Vicksburg was with him going to the assist in the purchase of land at Lauderdale for the establishment of hospital schools &c. for the Freedmen by the Executive Committee of Indiana Yearly Meeting. William Wales and his family of Minnesota are employed to assist in carrying on that institution. They also wish to secure the services of Dr. Edward Young from Ohio for that place. W. Wales & wife have seven children. I hear they intend to employ some of them as teachers.

~

1866. Tuesday, January 9.

I have really thought some of going to Lauderdale myself but I feel at the same time that my claims are almost irresistible in the home of my nativity, and had it not been that I have long felt a wish to assist if possible in ameliorating the condition of the human family and lifting up its degraded numbers to a higher plain of life, I would not now be found enduring the privations, which every true philanthropist must endure, in Jackson Miss and in many other places in the south. I can not go there though it sometimes looks pleasant.

~

1866. Wednesday, January 10.

We have both been quite well the most of the time since leaving home on the 4th of 12th mo last. Lizzie is more affected with sore throat and hoarseness, produced I think by cold and by singing with her pupils, which disqualifies her for the duties of the schoolroom. It is very hard for anyone who does not have a stentorian voice to sing with these children. They seem to be built up for singing and they delight in it, delight to raise their voices to the very highest pitch of power.

When Dillon Hayworth was here he objected to our teaching them to sing, I think without good reason.

Diary of Mary Jane Edwards, of Raysville, Indiana, January 1, 1866, to December 23, 1866. Transcription copyrighted by Marilyn Holloway Swander and Barbara Miller. A copy of the original diary is available at the Earlham College Archives, Richmond, Indiana.

CHANGES IN AFRICAN AMERICAN POPULATION

As many Hoosier Democrats feared, African Americans did begin arriving in Indiana during and after the war. The growth in population was concentrated along the Ohio; other counties, however, actively drove African Americans from their pre–Civil War homes.

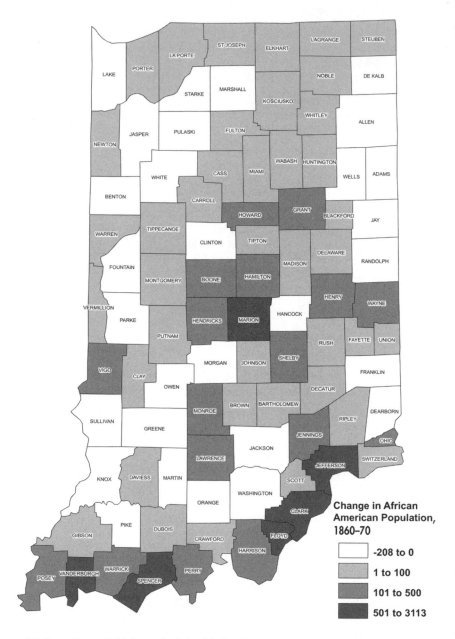

Change in African
American Population,
1860–70

☐ -208 to 0

☐ 1 to 100

☐ 101 to 500

■ 501 to 3113

U.S. Census Bureau, Eighth Census, *Population of the United States in 1860; Compiled from the Original Returns of the Eighth Census . . .* (Washington, D.C.: GPO, 1864), 109–11; and U.S. Census Bureau, Ninth Census, *Statistics of the Population of the United States . . .* (Washington, D.C.: GPO, 1872), 26–27.

"AT LEAST THEY OUGHT TO BE WILLING"

For the Republican editor of the Kokomo Howard Tribune, *passing the Fifteenth Amendment was the right thing to do. Howard County had had a small African American community since before the Civil War, with 165 African Americans in 1860 and 304 in 1870, so this proposal had a local effect. As the editorial mentioned, a limited but very real sense of the rights of African Americans had spread to parts of the North, although its impact in Indiana was felt far less than elsewhere.*

The Amendment.

The Constitutional Amendment has passed both houses of Congress by the requisite majority . . .

The opportunity is now afforded to the Indiana Legislature to ratify this amendment, and we hope that it may be done speedily. We believe that the people are ready, now that slavery has ceased to exist and impartial suffrage has been established in all the Southern States and about one half of the Northern States, to vote to make it universal. Iowa and Minnesota have within a year stricken the word "white" out of their suffrage laws by popular vote, and we cannot doubt that the people of Indiana would do so if their opportunity were afforded them, at least they ought to be willing. The Legislature should welcome this opportunity to put an end to the negro question, and to put down vulgar, insensate and tyrannical prejudice—Kansas ratified the Amendment on Saturday.

Kokomo Howard Tribune, March 4, 1869.

DEMOCRATIC REACTION TO THE FIFTEENTH AMENDMENT

Just as in the middle of the war, when Republicans abandoned the legislature so as to deny the Democratic majority a quorum, Democrats resigned in mass when faced with the passage of the Fifteenth Amendment giving African American males the right to vote. They then renominated their legislators after the mass resignation and instructed them to resign again.

Look it in the Face.

Let no man who considers himself the superior of the negro, allow any Radical negro worshiper to throw dust in his eyes to keep him from seeing the real issue by false and exaggerated statements about failures to pass appropriation or any other kind of bills, as proposition after proposition was made by the Democratic members for a postponement of the Suffrage Amendment, so as to give time and opportunity for the enactment of all laws, that the public interests demanded, and even after the resignations had been placed in the hands of the Governor, Mr.

Welborn, acting for the Democratic members, was approached by a leading and influential Radical of the State, and asked whether the Democrats would withdraw their resignations, provided the Radical members woud postpone action on the Amendment until the appropriation bills had been passed. Mr Welborn answered for his friends that they would do so cheerfully. And this being true, the judgment of every honest man must be that the responsibility of the breaking up of the Legislature rests upon the Radical members of that body.

The evils resulting from the sudden termination of the Legislature can only be temporary, and are small and insignificant in comparison with the evil of engrafting by knavish means, for knavish purposes, of an amendment upon the Federal Constitution to establish permanently, negro suffrage throughout the entire country; to force it upon all the States in the election of all their local officers and in the regulation of all their local affairs, to take from them a most momentous and vital right, which, as States, they have enjoyed unquestioned, from the earliest date of the existence of the Government, to wrench from them the powers and prerogatives without which they will not be States in any understood sense of term; to rob them of their whole distinctive character as States; in fine, to work a tremendous revolution in the nature of Republican institutions.

Brookville Franklin Democrat, March 19, 1869.

DIVIDED COMMUNITIES

The Civil War left some communities divided, and those divisions continued long after the war was over, seeping into churches. Eventually, the dispute below was resolved in the courts, with each splinter getting the use of the building two Sundays a month—fortunately, in their Baptist sect, they typically had home meetings only twice a month.[9]

Big Cedar.—Praise God from whom all blessings flow.—Brother Stout has charged one of our worthy citizens with being a "Rebel," to which mild imputation he has seen fit to reply as follows: "You are a liar," and the question will be determined some time this week. Of course the Ira-te individual who prefers the charges against his brother *"fit bled* and *died"* for the country in the way of a secret police for Springfield Township. We opine that the Stout individual will have many of his Conovers and "sich like" on the stand, and we say to all parties interested, stand from under, and look out for the *dirty* clothes of Mrs. Surratt.

Brookville Franklin Democrat, April 23, 1869.

~

Church Difficulty.

June 12th, 1869.

Mr. Bingham,—I propose to give you a short history of the difficulty that has arisen in the Big Cedar Grove Baptist Church. I am an unbiased, impartial looker-on, and consider that I can view it in the light of reason and justice.

Near the close of the Rebellion there was a Southern refugee (named Pardue) came into this neighborhood and represented himself to be a minister, and by the way, preached very successfully for a while. After a time the Copperhead members became disgusted with the gentleman because he always offered a prayer for those in authority and for the success of the Union arms. They thought that at their next election for Pastor they would oust him, but it proved to be the contrary. He was elected to fill the pulpit on the fourth Sunday. During the year Pardue was called to take a charge in Tipton County, and at once applied for a letter. It was granted, and he left for the new field of labor. In the course of a year Pardue returned and presented his letter for admittance to membership again in this Church. He was rejected on account of his missionary views. Charge were brought that he had sold this church out to the Missionary Baptists. His political creed was also a great obstacle in the way of re admission.

Since that time there has been a bad feeling in the church. At every election since, a thorough canvass has been made and every voter "brought to time." The Stout-Goudie imbroglio has opened the breach still wider, and will be the end of the church relation, if the Thurstonian revolutionists persist in the way they have begun, as the following will show.

. . .

[a table that shows a vote in which Stout clearly beats out Thurston]

. . .

The Thurstonian, Anti-Missionary, Copperhead element, not satisfied with the result, passed a resolution at their May meeting that at the June meeting they would have another election for Pastor. They carried their intention into execution. A thorough canvass was made, as much so as in a political contest. Some of the members spent a week or more riding about urging members to come out.

. . .

[The effort failed in the whole church, but the Thurstonians held their own election]

. . .

Thus the Church is divided into two parties, both claiming the Church property; and two Pastors, both claiming the 2nd Sunday in each month. The law and evidence will decide the former, and the latter may probably be decided by physical force. "Let justice be done, though the heavens fall."

Brookville Indiana American, June 25, 1869.

Timeline

1846

May   War against Mexico declared.

August   Wilmot Proviso introduced, prohibiting slavery in any territory acquired from Mexico; subsequently attached to other bills, it drives a wedge between the Northern and Southern wings of the Democratic Party.

1848

August   Free Soil Party formed, calling for the territories to be free from slavery.

November   Whig Zachary Taylor elected president; Lewis Cass carries Indiana with 49 percent of vote, while Free Soil nominee Martin Van Buren garners 5 percent.

1850

September   Compromise legislation, introduced in Congress by Henry Clay to work out sectional conflict over slavery, passed by Congress and signed by President Millard Fillmore.

October   Indiana Constitutional Convention assembles.

December   Governor Joseph A. Wright pledges that Indiana will be faithful to the Compromise legislation of 1850.

1851

February   Indiana Constitutional Convention adjourns and places the new constitution before the voters.

June   Maine enacts statewide prohibition on sale of alcoholic beverages.

October   A group of Indiana women forms a Women's Rights Association in Dublin, Wayne County, to demand rights for women.

November   New Indiana state constitution approved by voters; article excluding African Americans and providing funds to send African Americans to Liberia submitted separately to voters and overwhelmingly approved.

1852

August   Free Soil Party convention nominates U.S. Representative George
              W. Julian of Centreville, Indiana, as vice presidential candidate.

October   Democrat Joseph A. Wright elected governor. Democrats nearly
              sweep the congressional races (the Whigs win only one seat) and
              gain overwhelming control of the General Assembly.

November   Democratic Party candidate Franklin Pierce elected president,
              carrying Indiana with 52 percent of the vote; the Free Soil Party
              gains less than 4 percent, despite having Hoosier Julian on the
              ticket.

1853

January   Indiana Free Soil Party supporters form Free Democratic
              Association.

June   John Freeman, a free African American who has moved to Indiana
              from Georgia, arrested when a man claims Freeman is his runaway
              slave. Held in jail for nine weeks while court case proceeds,
              Freeman proves he is not a runaway slave. Case creates stir
              throughout state against fugitive slave law.

1854

January   Senator Stephen A. Douglas of Illinois introduces Kansas-Nebraska
              bill to admit those territories to statehood by popular sovereignty.
              Bill passes in May. Antislavery Democrats leave Democratic Party
              in protest over Kansas-Nebraska Act.

              Large temperance convention held in Indianapolis.

February   First Know Nothing lodge formed at Lawrenceburg following
              collapse of Whig Party and amid rise of anti-Catholicism in
              Indiana.

July   Convention meets in Indianapolis to protest the Kansas-Nebraska
              Act, attracting anti-Nebraska Democrats, former Whigs, Know
              Nothings, and Free Soilers. Group agrees on the name People's
              Party and calls for restoration of Missouri Compromise of 1820.

October   Newly formed Indiana People's Party wins large majorities in
              various Indiana elections, sweeps state offices, wins nine of

eleven congressional seats, and gains control of state House of Representatives.

1855

September   Antislavery settlers in Kansas repudiate fraudulent proslavery territorial legislature.

October   Antislavery Kansas settlers set up their own government; two governments in Kansas.

1856

May   Massachusetts Senator Charles Sumner severely beaten on the Senate floor by South Carolina Congressman Preston Brooks; Sumner requires three years to recover from wounds.

October   Democrat Ashbel P. Willard elected governor, narrowly defeating People's Party candidate Oliver P. Morton. Democrats win state offices, regain four congressional seats and control of the lower house of the General Assembly, but a coalition of the People's Party and Know Nothings controls the upper house.

November   Democratic Party candidate James Buchanan elected president over Republican Party candidate John C. Frémont; Buchanan takes over 50 percent of the Indiana vote.

1857

January   A group of Indiana African Americans meets in Indianapolis to appeal to Indiana General Assembly to rescind restrictions on testimony in state courts.

March   *Dred Scott* case handed down from U.S. Supreme Court rules that African Americans have "no rights that whites are bound to respect" and are not citizens under law. Also rules that Congress has no power to prohibit slavery in the territories.

October   Lecompton Constitutional Convention meets in Kansas; produces a rigged proslavery referendum process.

December   Proslavery Kansas Constitution vote prevails when antislavery supporters refuse to vote.

1858

March   U.S. Senate votes to accept Lecompton Constitution for Kansas; House votes to resubmit the matter to a vote.

May   "English Bill"—named after author Representative William English of Indiana—passes Congress to achieve compromise on Kansas.

August   Lecompton Constitution resubmitted to Kansas voters, who reject it. Kansas will remain a territory until 1861.

             Abraham Lincoln and Stephen A. Douglas hold a series of debates in Illinois while vying for a U.S. Senate seat. Slavery dominates their arguments.

1859

October   Radical antislavery leader John Brown leads violent raid on U.S. arsenal at Harpers Ferry, Virginia, in an attempt to foment slave insurrection. U.S. troops overcome raiders.

December   John Brown hanged after trial for murder.

1860

January   State Democratic convention nominates Thomas A. Hendricks as gubernatorial candidate. Rival Republican candidates for the gubernatorial nomination Henry S. Lane and Oliver P. Morton strike a deal to run together for governor and lieutenant governor respectively.

April   Democratic national convention in Charleston, South Carolina, breaks up when Southern delegates walk out in protest of insufficiently forceful protection of slavery.

May   Constitutional Union Party—formed of remnants of Whig and American parties, primarily from the South—nominate John Bell for president.

             Republican national convention in Chicago, Illinois, nominates Abraham Lincoln for president.

June   Democratic Party convention reconvenes in Baltimore with Southern delegates, who again walk out; nominates Stephen A. Douglas for president.

Southern Democrats nominate John C. Breckinridge for president. Indiana senators Jesse D. Bright and Graham N. Fitch support Breckinridge's ticket.

October   Republican Party candidate Henry S. Lane elected as governor over Democrat Hendricks. Republicans retain seven congressional seats and regain control of both houses of the General Assembly.

November   Lincoln elected president, taking a majority of the Indiana vote.

December   South Carolina secedes from the United States.

Senator J. J. Crittenden of Kentucky proposes compromise measures to settle sectional issues over slavery.

1861

January   Henry S. Lane sworn in as governor, Oliver P. Morton as lieutenant governor. Indiana General Assembly selects Lane as U.S. senator; Morton becomes governor.

Mississippi, Florida, Alabama, Georgia, and Louisiana secede from the United States. U.S. forts and arsenals in South seized.

February   Confederate States of America established; Jefferson Davis named provisional president. Texas secedes.

Abraham Lincoln, U.S. president-elect, en route to Washington, D.C., speaks in Indianapolis.

Washington peace conference, February–March.

March   Lincoln inaugurated.

Governor Morton visits Washington to obtain arms for state militia.

April   South Carolina troops bombard Fort Sumter in Charleston harbor; garrison surrenders.

Lincoln calls for 75,000 volunteers for three months. Indiana called on to raise 6,000 volunteers, who assemble and organize in Indianapolis.

Indiana General Assembly convenes in special session; authorizes war loan of two million dollars for military appropriations.

May   General Assembly reorganizes state militia as Indiana Legion; authorizes six additional regiments for twelve months' service.

Three-month volunteers depart for western Virginia.

Lincoln requests four Indiana regiments for three years or duration of war.

June   Battle of Phillippi, (western) Virginia, Federal victory; troops commanded by Indiana brigadier general Thomas A. Morris.

July   Battle of Bull Run, Virginia; rebels victorious.

August   Former Democratic governor Joseph A. Wright returns from Europe and endorses Lincoln's war policy.

September Confederate forces seize Columbus, Kentucky, violating Kentucky's "neutrality." Federal forces enter Kentucky.

October   Governor Morton appeals to patriotic women of Indiana to supply clothing and blankets for troops.

December By December, Indiana supplies 61,000 volunteers, exceeding its quota of 39,000.

1862

January   President Lincoln replaces Secretary of War Simon Cameron with Edwin M. Stanton.

Democratic convention at Indianapolis; Democrats enunciate policy positions that will be significant in their election victories in October.

February   Senator Jesse D. Bright, Democrat of Indiana, expelled from U.S. Senate after revelation that Bright has written to Confederate president Jefferson Davis. Governor Oliver P. Morton appoints prowar Democrat Joseph A. Wright to complete Bright's term.

Forts Henry and Donelson in Tennessee captured by U.S. naval and army forces; 15,000 rebel troops surrender; 3,000 prisoners sent to Camp Morton in Indianapolis and Lafayette.

Indiana Sanitary Commission/Indiana Military Agency created by Governor Morton to supply and distribute medical supplies and render aid to Indiana troops in the field and in army hospitals.

Federal troops occupy Nashville, Tennessee.

April	Battle of Shiloh, Tennessee; Union victory.
	Army of the Potomac under Major General George B. McClellan begins Peninsular Campaign in Virginia to capture Richmond.
	New Orleans captured by Union naval and army forces.
June	Robert E. Lee assumes command of rebel Army of Northern Virginia.
July	After a series of bloody battles, McClellan orders retreat of Army of the Potomac and ends Peninsular Campaign.
	U.S. Congress passes law to establish a federal arsenal at Indianapolis; construction begins in 1863.
	War Department issues call for 300,000 additional troops for three years' service.
	Rebel guerrilla raid on Newburgh, Warrick County, Indiana, results in capture of town and seizure of military stores. Governor Morton organizes a retaliatory effort to catch and punish guerrillas in western Kentucky.
August	War Department issues another call for additional 300,000 troops, and authorizes a draft for nine months' service to be administered by state authorities.
	Confederate armies under Generals Edmund Kirby Smith and Braxton Bragg invade Kentucky from eastern Tennessee.
	Battle of Richmond, Kentucky; Confederate victory. Several raw Indiana regiments captured.
September	Rebel troops threaten Cincinnati, Ohio, and Louisville, Kentucky; Governor Morton organizes Indiana troops to defend the cities.
	Battle of Antietam Creek, Maryland; Union victory ends Lee's invasion of Maryland.
	President Lincoln announces preliminary Emancipation Proclamation.
	Munfordville, Kentucky, garrisoned by Indiana troops, surrenders to Bragg's overwhelming forces.
	Several Democratic speakers and candidates arrested by military authority for speeches critical of war policy and the Lincoln

administration. Lincoln suspends the privilege of the writ of *habeas corpus* throughout the Northern states.

October   Battle of Corinth, Mississippi; Union victory.

Battle of Perryville, Kentucky; Union victory. Bragg and Kirby Smith retreat to Tennessee. Though victorious, Lincoln relieves Major General Don Carlos Buell of command of the Army of the Cumberland, replacing him with Major General William S. Rosecrans.

Draft occurs in Indiana. Draft riot in Hartford City, Blackford County, causing destruction of enrollment records, resulting in troops occupying the county and superintending draft. Troops posted at polling places in county to arrest rioters.

State elections in Indiana; Democrats win majority of seats in General Assembly and U.S. congressional seats.

November   Lincoln relieves McClellan of command of Army of the Potomac, replaces him with Indiana-born Ambrose E. Burnside.

December   Battle of Fredericksburg, Virginia; Confederate victory.

1863

January   Emancipation Proclamation takes effect.

President Abraham Lincoln relieves General Ambrose E. Burnside of command of Army of the Potomac, replaces him with General Joseph Hooker.

Indiana General Assembly convenes.

Troops sent to arrest deserters in Morgan County fired on by men on horseback.

February   Most Republican members of General Assembly "bolt," leaving Indianapolis for Madison, Indiana, denying quorum necessary for legislative business.

March   Enrollment Act passed by Congress establishes federal draft administered by military authority.

Brigadier General Henry B. Carrington appointed commander of the newly created military district of Indiana.

Troops called out to Rush County to arrest deserters.

General Assembly adjourns without passing a state appropriations bill necessary to fund state government.

Lincoln appoints General Burnside commander of the Department of the Ohio, encompassing Ohio, Indiana, Michigan, Illinois, and parts of Kentucky.

April   Battle of Thompson's Station, Tennessee; two Indiana regiments captured.

Major General Ulysses S. Grant crosses Mississippi River south of Vicksburg, Mississippi, to attack Vicksburg citadel from the south and east.

Riots in Brown and Hendricks counties.

Burnside announces General Orders 38, announcing military arrests for persons in Department of the Ohio who speak or publish criticism of the Lincoln administration's war policies or express sympathy for the rebellion.

Burnside replaces Carrington with Brigadier General Milo S. Hascall as commander of military district of Indiana. Hascall announces his General Orders 9, reiterating Burnside's General Orders 38 specifically for Indiana.

May   Battle of Chancellorsville, Virginia; Confederate victory.

Hascall arrests Indiana newspaper editors and orders their newspapers temporarily suspended for violating his General Orders 9.

Riots in Greensburg and Fort Wayne.

Governor Oliver P. Morton travels to Washington to confer with federal officials to depose Burnside and Hascall.

Ohio Democrat and leading antiwar critic of the Lincoln administration Clement L. Vallandigham arrested in Dayton by order of General Burnside for speeches critical of war policy. Tried by military commission and banished to Confederacy.

Democratic mass meeting in Indianapolis attracts thousands of Democrats, many of whom are armed. Troops are positioned around city during meeting. Disturbances between meeting attenders and soldiers occur. Democrats leaving by train shoot off their guns. General Hascall orders troops to halt trains and seize arms of passengers.

Federal forces under Grant surround Vicksburg and begin siege.

June   Hascall removed from command of District of Indiana by Burnside under pressure from Governor Morton. Replaced by Brigadier General Orlando B. Willcox.

Draft resistance in Sullivan, Rush, Johnson, Boone, Fulton, Jay, Monroe, Putnam, Greene, and other counties. Draft enrollment officers ambushed and shot dead in Sullivan and Rush counties. Troops sent to various points to arrest resisters, quell disturbance, and protect enrollment officials.

Small force of rebel cavalry under Captain Thomas H. Hines crosses Ohio River and marauds through several southern Indiana counties. Indiana Legion troops chase them down, killing and capturing most before they can recross the river.

Major General William S. Rosecrans, commander of the Army of the Cumberland, begins his advance into southern and eastern Tennessee, the "Tullahoma Campaign," to outmaneuver Confederate Braxton Bragg.

July   Confederate forces at Vicksburg surrender to Grant; Union forces now control the full length of the Mississippi River, thus cutting the Confederacy in half.

Battle of Gettysburg, Pennsylvania, between Army of the Potomac and Lee's Army of Northern Virginia. Union victory ends Lee's invasion of Pennsylvania.

Morgan's Raid into Indiana. State rallies en masse to repel invasion. Indiana troops and pursuing federal cavalry chase Brigadier General John Hunt Morgan's cavalry across southern Indiana eastward into Ohio. Morgan's force eventually disintegrates; most raiders captured in eastern Ohio.

War Department calls for troops to serve for six months' enlistment.

August   Burnside begins his East Tennessee campaign.

September	Battle of Chickamauga, Georgia; Confederate victory. Bragg counterattacks Rosecrans's army, forcing it to retreat to Chattanooga. Bragg besieges the federal army in the city.
October	Lincoln relieves Rosecrans of command of Army of the Cumberland; places all federal forces in West under command of General Grant, who takes command at Chattanooga.
	War Department makes call for 300,000 troops.
	Governor Morton suggests to War Department a plan to encourage veterans to reenlist; the plan is accepted with modification and put into effect by the army.
November	Battles of Chattanooga, Tennessee. Union forces under command of General Grant assault rebel positions on Missionary Ridge and Lookout Mountain, overlooking Chattanooga. Confederates driven back into Georgia.
	Burnside's army partially besieged by rebel forces at Knoxville, Tennessee.
December	General William T. Sherman and forces sent to relief of Burnside at Knoxville; Confederates end siege and retreat into Virginia.

1864

February	General William T. Sherman campaigns through Mississippi, destroying rebel infrastructure and supplies.
	Republican (Union) state convention in Indianapolis endorses Abraham Lincoln and Oliver P. Morton for president and governor, respectively.
	War Department calls in February and March for an additional 400,000 troops.
April	Governor Morton and Governor John Brough of Ohio devise plan to raise troops for one hundred days' enlistment; Indiana's quota to be 20,000 troops. Only 7,000 can be raised.
	Thirteenth Amendment to the U.S. Constitution banning slavery passes U.S. Senate.
May	Sherman begins his Georgia campaign, marching out of Chattanooga southward. Continuous fighting against rebels under

General Joseph E. Johnston until September in slow advance toward Atlanta.

Ulysses S. Grant, in overall command of U.S. Army, begins his Virginia campaign with Army of the Potomac. Battle of the Wilderness, Virginia.

June — Battle of Cold Harbor, Virginia; beginning of siege of Petersburg (to April 1865). Battle of the Crater.

July — Sherman reaches outskirts of Atlanta, Georgia. Atlanta partially besieged.

Democratic state convention meets in Indianapolis. Moderates who support prosecution of war control the affair and nominate Joseph E. McDonald and David Turpie to head the ticket.

War Department calls for an additional 500,000 troops.

Governor Morton authorizes publication of an expose of the secret Sons of Liberty organization in Indiana in the *Indianapolis Daily Journal*.

August — Planned uprising of Sons of Liberty organization fails to happen.

Army raid on warehouse of H. H. Dodd's Indianapolis printing business finds boxes marked "tracts" filled with revolvers.

Democratic national convention held in Chicago, Illinois. George B. McClellan chosen as candidate for president.

Governor Morton and Joseph McDonald begin series of joint debates around the state.

September — Federal troops enter city of Atlanta; Confederate troops retreat from city, destroy military stores resulting in much of the city burning.

Dodd arrested by military authority. Military commission trial of Dodd begins.

Draft in response to July call for troops begins.

October — Dodd escapes the federal prison in Indianapolis and flees to Canada. Dodd convicted of treason in absentia by military commission.

A second conspiracy trial begins against Lambdin Milligan, William Bowles, Andrew Humphries, and Stephen Horsey. All are convicted, and all except Humphries are sentenced to die.

State elections in Indiana result in large Republican victories; Morton elected governor, Conrad Baker elected lieutenant governor; Republicans win control of both Assembly chambers and majority of congressional races.

Confederate army under General John Bell Hood marches west and north to cut Sherman's communication and supply lines.

November   Sherman begins march to Savannah, Georgia (the "March to the Sea").

Presidential election results in landslide victory for Lincoln over McClellan; Lincoln takes about 53.5 percent of the vote in Indiana.

Hood's Confederate army advances into southern Tennessee, defeated by General George H. Thomas's forces at the battle of Franklin, Tennessee.

December   War Department calls for 300,000 troops.

Sherman reaches Savannah, Georgia, makes contact with U.S. Navy. Rebel forces in Savannah retreat northward into South Carolina.

Hood advances northward. Battle of Nashville, Tennessee; Union victory. Hood's army destroyed.

1865

January   General William T. Sherman's army advances north into South Carolina.

Thirteenth Amendment to U.S. Constitution banning slavery passes U.S. House.

February   Indiana General Assembly ratifies Thirteenth Amendment to U.S. Constitution banning slavery.

Sherman's army advances into North Carolina, pushing rebel forces ahead of them.

March   Abraham Lincoln sworn in to serve his second term as president.

April	General Robert E. Lee's Army of Northern Virginia evacuates Richmond, Virginia. Jefferson Davis and Confederate cabinet flee. Lee surrenders his army.
	President Lincoln shot and killed by assassin in Washington, D.C. Andrew Johnson sworn in as president.
	General Joseph E. Johnston surrenders his army in North Carolina two weeks after Lee's surrender.
May	Fighting continues in Texas; battle of Palmetto Ranch, Texas. Last Union soldier killed in action is from Indiana.
	Condemned conspirators file suit demanding release because they have not been indicted by a civilian grand jury.
	Confederate president Jefferson Davis captured in Georgia.
	Death sentence on Lambdin Milligan, William Bowles, and Stephen Horsey commuted to life imprisonment.
October	Indiana African Americans convene in Indianapolis to request repeal of laws limiting rights of African Americans to testify in court and access to schools.
December	Thirteenth Amendment to U.S. Constitution banning slavery ratified by three-fourths of states.

1866

March	Congress creates Freedman's Bureau under War Department to help impoverished African American former slaves.
April	U.S. Supreme Court decides in *Ex parte Milligan* that the conviction of the conspirators was unconstitutional.
	Congress passes Civil Rights Act over veto of President Andrew Johnson granting citizenship to all native-born persons except Indians.
	Indiana Supreme Court invalidates African American exclusion article of Indiana Constitution.

1868

January	Indiana General Assembly ratifies Fourteenth Amendment to the U.S. Constitution granting equal protection and citizenship to African Americans.

1869

May   Indiana General Assembly passes law to require local governments to establish separate schools for African American children if there is a sufficient number of children to justify it.

May   Indiana General Assembly votes to adopt Fifteenth Amendment to the U.S. Constitution giving vote to African American men.

Discussion Questions

CHAPTER 1: THE POLITICS OF SLAVERY

1. What were the attitudes of white Indiana residents toward African Americans? Was Indiana a safe place for those escaping from slavery? For African Americans who were legally free?

2. How did Hoosiers react to the controversies over slavery in the territories? Why were many Indianans willing to compromise?

3. How did slavery divide the Indiana Democratic Party? Identify the distinct positions of different Hoosier Democrats, including those who left the party over slavery.

CHAPTER 2: THE ELECTION OF 1860 AND SECESSION

1. What geographical patterns are evident in the voting for the 1860 election? What explains these patterns?

2. How did Republicans define freedom? Northern Democrats? Southern Democrats?

3. How did Hoosiers react to the threats of secession? Did those reactions change over the months between the election and the beginning of the war?

4. How well prepared was Indiana for a civil war?

CHAPTER 3: CHOOSING SIDES, MAKING AN ARMY

1. How did the cause of "Union" unite Hoosiers after Fort Sumter? What were the various meanings that Hoosiers attached to the cause of "Union"?

2. Read the article from the *Angola Steuben Republican* about Sojourner Truth's visit and then find Steuben County on the maps detailing the vote for African American exclusion and the Republican 1860 vote. Why does this Republican newspaper appear so reluctant to embrace her message?

3. Why did some Hoosier men volunteer? Why did others choose to remain at home? How could one be loyal and not volunteer?

4. What difficulties did the government face in attracting volunteers to the army? Why did these difficulties increase over the course of the war?

CHAPTER 4: THE FRONT LINES

1. What were the conditions of day-to-day life in the army?

2. How did soldiers react to being away from home, many for the first time in their lives? How was a soldier's morale affected by news from home?

3. What was the attitude of soldiers toward battle? Did this attitude change over the course of the war? By the end of the war, what were soldiers fighting for?

CHAPTER 5: THE HOME FRONT

1. How did their husbands' enlistment affect women in Indiana emotionally? Materially?

2. Compare J. W. Gordon's letter with the letter from D. Holmes on the death of James Marquise and recall that 24,000 families in Indiana went through similar experiences. To what did the survivors cling?

3. How did the political conflicts of the war spill into ordinary daily life at home?

CHAPTER 6: RACE, SLAVERY, AND THE EMANCIPATION PROCLAMATION

1. How did Hoosiers react to the Emancipation Proclamation? How did Republicans defend it?

2. Why did the proposal to recruit African American troops anger some Hoosiers?

3. Why did Hoosiers of African descent like William Edrington and Benjamin Trail choose to fight despite being treated as second-class citizens?

CHAPTER 7: THE BATTLE TO CONTROL STATE GOVERNMENT

1. Why did the state swing dramatically to the Democratic Party in the 1862 election? What expectations did the Democrats take into their legislative session?

2. How did Democrats react to the Republicans' bolt? How did it reinforce their belief that the Republicans were exercising arbitrary power?

3. How did Governor Morton navigate between demands of Democrats and dissenters on the one hand and the army's attempt to control the state of Indiana on the other?

4. Was the state government a threat to Hoosiers' civil liberties? Was the military?

CHAPTER 8: THE MORGAN RAID

1. How did Indiana react to Morgan's raid?

2. Look at the engraving of Morgan's raid in Salem. What can the picture tell us about the raid? In what ways are images trustworthy or not?

CHAPTER 9: DISSENT, VIOLENCE, AND CONSPIRACY

1. What bred the distrust on the home front? How did Hoosier Democrats perceive their Republican neighbors? How did Hoosier Republicans view their Democratic neighbors?

2. Why did this distrust become violent? Did Hoosiers of all stripes overreact, or did their neighbors with different political views really represent an extreme danger to their way of life?

3. Compare the various accounts in this chapter. Which do you find the most trustworthy? Why? Which the least? Why? Do you find yourself choosing one side or the other?

4. Do you believe there was a conspiracy? Can we make a distinction between those Hoosiers who organized to resist threats to their liberties and those who organized to actively revolt against the federal and state governments? Was it possible for the government and military at the time to make such a distinction?

5. Why did many Hoosier soldiers enter the war as Democrats but leave it as Republicans?

6. Compare the maps of the 1860 and 1864 Republican vote (maps 2.1 and 9.1). Where did the Republicans pick up votes?

CHAPTER 10: WAR'S END

1. How did Hoosiers react to Lincoln's death? How did it invest the war with additional meaning?

2. Why did the Supreme Court strike down the convictions of the conspirators?

3. What motivated people like Mary Jane Edwards to go South to aid the freed-people?

4. Why did the Democratic Party fight the Fifteenth Amendment?

5. How was Indiana changed by the war?

OVERALL

1. What was the role of religion in shaping responses to the Civil War and the events surrounding it? How did Hoosiers use religion to make sense of the events? To give them comfort?

2. Was Oliver P. Morton the right leader for Indiana in the Civil War?

Notes

INTRODUCTION

1. Charles Kettleborough, *Constitution Making, in Indiana,* 3 vols. (Indianapolis: Indiana Historical Commission, 1916–30), 1:122, 117.

2. Gregory S. Rose, "Upland Southerners: The County Origins of Southern Migrants to Indiana by 1850," *Indiana Magazine of History* 82 (September 1986): 242–63; Rose, "Hoosier Origins: The Nativity of Indiana's United States–Born Population in 1850," *Indiana Magazine of History* 81 (September 1985): 201–32; and Rose, "The Distribution of Indiana's Ethnic and Racial Minorities in 1850," *Indiana Magazine of History* 87 (September 1991): 224–60.

3. Letter from B. Whitson, "Indianans Be Vigilant," *Salem Indiana Farmer,* July 4, 1823.

4. United States Census Office, *The Seventh Census of the United States, 1850* (1853; reprint, New York: Arno Press, 1976), 756–57.

5. Sharon Baptist Church, Washington Township, Washington County, Indiana, August 3, 1822; and Minutes of Sinking Spring Baptist Church, Posey Township, Washington County, Indiana, 3rd Saturday, April 1827, transcript; Baptist Church Records, Washington County Historical Society, Salem, Indiana.

6. Tilghman Howard, "An Indiana Democrat of Southern Origin Speaks for the Union, 1832," ed. Chase Mooney, *Indiana Magazine of History* 58 (June 1962): 143–44.

7. United States Census Office, *Population of the United States in 1860* (Washington, D.C.: GPO, 1864), 111.

CHAPTER 1: THE POLITICS OF SLAVERY

1. United States Census Office, *The Seventh Census of the United States, 1850* (1853; reprint, New York: Arno Press, 1976), 756–57.

2. Donald F. Carmony, *Indiana, 1816–1850: The Pioneer Era,* vol. 2 of *The History of Indiana* (Indianapolis: Indiana Historical Bureau and Indiana Historical Society, 1998), 626–28.

3. *Brookville Indiana American,* June 27, 1856.

4. William Noel, Rockville, Indiana, to John G. Davis, February 27, 1854, John G. Davis Papers, Indiana Historical Society, Indianapolis, Indiana.

5. [Jesse] Bright, [Washington, D.C.], to William H. English, March 9, 1858, William H. English Collection, Indiana Historical Society, Indianapolis, Indiana.

CHAPTER 2: THE ELECTION OF 1860 AND SECESSION

1. *Indianapolis Indiana Daily Journal,* November 10, 1860.

2. *Paoli American Eagle,* January 10, 1861.

3. Robert Dale Owen, Indianapolis, to Samuel Hall, Indianapolis, February 10, 1861, Samuel Hall Papers, Indiana Historical Society, Indianapolis, Indiana.

4. Emma Lou Thornbrough, *Indiana in the Civil War Era, 1850–1880,* vol. 3 of *The History of Indiana* (Indianapolis: Indiana Historical Society, 1965), 99–103.

5. See the 1860 letters by and about Thompson in the Abraham Lincoln papers, American Memory Project, Library of Congress (http://memory.loc.gov/ammem/alhtml/malhome.html).

CHAPTER 3: CHOOSING SIDES, MAKING AN ARMY

1. *Indianapolis Daily Journal,* April 5, 1861.

2. W. H. H. Terrell, *Indiana in the War of the Rebellion: Report of the Adjutant General* (1869; reprint of vol. 1. Indianapolis: Indiana Historical Bureau, 1960), 5–21, 561–66; and United States Census Office, *Population of the United States in 1860* (Washington, D.C.: GPO, 1864), 106–13.

3. Letter from E. Martinelli and A. J. Harrison to O. P. Morton, January 30, 1861, Governor Oliver P. Morton Papers, Indiana State Archives, Indianapolis, Indiana; see also the many letters from county officials in this period in these files.

4. Terrell, *Indiana in the War,* 21–68, 561–66; and Thomas E. Rodgers, "Republicans and Drifters: Political Affiliation and Union Army Volunteers in West-Central Indiana," *Indiana Magazine of History* 92 (December 1996): 321–45.

5. Terrell, *Indiana in the War,* 49–68, 561–66; James W. Geary, *"We Need Men": The Union Draft in the Civil War* (DeKalb: Northern Illinois University Press, 1991), 78–102; and Peter Levine, "Draft Evasion in the North during the Civil War, 1863–1865," *Journal of American History* 67 (March 1981): 816–34.

6. *New York Times,* June 29, 1888.

7. See Jacquelyn S. Nelson, *Indiana Quakers Confront the Civil War* (Indianapolis: Indiana Historical Society, 1991).

8. The *Broad Axe of Freedom,* a newspaper published in Richmond, Indiana, supported the Republican Party and was strongly abolitionist in its editorial position.

CHAPTER 4: THE FRONT LINES

1. James M. McPherson, *Battle Cry of Freedom: The Civil War Era* (New York: Oxford University Press, 1988), 485.

2. Telegraph from O. P. Morton to M. C. Meigs, December 6, 1862, Governor O. P. Morton Telegraphic Correspondence, vol. 16, 18, Indiana State Archives, Indianapolis, Indiana.

3. See Ella Lonn, *Desertion during the Civil War* (Gloucester, Mass.: American Historical Association, 1928; reprint, Lincoln: University of Nebraska Press, 1998).

4. Hotz may have been referring to German Baptists, often called the Dunkards in the United States, who were conscientiously exempt from the draft.

5. See Iver Bernstein, *The New York City Draft Riots: Their Significance for American Society and Politics in the Age of the Civil War* (New York: Oxford University Press, 1990).

6. "Contrabands of war" was the term for runaway slaves who flocked to the safety of army camps coined by Union general Benjamin Butler in 1861.

7. Frank Moore, *Women of the War: Their Heroism and Self Sacrifice* (Hartford: S. S. Scranton, 1867), 333–40.

8. Erysipelas was a painful bacterial skin infection often contracted in army camps.

CHAPTER 5: THE HOME FRONT

1. United States Census Office, *Population of the United States in 1860* (Washington, D.C.: GPO, 1864), 656–80.

2. Alan Olmstead, "The Mechanization of Reaping and Mowing in American Agriculture, 1833–1870," *Journal of Economic History* 35 (June 1975): 327–52.

3. Thomas E. Rodgers, "Hoosier Women and the Civil War Home Front," *Indiana Magazine of History* 97 (June 2001): 105–28.

4. Emma Lou Thornbrough, *Indiana in the Civil War Era, 1850–1880*, vol. 3 of *The History of Indiana* (Indianapolis: Indiana Historical Society, 1965), 414.

5. W. H. H. Terrell, *Indiana in the War of the Rebellion: Report of the Adjutant General* (1869; reprint of vol. 1, Indianapolis: Indiana Historical Bureau, 1960), 563.

CHAPTER 6: RACE, SLAVERY, AND THE EMANCIPATION PROCLAMATION

1. Kenneth M. Stampp, *Indiana Politics during the Civil War* (Indianapolis: Indiana Historical Bureau, 1949; reprint, Bloomington: Indiana University Press, 1978), 132.

2. See V. Jacque Voegeli, *Free but not Equal: The Midwest and the Negro during the Civil War* (Chicago: University of Chicago Press, 1967).

3. See Ira Berlin, *Generations of Captivity: A History of African-American Slaves* (Cambridge, Mass.: Belknap Press, 2003), 252–53.

4. I. H. Rowland, Jackson, Tennessee, to E. N. Shelliday, January 15, 1863, Rowland-Shilliday papers, Indiana Historical Society, Indianapolis, Indiana.

5. See William Forstchen, "The Twenty-Eighth United States Colored Troops: Indiana's African Americans Go to War, 1863–1865," Ph.D. diss., Purdue University, 1994.

6. John Hardin, Vicksburg, Mississippi, to John and Luly A. Hardin, October 11, 1863, John Hardin letters, Sesquicentennial Manuscripts, William Henry Smith Memorial Library, Indiana Historical Society, Indianapolis, Indiana.

7. Dudley Taylor Cornish, *The Sable Arm: Negro Troops in the Union Army, 1861–1865* (New York: Norton, 1966), 258, and Joseph T. Glatthaar, *Forged in Battle: The Civil War Alliance of Black Soldiers and White Officers* (New York: Meridian, 1990), 165–66.

8. According to the biblical books Leviticus and Deuteronomy, every fifty years God's people were to celebrate by restoring land, wiping out debts, and freeing all indentured servants.

9. Lincoln wrote: "My paramount object in this struggle is to save the Union, and is not either to save or to destroy slavery. If I could save the Union without freeing any slave I would do it, and if I could save it by freeing all the slaves I would do it; and if I could save it by freeing some and leaving others alone I would also do that. What I do about slavery, and the colored race, I do because I believe it helps to save the Union; and what I forbear, I forbear because I do not believe it would help to save the Union." See Lincoln to Horace Greeley, August 22, 1862, in *The Collected Works of Abraham Lincoln*, ed. Roy P. Basler, 9 vols. (New Brunswick, NJ: Rutgers University Press, 1953–55), 5:388–89.

10. Kentucky politician J. J. Crittenden had offered a compromise solution in the Congress early in 1861 that would have protected slavery but restricted its geographical reach. It failed.

11. See Stephen A. Vincent, *Southern Seed, Northern Soil: African-American Farm Communities in the Midwest, 1765–1900* (Bloomington: Indiana University Press, 1999), 102.

CHAPTER 7: THE BATTLE TO CONTROL STATE GOVERNMENT

1. Kenneth M. Stampp, *Indiana Politics during the Civil War* (Indianapolis: Indiana Historical Bureau, 1949; reprint, Bloomington: Indiana University Press, 1978), 130–33. See also Emma Lou Thornbrough, *Indiana in the Civil War Era, 1850–1880*, vol. 3 of *The History of Indiana* (Indianapolis: Indiana Historical Society, 1965), 120.

2. Thornbrough, *Indiana in the Civil War Era,* 190–96.

3. See Thomas E. Rodgers, "Liberty, Will, and Violence: The Political Ideology of the Democrats of West-Central Indiana during the Civil War," *Indiana Magazine of History* 92 (June 1996): 139, and "Republicans and Drifters: Political Affiliation and Union Army Volunteers in West-Central Indiana," *Indiana Magazine of History* 92 (December 1996): 321–45.

4. Stampp, *Indiana Politics,* 158–85, and Thornbrough, *Indiana in the Civil War Era,* 185–87.

5. Lazarus Noble served as adjutant general of Indiana from 1861 to 1864, and was a close ally of Governor Morton.

6. The first battle at Manassas, Virginia, also known as Bull Run, was fought on July 21, 1861, and was a Confederate victory.

7. Missouri saw severe conflict, which devolved into ruthless guerrilla warfare early in the war. Military authorities enacted strict policies in an attempt to govern lawlessness and guerrilla activity. See Michael Fellman, *Inside War: The Guerrilla Conflict in Missouri during the Civil War* (New York: Oxford University Press, 1989).

8. Referring to the antiwar platform which emerged from the January 8, 1862, Indiana Democratic Party convention.

9. Democrat Thomas A. Hendricks had served in the U.S. House of Representatives in the 1850s, and lost the gubernatorial race to Morton in 1860. He was the leading figure in the Indiana Democratic Party.

10. Emma Lou Thornbrough, "Judge Perkins, the Indiana Supreme Court, and the Civil War," *Indiana Magazine of History* 60 (1964): 79–96.

11. The Democratic majority selected Thomas A. Hendricks to serve as U.S. senator.

12. See Stephen Towne, "Killing the Serpent Speedily: Governor Morton, General Hascall, and the Suppression of the Democratic Press in Indiana, 1863," *Civil War History* 52 (March 2006): 41–65.

CHAPTER 8: THE MORGAN RAID

1. For works on guerrilla war and political conflict in Kentucky, see Stephen D. Engle, *Struggle for the Heartland: The Campaigns from Fort Henry to Corinth* (Lincoln: University of Nebraska Press, 2001); Earl J. Hess, *Banners to the Breeze: The Kentucky Campaign, Corinth, and Stones River* (Lincoln: University of Nebraska Press, 2000); B. Franklin Cooling, *Fort Donelson's Legacy: War and Society in Kentucky and Tennessee,*

1862–1863 (Knoxville: University of Tennessee Press, 1997); and Lowell H. Harrison, *The Civil War in Kentucky* (Lexington: University Press of Kentucky, 1975).

2. James A. Ramage, *Rebel Raider: The Life of General John Hunt Morgan* (Lexington: University Press of Kentucky, 1986).

3. The National Road, built by the federal government over several decades in the early nineteenth century, provided a route for settlers to travel west into the Old Northwest. It bisected Indiana from Richmond west through Indianapolis to Terre Haute.

4. William Marvel, *Burnside* (Chapel Hill: University of North Carolina Press, 1991), 257.

CHAPTER 9: DISSENT, VIOLENCE, AND CONSPIRACY

1. O. P. Morton to A. Lincoln, March 6, 1863, Abraham Lincoln Papers, Library of Congress, Washington, D.C.

2. *Covington People's Friend,* June 17, 1863. Hascallian refers to Brigadier General Milo S. Hascall, who had been commander of the military district of Indiana. Hascall had arrested Democratic newspaper editors for publishing criticisms of the war effort.

3. Jean Baker, *Affairs of Party: The Political Culture of Northern Democrats in the Mid-Nineteenth Century* (Ithaca: Cornell University Press, 1983), 286–87.

4. See Mark C. Carnes, *Secret Ritual and Manhood in Victorian America* (New Haven, Conn.: Yale University Press, 1989), and Mary Ann Clawson, *Constructing Brotherhood: Class, Gender, and Fraternalism* (Princeton, N.J.: Princeton University Press, 1989).

5. Current literature on Democratic secret societies during the Civil War is dominated by the work of Frank L. Klement, who wrote a series of books and articles over a number of years. Klement denied the existence of revolutionary conspiracies and argued that Republican politicians and military commanders knowingly fabricated reports of Democratic plots and disloyalty for partisan purposes. Klement's thesis has dominated the literature of Northern politics for many years. Among his works, see *The Copperheads in the Middle West* (Chicago: University of Chicago Press, 1960); "Carrington and the Golden Circle Legend in Indiana during the Civil War," *Indiana Magazine of History* 61 (1965): 31–52; *The Limits of Dissent: Clement L. Vallandigham and the Civil War* (Lexington: University Press of Kentucky, 1970); and *Dark Lanterns: Secret Political Societies, Conspiracies, and Treason Trials in the Civil War* (Baton Rouge: Louisiana State University Press, 1984). See also G. R. Tredway, *Democratic Opposition to the Lincoln Administration in Indiana.* Indiana Historical Collections, volume 48 (Indianapolis: Indiana Historical Bureau, 1973). For a countering view of the antiwar Democrats, see Jennifer L. Weber, *Copperheads: The Rise and Fall of Lincoln's Opponents in the North* (New York: Oxford University Press, 2006).

6. Mark E. Neely Jr., *The Fate of Liberty: Abraham Lincoln and Civil Liberties* (New York: Oxford University Press, 1991), 51–65.

7. "Pi" was a printer's term meaning complete disorder.

8. In September, 1862, some river county Indiana Legion troops crossed the Ohio River and fought small battles against rebel guerrilla forces in Kentucky, including a fight at Owensboro.

9. Earlier in April, 1863, Major General Ambrose E. Burnside, commander of the Department of the Ohio encompassing the states of Ohio, Indiana, Michigan, Illinois, and parts of Kentucky, announced a military order, General Orders 38, which prohibited anti-administration speech or speech that gave "aid and comfort" to the rebels.

10. By 1863 several exposés of the Knights of the Golden Circle had been published. Dodd probably referred to a locally published title. See Charles O. Perrine, *An Authentic Exposition of the "K.G.C.," "Knights of the Golden Circle"; or, A History of Secession from 1834 to 1861* (Indianapolis: C. O. Perrine, 1861).

CHAPTER 10: WAR'S END

1. Kenneth M. Stampp, *Indiana Politics during the Civil War* (Indianapolis: Indiana Historical Bureau, 1949, repr. Bloomington: Indiana University Press, 1978), 251.

2. B. M. Mills, Vicksburg, Mississippi, to his mother [Sarah Mills], April 19, 1865, "Letters of Caleb Mills Written to His Son, Lieutenant Benjamin Marshall Mills, 49th U.S. Colored Infantry, 1864–1865: Letters of the Son to His Parents during That Period," 84, bound typescript, Indiana Historical Society, Indianapolis, Indiana.

3. *Indianapolis Daily Sentinel,* April 17, 1865.

4. Megan J. McClintock, "Civil War Pensions and the Reconstruction of Union Families," *Journal of American History* 83 (September 1996): 456–80; and Chulhee Lee, "Wealth Accumulation and the Health of Union Army Veterans," *Journal of Economic History* 65 (2005): 352–85.

5. Richard Franklin Bensel, *Yankee Leviathan: The Origins of Central State Authority in America, 1859–1877* (Cambridge: Cambridge University Press, 1990); and Heather Cox Richardson, *The Greatest Nation of the Earth: Republican Economic Policies during the Civil War* (Cambridge: Harvard University Press, 1997).

6. Letter from Lane, Crawfordsville, Indiana, to the President of the U.S. [Andrew Johnson], May 21, 1865, typescript, H. S. Lane mss, Lilly Library, Indiana University, Bloomington, Indiana.

7. Emma Lou Thornbrough, *Indiana in the Civil War Era, 1850–1880,* vol. 3 of *The History of Indiana* (Indianapolis: Indiana Historical Society, 1965), 219–20.

8. Thornbrough, *Indiana in the Civil War Era,* 242–45.

9. *Brookville Franklin Democrat,* October 6, 1871.

Selected Bibliography

GENERAL

McPherson, James M. *Battle Cry of Freedom: The Civil War Era*. New York: Oxford University Press, 1988.

Nation, Richard F. *At Home in the Hoosier Hills: Agriculture, Politics, and Religion in Southern Indiana, 1810–1870*. Bloomington: Indiana University Press, 2005.

Nelson, Scott Reynolds, and Carol Sheriff. *A People at War: Civilians and Soldiers in America's Civil War, 1854–1877*. New York: Oxford University Press, 2007.

Terrell, W. H. H. *Indiana in the War of the Rebellion: Report of the Adjutant General*. 1869. Reprint of vol. 1. Indianapolis: Indiana Historical Bureau, 1960.

Thornbrough, Emma Lou. *The Negro in Indiana before 1900: A Study of a Minority*. 1957. Bloomington: Indiana University Press, in association with the Indiana Historical Bureau, 1985.

———. *Indiana in the Civil War Era, 1850–1880*. Vol. 3 of *The History of Indiana*. Indianapolis: Indiana Historical Society, 1965.

Towne, Stephen. "Scorched Earth or Fertile Ground: Indiana in the Civil War, 1861–1865." In *The State of Indiana History 2000*, edited by Robert M. Taylor. Indianapolis: Indiana Historical Society, 2001.

INTRODUCTION

Berwanger, Eugene H. *The Frontier against Slavery: Western Anti-Negro Prejudice and the Slavery Extension Controversy*. Urbana: University of Illinois Press, 1967.

Carmony, Donald F. *Indiana, 1816–1850: The Pioneer Era*. Vol. 2 of *The History of Indiana*. Indianapolis: Indiana Historical Bureau and Indiana Historical Society, 1998.

Finkelman, Paul. "Evading the Ordinance: The Persistence of Bondage in Indiana and Illinois." *Journal of the Early Republic* 9 (Spring 1989): 21–51.

———. "Fugitive Slaves, Midwestern Racial Tolerance, and the Value of 'Justice Delayed.'" *Iowa Law Review* 78 (1992): 89–141.

Hamm, Thomas D., April Beckman, Marissa Floriv, Kirsti Giles, and Marie Hopper. "'A Great and Good People': Midwestern Quakers and the Struggle against Slavery." *Indiana Magazine of History* 100 (2004): 3–25.

CHAPTER 1: THE POLITICS OF SLAVERY

Baker, Jean. *Affairs of Party: The Political Culture of Northern Democrats in the Mid-Nineteenth Century*. Ithaca: Cornell University Press, 1983.

Foner, Eric. *Free Soil, Free Labor, Free Men: The Ideology of the Republican Party before the Civil War*. New York: Oxford University Press, 1970.

Gienapp, William E. *The Origins of the Republican Party, 1852–1856*. New York: Oxford University Press, 1987.

Holt, Michael. *The Political Crisis of the 1850s*. New York: Norton, 1978.

Hunter, Carol. "The Rev. Jermain Loguen: As a Slave and as a Freeman; A Narrative of Real Life." *Afro-Americans in New York Life and History* 13, no. 2 (1989): 33–46.

Kotlowski, Dean J. "'The Jordan is a hard road to travel': Hoosier Responses to Fugitive Slave Cases, 1850–1860." *International Social Science Review* 78, nos. 3–4 (2003): 71–78.

Morrison, Michael A. *Slavery and the American West: The Eclipse of Manifest Destiny and the Coming of the Civil War.* Chapel Hill: University of North Carolina Press, 1997.

Nation, Richard F. "Violence and the Rights of African Americans in Civil War–Era Indiana: The Case of James Hays." *Indiana Magazine of History* 100 (2004): 215–30.

Potter, David M. *The Impending Crisis, 1848–1861.* Completed by Don E. Fehrenbacher. New York: Harper Torchbooks, 1976.

CHAPTER 2: THE ELECTION OF 1860 AND SECESSION

Calhoun, Charles W. "'Incessant Noise and Tumult': Walter Q. Gresham and the Indiana Legislature during the Secession Crisis." *Indiana Magazine of History* 74 (1978): 223–51.

Elbert, E. Duane. "Southern Indiana in the Election of 1860: The Leadership and the Electorate." *Indiana Magazine of History* 70 (March 1974): 1–23.

CHAPTER 3: CHOOSING SIDES, MAKING AN ARMY

Geary, James W. *"We Need Men": The Union Draft in the Civil War.* DeKalb: Northern Illinois University Press, 1991.

Levine, Peter. "Draft Evasion in the North during the Civil War, 1863–1865." *Journal of American History* 67 (March 1981): 816–34.

Rodgers, Thomas E. "Republicans and Drifters: Political Affiliation and Union Army Volunteers in West-Central Indiana." *Indiana Magazine of History* 92 (December 1996): 321–45.

CHAPTER 4: THE FRONT LINES

Frank, Joseph Allan. *With Ballot and Bayonet: The Political Socialization of American Civil War Soldiers.* Athens: University of Georgia Press, 1998.

Hesseltine, William B. *Civil War Prisons: A Study in War Psychology.* New York: F. Ungar, 1964.

Linderman, Gerald F. *Embattled Courage: The Experience of Combat in the American Civil War.* New York: Free Press, 1987.

McPherson, James M. *For Cause and Comrades: Why Men Fought in the Civil War.* New York: Oxford University Press, 1997.

Mitchell, Reid. *Civil War Soldiers.* New York: Viking, 1988.

———. *The Vacant Chair: The Northern Soldier Leaves Home.* New York: Oxford University Press, 1993.

Nelson, Jacquelyn S. *Indiana Quakers Confront the Civil War.* Indianapolis: Indiana Historical Society, 1991.

Schultz, Jane E. *Women at the Front: Hospital Workers in Civil War America.* Chapel Hill: University of North Carolina Press, 2004.

Seigel, Peggy Brase. "She Went to War: Indiana Women Nurses in the Civil War." *Indiana Magazine of History* 86 (1990): 1–27.

Urwin, Gregory J. W., ed. *Black Flag over Dixie: Racial Atrocities and Reprisals in the Civil War.* Carbondale: Southern Illinois University Press, 2004.

CHAPTER 5: THE HOME FRONT

Bensel, Richard Franklin. *Yankee Leviathan: The Origins of Central State Authority in America, 1859–1877.* Cambridge: Cambridge University Press, 1990.

Marshall, Joan E. "Aid for Union Soldiers' Families: A Comfortable Entitlement or a Pauper's Pittance? Indiana, 1861–1865." *Social Science Review* (June 2004): 207–42.

Richardson, Heather Cox. *The Greatest Nation of the Earth: Republican Economic Policies during the Civil War.* Cambridge: Harvard University Press, 1997.

Rodgers, Thomas E. "Hoosier Women and the Civil War Home Front." *Indiana Magazine of History* 97 (June 2001): 105–28.

Silber, Nina. *Daughters of the Union: Northern Women fight the Civil War.* Cambridge: Harvard University Press, 2005.

CHAPTER 6: RACE, SLAVERY, AND THE EMANCIPATION PROCLAMATION

Berlin, Ira, Joseph P. Reidy, and Leslie S. Rowland, eds. *Freedom's Soldiers: The Black Military Experience in the Civil War.* New York: Cambridge University Press, 1998.

Cornish, Dudley T. *The Sable Arm: Negro Troops in the Union Army, 1861–1865.* New York: Norton, 1966.

Miller, Edward A. Jr. "Garland H. White, Black Army Chaplain." *Civil War History* 43 (September 1997): 201–18.

CHAPTER 7: THE BATTLE TO CONTROL STATE GOVERNMENT

Klement, Frank L. *The Copperheads in the Middle West* (Chicago: University of Chicago Press, 1960.

————. *The Limits of Dissent: Clement L. Vallandigham and the Civil War.* Lexington: University Press of Kentucky, 1970.

Marvel, William. *Burnside.* Chapel Hill: University of North Carolina Press, 1991.

Rodgers, Thomas E. "Liberty, Will, and Violence: The Political Ideology of the Democrats of West-Central Indiana during the Civil War." *Indiana Magazine of History* 92 (June 1996): 133–59.

Silbey, Joel. *A Respectable Minority: The Democratic Party in the Civil War Era, 1860–1868.* New York: Norton, 1977.

Stampp, Kenneth M. *Indiana Politics during the Civil War.* 1949. Bloomington: Indiana University Press, in association with the Indiana Historical Bureau, 1978.

Tredway, G. R. *Democratic Opposition to the Lincoln Administration in Indiana.* Indiana Historical Collections 48. Indianapolis: Indiana Historical Bureau, 1973.

Weber, Jennifer. *Copperheads: The Rise and Fall of Lincoln's Opponents in the North.* New York: Oxford University Press, 2006.

CHAPTER 8: THE MORGAN RAID

Ramage, James A. *Rebel Raider: The Life of General John Hunt Morgan.* Lexington: University Press of Kentucky, 1986.

Roller, Scott. "Business as Usual: Indiana's Response to the Confederate Invasions of the Summer of 1863." *Indiana Magazine of History* 88 (March 1992): 1–25.

CHAPTER 9: DISSENT, VIOLENCE, AND CONSPIRACY

Churchill, Robert. "Liberty, Conscription, and a Party Divided: The Sons of Liberty Conspiracy of 1863–1864." *Prologue* 30 (1998): 294–303.

Klement, Frank L. *Dark Lanterns: Secret Political Societies, Conspiracies, and Treason Trials in the Civil War.* Baton Rouge: Louisiana State University Press, 1984.

Neely, Mark E., Jr. *The Fate of Liberty: Abraham Lincoln and Civil Liberties.* New York: Oxford University Press, 1991.

Towne, Stephen E. "Killing the Serpent Speedily: Governor Morton, General Hascall, and the Suppression of the Democratic Press in Indiana, 1863." *Civil War History* 52 (March 2006): 41–65.

———. "Works of Indiscretion: Violence against the Democratic Press in Indiana during the Civil War." *Journalism History* 31 (2005): 138–49.

Wertheim, Lewis J. "The Indianapolis Treason Trials, the Elections of 1864 and the Power of the Partisan Press." *Indiana Magazine of History* 85 (1989): 236–50.

CHAPTER 10: WAR'S END

Beck, Scott A. L. "Freedmen, Friends, Common Schools and Reconstruction." *Southern Friend* 17 (1995): 5–31.

Richardson, Heather Cox. *The Death of Reconstruction: Race, Labor, and Politics in the Post–Civil War North, 1865–1901.* Cambridge: Harvard University Press, 2001.

Index